TERROR TRACKER

TO MUM, DAD AND STEVE

TERROR TRACKER

AN ODYSSEY INTO PURE FEAR

NEIL DOYLE

MAINSTREAM
PUBLISHING
EDINBURGH AND LONDON

First published in Great Britain in 2004 by
MAINSTREAM PUBLISHING COMPANY (EDINBURGH) LTD
7 Albany Street
Edinburgh EH1 3UG

ISBN 1 84018 874 X

All images courtesy of ND archive (www.neildoyle.com)

A catalogue record for this book is available from the British Library

Typeset in Apollo and Electra
Printed and bound in Great Britain by
Antony Rowe Ltd, Chippenham, Wiltshire

ACKNOWLEDGEMENTS

My deep and sincere thanks go to everyone who helped in the making of this book. Some of you are named and some of you couldn't be named. Special thanks go to Mr S. A big thank you goes to my family, Jean, Peter, and my friends for their encouragement and unstinting support. A final vote of appreciation goes to Rosie, for reminding me to take regular screen breaks.

CONTENTS

List of Abbreviations 9

Glossary 11

Author's Note 12

Prologue 13

Towering Inferno 17

Second Base 36

Anthrax Faxes 56

Nukedom 77

The Missing Link 99

Baghdad Olympiad 122

Al-Qaeda Exposed 138

The Hamza Videos 161

Meeting Mrs Galt 183

The Hoist 203

Epilogue 233

Index 236

LIST OF ABBREVIATIONS

ADM – Atomic Demolition Munitions
ATF – Bureau of Alcohol, Tobacco, Firearms and Explosives
BCE – Before Common Era
CIA – Central Intelligence Agency
CIRA – Continuity Irish Republican Army
CPS – Crown Prosecution Service
DA – District Attorney
DEFCON – Defence Condition
DFLP – Democratic Front for the Liberation of Palestine
DMZ – Demilitarised Zone (Korea)
DTI – Department of Trade and Industry
FBI – Federal Bureau of Investigation
ECGD – Export Credit Guarantees Department
EMAP – East Midlands Allied Press
FEMA – Federal Emergency Management Agency
GIA – Armed Islamic Group (Algeria)
GRU – Glavnoye Razvedovatel'noye Upravlenie (Russian military intelligence agency)
IOC – International Olympic Committee
IP – Internet Protocol
IRA – Irish Republican Army
ISI – Directorate for Inter-Services Intelligence (Pakistan)
LIHOP – [They] Let It Happen On Purpose (theory about 11 September)
LTTE – Liberation Tigers of Tamil Eelam
MASCAL – Mass Casualty Exercise
MI5 – British Security Service (domestic)

MI6 – British Secret Intelligence Service (foreign)
NASA – National Aeronautics and Space Administration
NORAD – North America Aerospace Defense Command
NRO – National Reconnaissance Office
NSA – National Security Agency
NYPD – New York Police Department
OPM – Organisation for the Preparation of Mujahideen
PDF – Portable Document Format
PDFLP – Popular Democratic Front for the Liberation of Palestine
PLO – Palestinian Liberation Organisation
RPG – Rocket-propelled Grenade
SAS – Special Air Service
SBS – Special Boat Service
SDECE – Service de Documentation Extérieur et de Contre-Espionnage (French intelligence agency)
UAV – Unmanned Aerial Vehicle
WMD – Weapons of Mass Destruction
WTC – World Trade Center

GLOSSARY

Allah	God
bayat	pledge of allegiance
burka	loose garment covering the whole body
inshallah	'if Allah wills it'
intifada	uprising
jihad	holy war by Muslims against unbelievers
Koran	the Islamic sacred book
madrassa	college for Islamic instruction
masjid	mosque
Mujahid	person who fights a jihad
Mujahideen	guerrilla fighters
shaheed	Muslim martyr
sharia	Islamic canonical law
Shi'a	one of the two main branches of Islam that regards Ali, the fourth caliph, as the true successor to the Prophet Mohammad
Sunna	traditional portion of Muslim law based on Mohammad's words or acts
Sunni	one of the two main branches of Islam and differing from Shi'a in its understanding of the Sunna and in its acceptance of the first three caliphs
ummah	the whole community of Muslims
zakat	obligatory payment made annually under Islamic law and used for charitable and religious purposes

AUTHOR'S NOTE

The quotations used in the text are reproduced verbatim wherever possible. At first glance, some of the reported speech of people for whom English is not their first language might appear a little odd. I've refrained from cleaning these up and stuck to the quotes as they appear in court documents and other transcripts. It would appear even stranger if everyone was talking in perfect Queen's English, I feel.

If you'd like to read more about the subjects covered here, I've included a notes page on my website where you can browse through some of the source materials that I've gathered. There's also a multimedia section where you can watch video clips and listen to audio recordings. Your login details are – username: reader102 password: access901. Some of the characters you'll be encountering are hanging out in the discussion forum at www.neildoyle.com.

PROLOGUE

I was lounging in the office of a senior diplomat when it happened. We'd just returned from a very good lunch at a restaurant near Marble Arch in London and were continuing our discussion about military intelligence and the rise of international terrorism at the embassy. He'd cleared his diary for the day so we could talk at length and get to know each other, for which I was very grateful.

We were in the middle of a conversation when an elderly gentleman opened the door and walked in. Our host's face lit up with a broad, surprised smile, and he rushed forward to guide the man towards one of the seats around the coffee table. Judging by his obvious delight, I suspected that we had a very important visitor in our midst. I instinctively stood up, to attention almost, and waited to be introduced. I was one of three guests in the office, and we were introduced and shook hands in turn.

The visitor took his seat, and we were proudly told that he was 82 years old. He certainly was a VIP, as we learned that he was the retired former vice-chief of the country's army. Now I understood why our host was so delighted to see him. Our new companion was also a distinguished military historian, and as soon as he started answering questions his erudition was immediately apparent.

More than slightly awed, I was invited to ask the General a question. I desperately racked my brains to come up with something that might sound vaguely intelligent. After a pregnant pause, I asked him whether he thought that an event like 11 September might happen again.

Before I'd even finished the sentence, he said: 'Yes, yes, yes,' nodding vigorously in what I took to be an almost impatient manner. 'Many times over,' he added. It was almost as if I'd asked the very dumb question that I had been trying so hard to avoid. He was staring up at the ceiling as he talked, and I feared I had made a faux pas. I followed up by asking if he thought that we were in the very early stages of this so-called 'war on terror' and his reaction was very similar.

'Conor Cruise O'Brien said after he retired [as a high-ranking UN diplomat] that militant Islam posed a greater threat to the world than communism.' He paused there deliberately, giving us all a chance to let this prophecy sink in. He clearly believed it was coming true. As long ago as the late 1980s, one of Ireland's elder statesmen had foreseen the situation in which we now found ourselves. It was a remarkable premonition and a terrifying indicator of the size of problem that we might be facing.

'And I'm a socialist,' he proudly declared. It was his way of indicating that he didn't share the scepticism about the nature of the risk posed by al-Qaeda that is common on the left of the political spectrum. We laughed politely and he smiled, too; but the General was serious. 'I'm not a pessimist, but I just don't see any cause for hope at the moment,' he said.

Later, he explained that he was in London for a medical appointment. 'Prostate cancer. It travels up the spine until it reaches the brain,' he said solemnly. I suspect he thought it was an apt metaphor for the matter at hand.

As the meeting ended, I was presented with a gift. It was a book written by a high-ranking army officer about the struggle against international terrorism. I started to read it on the Underground on the way home. The author held similar views to the General it seemed: he predicted that the struggle between the West and militant Islamist groups would continue for generations – perhaps spread out over 100 years or more.

It's a matter of hot dispute as to whether the scenes we witness on the news of the aftermaths of terrorist bombings constitute a war at all; maybe it is all a convenient myth that benefits politicians. Whatever the truth is, according to my calculations we should expect to see an average of just under 14 al-Qaeda-sponsored suicide bomb attacks against Western interests every day before we will know that a war is in full swing. Let's hope it never gets to that stage, because by then it may be too late to affect the outcome.

What follows is the story of how I meandered towards being in a position to be able to make the above calculation.

neil@neildoyle.com

TOWERING INFERNO

There it was, right before our very eyes, on the TV in the office. A crowd had gathered to watch the giant silver building spewing black smoke and witness Hollywood fiction transform into real life. An ominous black plume was billowing from the north tower of the World Trade Center in New York City, but most people (those on the news desk especially) were sporting big smiles.

We were, after all, journalists and this was a major breaking story – a bit of a relief after a few slow news weeks. It had come out of nowhere and we stood around shaking our heads, though at the same time grinning like fools, because significant damage had obviously been inflicted.

It was in the back of everyone's mind that the tower might even topple over. You could almost feel the collective will-power pushing on the building, people imagining huge cracks forming and it crashing into the East River, throwing a vast sheet of white spray over the entire city; maybe even followed by something in the way of a tidal wave. It would be hard to beat a combined skyscraper collapse/tsunami event. Yes, that would be a very tasty story indeed.

It was 26 February 1993 and I was an ambitious reporter for a construction magazine at the time. Minor details like human casualties were confusing matters for those of us who were much more interested in the structural engineering angles to this story.

'One woman has been killed, apparently,' I said to someone who'd just sidled up to me to watch the pictures.

'Fuck the people. What's the damage like?' he responded.

The bosses were circling around now, so it was obviously getting

17

near the time when the editor would decide, as was customary during times of disaster, which one of us would be sent to report from the scene. I was a veteran of the Gulf War and an IRA bomb attack in the City of London, and I was already mentally packing my bags.

It was going to be a close call, though. He returned to his office and stood there, staring out of the window with a frown on his face. It was obvious that he was pondering whether the scale of the damage justified the expense involved in funding a foreign expedition. I could appreciate how at times the editor's dual roles of content overseer and bean counter would come into conflict and send his brain into a swirling torment of contradictory thoughts.

It soon emerged that the tower was probably structurally sound, but the desire for a sexy story triumphed over monetary concerns. As the deputy news editor and disaster specialist, I was summoned to an audience in the goldfish bowl.

My orders were: make haste for New York, go straight to the World Trade Center, phone in as soon as I got back to the hotel and don't dare to even consider attempting to return without stories so good that they might one day come to be viewed as holy scripture. The last point was emphasised in various ways, but the basic message was: 'Come back without a good story and you can start looking for a new job.'

There was a large element of naked bluff in this, as always, but an accidental balls-up could well trigger off such an event. Employment regulations don't seem to apply to publishing companies, which means working on the assumption that you could be frogmarched out of the building by two security guards at any time and without warning.

It's always possible that a small error in timing could trip you up. Diarmaid, a reporter colleague, once had to resort to feigning a possible heart attack in order to get stretchered off a flight that was about to take off from Hong Kong. As the plane was taxiing towards the runway, he suddenly realised that he would have narrowly missed his deadline by the time he landed in London. It was the only way that he could get off the plane; he had had no other option if he was to file his story on time. It was an impressive demonstration of commitment, although I doubt the airline would have had such charitable thoughts if they knew the truth.

Necessity really has to be the mother of invention when it comes to avoiding an embarrassing violation of the most basic rule of the trade: meet your deadline, whatever the circumstances. To date, I've missed a plane to Germany once, but I only had to wait two hours for the next flight. Probably my worst mistake in the sphere of travel arrangements was when I arrived a day too early for a flight, which is another story entirely.

My flight to New York was utterly uneventful. All I can really recall about it is a female member of the cabin crew taking a shine to me and letting me help myself to the drinks trolley behind the curtain as everyone else dozed or watched the film.

My first brush with the law came at immigration. There were five long queues, each leading up to a little blue kiosk, and a long yellow line painted on the floor just in front. Numerous warning signs suggested that I should not step over the line until I was called forward. And they meant it. One officer was policing the yellow line and keeping a close eye on the feet of the first person in each queue, growling and gesturing occasionally at people, even where the transgression could be measured in millimetres.

'Jesus. Welcome to America. Haven't these people got anything better to do?' I thought. I suddenly felt conspicuously foreign, and it's not a nice feeling. Smart-arse British journalist or not, I was a potential terrorist as far as these people were concerned, and they were very nervy. They were obviously not in the mood to put up with any nonsense.

Sure enough, after ten minutes of slow shuffling, all heads turned to watch a tall man of Middle Eastern appearance, hands cuffed behind his back, being steered across the hall by two men in uniform. He was more or less shoved into a large room with half-glazed partitions at the end of the hall to my left. I watched him sit down, encouraged by the officers pushing down on his shoulders. Then I noticed that there were others in the room, and it dawned on me that anyone looking Asian or Middle Eastern was being yanked out of the queues and taken aside for questioning.

I caught the gaze of a woman who was already in there. She was wearing a headscarf, and she stared back at me with a look that told me that she was outraged at how she was being treated but was forced to keep quiet and play along. As the queue shuffled forward, I glanced at her again. We locked eyes briefly, and she transmitted the full force of her feelings of sadness and deep rage to me.

It looked like they were rounding up any dusky, foreign-looking people as soon as they stepped off the planes. They didn't even have to look shifty. It seemed to be racism to me, and I did feel an instinctive upwelling from the gut telling me to do something. But there was nothing useful that a foreigner could do in the face of armed officials who were jumpy and on red alert.

These weren't auspicious omens, and, in any case, I was in danger of forgetting that every minute spent in the queue was increasing the risk that I might miss the sight of a skyscraper crashing into a river. I'd been cut off from the news for half a day and the thing could be listing dangerously at this very minute for all I knew. Bureaucratic procedures were threatening to get me the sack.

The kiosk woman finally gestured to indicate that I had clearance to stride forth and cross the holy yellow line. I approached.

'Business or pleasure?'

'A bit of both, hopefully,' I said, grinning, before realising that it was probably around the ten millionth time she'd heard that.

She shot me a look that I took to be threatening, in a blank kind of way.

'Well, business, mainly. I'm a journalist. I'm on my way to the World Trade Center,' I said, a little more solemnly this time.

Her eyes darted away from the screen, and she looked at me menacingly again. I was worried that my jocular response might have been construed as suspicious somehow.

After a few seconds of embarrassment, she offered me my passport back without looking at me or speaking. It appeared that I was free to proceed with my journey into the belly of the Great Satan, as some might say.

I wasn't feeling particularly enamoured of the place, but I soon had what can only be called a 'eureka moment' during the cab drive into town. I was hoping for a traditional yellow taxi, but ended up in a people-carrier, and the disappointment only added to my growing dismay: so far it seemed like a let-down all around. The streetscape outside the airport, the little that I'd seen so far, seemed to confirm that. Everything around me looked grimy and distinctly utilitarian. The light was going and just as I was thinking that the familiar skyline I'd seen so many times on TV and on film might be just a cruel optical illusion, we levelled out at the top of a hill approaching a bridge. I was instantly dumbstruck. Manhattan rose from the ground to fill the windscreen.

I could almost hear an orchestra strike up Gershwin. In the twilight, it looked like a monstrous glittering black tiara. The Empire State Building, the Chrysler Building and the twin towers of the World Trade Center were clearly visible. I couldn't see any signs of smoke, and there was no visual evidence that the north tower was leaning from the perpendicular.

The rest of the ride was just a blur of headlights and heavy traffic as we forged our way into the heart of the city. All I knew was that my hotel was near Central Park, and I assumed that was where we were heading. I didn't get any sense that the driver was going to rob me and turf me out in the middle of the Bronx or somewhere, although, if we had been heading for the Bronx, I wouldn't have had a clue. I relaxed, tried to enjoy the ride and acclimatise to my new surroundings.

The plan was to drop off my bags, get down to the World Trade Center and see what was happening, then phone the editor when I got back to the hotel – as instructed. I had had a quiet word with the office secretary when she was making the travel arrangements, to ask if she could do me a favour and book me into a half-decent hotel. She promised to do what she could. The editorial budget had recently been slashed, and I feared that penny-pinching would see me stuck in a cheap filthy hole. But a hotel close to Central Park sounded good to me at the time, and I was relishing the thought of indulging in room service and the minibar at the end of the day.

I was in for a big disappointment. The lobby of the hotel was tiny and so was the room. There was a two-foot gap around the bed and a close-up view of a brick wall outside the window. It was cheerless and greasy looking, with a green and white colour scheme, comparable perhaps to a cheap bed and breakfast place for asylum seekers in King's Cross back in London. I started to consider moving out but quickly discounted the possibility. Time was ticking away and I needed to crack on with the job in hand. I'd just have to put up with it.

I switched on the TV and found the local news channel. Nothing much seemed to have changed – the only real news was that engineers were still surveying the extent of the damage to the WTC's massive foundations. Apparently, a breach could let in the river and flood the city's subway system.

This reminded me that there was no time to dwell on my

unexpectedly seedy surroundings. I needed to get down there pronto. So, after checking my kit and making sure I had plenty of camera film, I left the room and went to find the lift.

I approached the man at the counter in the lobby and asked for directions to the World Trade Center, to his obvious amusement. He lost me during his lengthy description and gesticulations, although I gathered that it was quite some distance away and at least got a sense of the direction I should be heading in. I thanked him, slung my rucksack over my right shoulder and proceeded to step out into the street to begin my mission in earnest.

I hadn't appreciated how cold it would be, and I wasn't really dressed for it because I hadn't considered the weather at all. The first thing to hit me when I opened the door was a stinging icy blast of wind as I got my first real glimpse of New York City from the ground. Snow was piled up along the pavements. It was dark now, and it looked like everything was shut. I was surrounded by mid-rise office buildings and there was hardly anyone about, so I headed up the wide sidewalk for the moving lights of a busy street that I could see in the distance ahead of me.

I finally reached the road I was aiming for, and I was pretty sure it was Second Avenue. I got my first close-up look at New York in full swing. It looked much like the West End of London, bar all the yellow cabs, the wide roads and the tall buildings. I marvelled for a while at the blizzard of lights, the bustle of people hurrying along the wide sidewalks and the tramps with their shopping trolleys on the intersection, before I decided to hail a cab. One pulled up almost as soon as I raised my arm, and, although I wasn't entirely sure what the driver said, due to a heavy Russian-sounding accent, he nodded when I said, 'World Trade Center', and we were off.

He dropped me off a little way down the road, and at first I wondered where the twin towers were. After my eyes had adjusted to the dark sky, I saw them. There were only a few lights on, as the bomb had severed the main power supply, and from a distance they looked like two impossibly huge columns of basalt stretching up into the low cloud blanket. I was professionally eager to get on with things now that my goal was in sight, and I strode onwards, keeping my eyes glued to the towers and scanning them in vain for any signs that things were not quite right. There was a distinct occasional crunch of ice breaking underfoot as I walked quickly up the road past numerous parked fire trucks and ambulances towards where I guessed the core of the action would be.

I knew I was in the right place because I passed a large garage door that was bent outwards and blackened, and recognised this as being the entrance to the B-2 sub-basement car park where the Ryder hire truck packed with 90 kg of suspected C-4 plastic explosive had blown up. It had been parked in the lot reserved for the Secret Service, which had an office in Building Six in the complex. Officials were refusing to comment on how the terrorists had managed to park in an area that required special access.

The garage door had been deformed and forced towards horizontal by the power of the blast, and I recalled the television images that had shown black smoke belching out of this entrance. I stopped in front of the door and stared at the scene for a while, remembering that perhaps six people had died in the explosion, very likely near this spot. I stood still, trying to see if I could pick up any kind of intuitive signals, maybe just an odd ghostly feeling to hint that six souls had recently departed from this place. But there was nothing bar a faint hint of something on the wind, like a cross between sulphur and bleach, which I put down to smoke.

I snapped out of it and started to ponder my next move. The north tower loomed large and tapered into the blackness above me, utterly awe-inspiring despite its disabled state, or perhaps because of it. There was the occasional tinkle of falling broken glass, and as I became aware that I was losing the feeling in my feet, I also realised that there was a distinct lack of people on the ground given that it was a major incident scene. I could see some policemen guarding a cordon in the distance, but there were no obvious signs of the press pack. I set off to find it. Maybe I'd inadvertently wandered into the anticipated Drop Zone – the area where the building would most likely fall were it to collapse.

As I headed for the policemen, I came across what looked like a command trailer with light coming through its half-open door. I stuck my head inside and found two men sitting there staring at TV monitors. They turned to look at me. I asked if they knew whether a media centre had been set up, but they shrugged and shook their heads, then looked back at the TV monitors. They were obviously too wrapped up in what they were doing to be bothered with passing strangers, which was fair enough. I stepped down from the little stairway on the back of the truck and proceeded on towards the cops.

They were just as unhelpful. No, he didn't know anything about a media centre, said the first one. Another officer who was standing nearby wandered over to see what was going on. They were frowning down at me and fingering their belts as I explained where I'd come from and what I was doing. When I said that I needed to get inside the Trade Center, they started to look mildly pissed off.

'That is a crime scene. Put a foot over that line and you'll be busted,' said the first cop.

I tried to explain that I just wanted to find out where the press conferences were being held, but they both looked like they weren't hearing me and stared into the distance in opposite directions, making shooing gestures to indicate that I should move along now.

This is always the major challenge at the scene of a bombing: getting inside the police cordon and sneaking a peak at the crater. There are various subterfuges that I'd used successfully in the past – all legal and just the right side of ethical. This time, however, the scale of the task was far greater, I figured, considering the group of heavily armed and futuristically black-attired ATF (Alcohol, Tobacco, Firearms and Explosives) officers I'd just seen scurrying around the base of one of the towers. There was far too much firepower on hand for me to risk a casual amble in the direction of the crime scene, hoping that no one would notice me. ATF, FBI, NYPD, CIA, SWAT teams, Secret Service – they were all milling around in the dark in there somewhere, and were at battle stations. It was obvious that a trespasser really would be risking death as a terrorist suspect in a very one-sided shoot-out in the smoky murk somewhere in the bowels of the building. Dying for a story is all well and good, but this would be a mad death for no reason, as there was no story yet.

I would need daylight at the very least to be able to judge where any weak points in the defences were. If direct access is out of the question, then 'sponsored entry' is usually the solution. I needed to find the WTC's chief engineer, butter him up and get him to wave his ID around and get his important guest inside the complex.

As I walked away from the cops, I was literally scratching my head over my next move. I knew there must be a makeshift emergency response centre in one of the giant office buildings that surrounded me; it was just a question of finding it.

I spotted a guy carrying a large microphone: obviously a radio reporter. I flagged him down and asked him if he could tell me where the press conferences were being held.

'You want the Marriott Hotel. It's less than a block down. We're all in there,' he said, pointing over his shoulder.

It was my first break, and I figured that at least I should be able to find a PR person to bring me up to speed on the basics, after which I could track down the engineer. Coffee and general warmth were also beginning to become top priorities. The temperature was well below zero, I judged. I thanked him and headed for a gaggle of fire trucks that I could see flashing in the middle distance.

As I climbed the spiral staircase to the first floor of the Marriott, it was clear that I was in the right place. I was confronted by a *mélange* of suited media representatives and uniformed public service personnel who had obviously just spilled out from the main conference hall. They all seemed to be haggling with one another in the chandeliered lobby area just outside. As I got closer, it seemed like the chaotic aftermath you can get at the end of a press conference: there were interviews going on, camera lights moving around, people taking notes while gathered around official personnel wearing name badges, lots of frowning and men and women jogging around with microphones.

The largest of several gaggles was gathered around a name-badged man in shirtsleeves, who was gesturing with an arm that was grasping a walkie-talkie. There seemed to be an argument going on, and the man kept closing his eyes and pointing his nose in the air, his body language indicating that he wasn't going to budge. The last thing I'd seen on the TV news before leaving the hotel was that the media hadn't yet been allowed inside, and now it seemed that I'd arrived in the middle of the entry negotiations.

Every news editor in the land must have been bombarding those officials with phone calls demanding access to the crater. The focus of this delegated fury was now centred on the PR guy from the Port Authority of New York, it said on the badge, whose line of defence was that it was a crime scene and they couldn't risk evidence being disturbed.

So when could the media take a look? He didn't know. It would have to wait until forensics had finished their work, which could be days or even weeks. A muted yell of frustration went up from the media crowd around him; some people looked away in disgust; hands were thrown up. Weeks!? This was the hard core of the press pack, for sure, and as he tried to get away, two guys with cameras followed him, trying to appeal to his better nature.

He stopped, turned and held his hands up, as if to say 'OK, OK! I'll get back to you.' Then he looked at me, which was momentarily embarrassing. I was aware that I had been smiling as I soaked in the scene, and I felt like I'd been caught out. He held me in his unsmiling glare for a couple of seconds, then turned and hurried down the stairs.

While I had been watching this mêlée, most of the gathered journalists seemed to have wandered off into the various smaller rooms lined up opposite the conference hall. Interviews were still being conducted in the lobby, but things seemed to be calming down. The largest of the lecture rooms looked to be the busiest, and it turned out to be the new temporary base for the Port Authority's public relations team. I wanted to get a briefing on the day's events, to try and get an idea of what I'd missed, but it wasn't easy. There were three desks manned by PRs with small, ill-formed queues of press people in front of each one. I took my place in one of the queues and waited my turn as my colleagues placed requests for interviews, checked who would be present at a press conference scheduled for the following day, tried to pre-book places on any tour inside the WTC and so on.

I finally got my turn and was greeted by a kindly looking man called Wayne, who had white hair and a matching moustache. He looked extremely tired, and he almost winced when I said I'd just arrived from England and asked if I could get a quick rundown on the current state of play. He said he had a lot on his plate at the moment, although he'd do his best for me later on if I could wait a while. I took him at his word, found a seat at the side of the room and waited. It seemed to take forever, although it was probably only an hour or so. The room steadily emptied while I sat there, and every now and again the reluctant tour guide with the walkie-talkie would wander in and I would approach him. He wouldn't say anything, though, and wouldn't even look at me. He obviously hadn't taken a shine to me at first sight.

The room was virtually deserted when I approached Wayne at the desk yet again and reminded him that I was still waiting. He grimaced, looked away and let out a huge sigh. He pushed up his glasses and rubbed his eyes, then smiled and explained that he'd been working for 72 hours non-stop. He gestured at the chair in front of the desk. What did I want to know? He offered me a cup of coffee, and I gladly accepted.

For the next half an hour we sat and talked, and he gradually got me up to speed and filled me in on the background basics. The tower seemed to be in little danger of collapse, as no major damage to the building's foundations had been detected during a preliminary survey. A detailed inspection was under way, however, because they also held back the waters of the river and, as there was a major subway interchange under the complex, there was still a potential risk of flooding to the New York subway network if there was an undetected leak somewhere. He explained that the subsurface structure that supported the centre was known as 'the Bathtub'.

He went on to explain that most of the windows in the north tower had been broken by people trying to vent away the smoke as it poured up the building's core from the basement, rather than by the blast wave. The electricity substation that supplied power to the building and all the environmental controls were located in the basement close to where the truck bomb had been parked, which was why the lifts had stopped working. People evacuating from the upper floors had done so in total darkness, all holding hands and forming long human chains, coughing and choking as they felt their way down the staircases.

The big question was: who did this? There were no real clues at this stage, but as the attack had taken place two days before the second anniversary of the ceasefire that marked the end of the Gulf War, there was some media speculation about a link with Saddam Hussein. Wayne said that, in reality, no one had a clue. The body count so far was six, and a thousand people had suffered injuries.

It was late evening by now, and Wayne said there was little point in hanging around any more today, as there would be nothing to see. The scene of the crime was still off-limits to journalists and would be until they got the go-ahead from the FBI. We wrapped it up, and he slapped both hands on the desk, stood up, took his coat off the back of his chair and announced that he was looking forward to a long soak in the bath and a good sleep. He asked where I staying then offered to share a cab with me as he was heading in that direction.

He was intrigued as to why a construction journalist from

England had travelled so far to cover this story. I explained that most of the magazine's readers were civil or structural engineers, and they had a professional interest in how the building had performed during the explosion, as there could be major repercussions for the design of future skyscrapers. In any case, the magazine – *New Civil Engineer* – had a long tradition of sending reporters to major disasters all over the world. It had been the springboard for many journalists who'd later gone on to join national newspapers and TV companies.

I'd forgotten how cold it was outside, and it was a bleak scene as we walked from the hotel towards the main road. It was deserted and didn't look like a disaster site, although I could see some floodlit firefighters in the distance, going into the cordoned-off area. They were still damping down small fires inside the tower, Wayne said, as we walked on and picked our way through the rivers of cables and hoses, accompanied by the loud background clatter of portable generators.

In the taxi, he pointed out the landmarks as we made our way through the traffic, heading north. I was grateful for the hospitality he was showing me, but to my untrained eye Greenwich Village just looked like another lot of lights outside the window. However, I raised my eyebrows and tried to look appropriately interested at the right moments. We bid each other a cheery goodbye when we arrived at the hotel, knowing we'd probably cross paths again the next day. I certainly felt more cheerful as I made my way to my room, as I already had some good material and some promising leads to follow up. Maybe public relations people weren't all evil after all. I decided to skip dinner and get an early night, after watching a bit of TV news just to make sure I hadn't missed anything.

Those poor bastards. The situation hadn't really changed throughout the day, yet the local news channel reporters were still breathlessly reporting live from the scene as if the bomb had just gone off. The same old stuff was being repeated over and over. TV shopping channel presenters had nothing on these people. I'd been chatting to a reporter at the Marriott and it turned out that the channel had a reputation for being a cheapskate outfit. Reporters tripled-up as camera and sound operators, and they often had to hold the camera at arm's length in front of them and film themselves to make it look like there was crew behind them. I remember we both shook our heads and smiled in unison at the thought of it.

Acting in accordance with my orders, I phoned the editor at home. He probably regretted asking me to do this when I called, as it was four or five in the morning over there. A woman answered the phone and passed it over to him. I reeled off a situation report, but as he'd just woken up I could have been reciting a nursery rhyme, because he wasn't fully conscious during the call. Somewhere during all the yawning, I think I heard mumbled sounds that indicated satisfaction. 'Everything's going according to plan,' I reassured him, and hung up.

Confident that I was on top of the game, I decided to turn in.

By the following morning I was refreshed and keen to get moving. Keen enough to decide to try out the subway, which looked pretty grim and dirty. I emerged at Canal Street station and headed towards the World Trade Center once more. It looked like I'd got there just in time, as I could see a large throng of cameras and reporters gathered right outside the north tower where I'd been moved on the previous day. They all seemed to be expecting something, so I joined them and wove my way to the front of the crash barriers towards one side of the pack.

Suddenly, there was a huge crashing noise, and everyone instinctively started moving backwards, some breaking into a run, away from the noise. The wind had picked up and was dislodging huge sheets of broken window glass. It happened again, twice in quick succession, and I could see the next ones tumbling down from high up the building. Another six feet or so closer and there would have been injuries, because the barriers had been set up too close to the tower, patently. Four policemen, all looking up and behind them nervously as they were doing it, then shuffled the barriers forward beyond the danger zone.

This was a major league press pack. I was crammed in with maybe 150 fellow professionals and marvelling at the scale of it. There was also a certain amount of pride about being at the very heart of a major breaking world news story. There was a lot of jostling for position, and I could feel the sheer naked power of the crush when the pack shifted. The only other situation I'd been in that I could compare it to was when I was standing on the terraces at the old Wembley stadium during an FA Cup final as a teenager and narrowly avoided being trampled during one of many crowd-shifts during the game.

Then came the sound of a helicopter in the distance. The noise slowly built into a roar, and more cameramen and journalists came running to join the pack. Something was happening, and I asked the guy next to me what was going on. It was the Mayor and the Governor coming in on an official visit, and I gathered that their names were, respectively, David Dinkins and Mario Cuomo. Dinkins, I discovered later on, was up for re-election that year and was facing a stiff challenge from a guy called Rudolph Giuliani.

I couldn't see the chopper, but I could sure hear it. The pack became hyper-excited as the din became deafening, and the jostling turned into near-fighting as the cameramen surged forward to secure a clear line of sight. Reporters were elbowing each other out of the way; arguments broke out between TV cameramen and press photographers; and I was slowly being eased out to the margins of the pack, as I wasn't joining in with the scrapping. I was yielding because I had no real interest in the statements that the politicians were presumably about to deliver, although it was obviously going to be hot news for my American colleagues. I was feeling weirdly guilty that I might be depriving someone more deserving of their rightful place in the rowdy congregation.

I decided to save myself from being stomped and moved right out to the sidelines, when I saw the undercarriage of the aircraft above us as it started dropping down for a landing less than fifty metres to our right.

Soon, two men were walking towards the crowd from the chopper, followed by an entourage of maybe twenty others who were hanging back. The pack went into an utter frenzy, and I was glad that I'd got out of the way. I craned my neck from time to time to get a glimpse of the action, and I could see the two visiting dignitaries gesticulating while they addressed the crowd. I could hardly make out what they were saying, however; I only caught the odd word as I waited to see what would happen next.

After less than ten minutes, the visitors started walking away. The pack relaxed and slowly the pressmen started to drift off, while I pondered what to do next. I overhead two guys talking about the 'emergency control centre at City Hall', and this seemed like the logical next move. I checked the map and saw that it was close by, to the north-west of the WTC complex, so I started heading in that direction.

A rising sense that time was ticking on was nagging at me now,

30

because I hadn't really got any decent story leads as yet. Returning home with nothing much to report was unthinkable, and an image in my head of an angry editor blowing his gasket was starting to haunt me. Maybe I'd have some luck at City Hall.

Inside the City Hall building, I found the NYC emergency centre when I turned a corner and saw a long line of reporters and cameramen sitting on the floor looking bored, or otherwise just hanging around doing nothing in particular. It seemed that the governor and the mayor were inside on a tour of inspection and the media people were waiting outside for them to re-emerge. The door to the room at the end of the corridor was guarded by three police officers. I decided to hang around for a bit to see what I could pick up.

After around 20 minutes of absolute inaction, I was getting impatient. Every now and then an official emerged, usually frowning, and scurried off somewhere. I was intrigued, because, judging by the odd glimpse I got through the doorway, it looked like there were no lights on in the room.

When you're having no luck, you have to start thinking about making some. I walked to the end of the corridor, flashed my press card (which was out of date) and explained to the policemen that I was a journalist from England. Would they mind if I took a quick peek inside?

To my mild astonishment, they agreed. I could have a quick look, as long as I didn't actually enter the room. One of the cops raised an arm and opened the door wide enough for me to stick my head through the gap. I was right: the place was in darkness apart from a very dim red glow of emergency lighting. If the governor and the mayor were doing the rounds inside, I had no chance of identifying them in the eerie ruby gloom.

It was much larger than I had anticipated – cavernous, even – and it looked for all the world like a scene from mission control at NASA: rows of people sitting at computer terminals below a series of giant display screens. I couldn't make any sense of the diagrams on the screens, although I guessed they were city-wide maps of communications, utilities and transport networks. I knew that virtually all TV broadcasts in the city were cut off on the day of the attack as the WTC building housed transmitters used by all the big networks. It was an impressive display of high technology, and I wondered just how practical the place was. The bomb destruction was limited and confined to a very small part of the city, and I got the feeling that there was a large element of show about all this.

Hanging around here for much longer would be pointless, I thought, as I didn't get the feeling that this was the right place for major news story leads. Time for my next move. The Marriott Hotel beckoned once more, and I retraced my steps. I returned to find a press conference under way, but there was little of huge importance being said, until a journalist asked about an engineering report that had been commissioned about the towers some years previously. It had noted that all of the building's incoming utilities were grouped together in the basement, which made it vulnerable to a terrorist attack. It recommended that the services should be separated out and dispersed in different locations and on different floors to minimise the risk that they'd all be knocked out simultaneously by a bomb. The owners of the building, the Port Authority of New York, obviously hadn't acted on the recommendations, which might have reduced injuries. An official was forced to admit, in vague terms, that, no, they hadn't acted on it, but there were plans to do so. That was a great lead for me, and I wondered why the reporter had announced his findings at a press conference, effectively giving away his exclusive to everyone: a free story. 'Thanks very much,' I thought, as I started scribbling away.

After the conference broke up, I wandered back into the PR office – just in time to hear that small groups of journalists would now be escorted on trips inside the damaged tower, one group at a time. Each group would be no larger than five people, said the PR man who had seemed to take a dislike to me. Five people immediately stepped forward to sign up, and I followed. He started to jot down their names and affiliations, but when I started to give my details, he said, sorry, six was too many. I protested, pointed out that I'd flown over from England especially to see this, and generally tried to appeal to his better nature and to appear anguished. I think he just liked to annoy people, because he finally agreed and I'd be on the very first away team. His only advice was to keep together as a group, follow him and try not to disturb anything, as it was still very much a crime scene. He seemed to be looking at me for most of the time when he was reeling this off. Perhaps he had an inkling that my intention was to melt away from the group once we were inside and 'get lost', so I could conduct my own investigations.

We were led into the building and along a series of dark corridors until we turned and started along a passage that was lined with festoons of brightly shining bare light bulbs strung along yellow cables. We'd arrived at the portal to the crater site, which was a doorway covered by a tarpaulin. Our guide said we could take turns to have a quick look at the crime scene, but we couldn't enter. We could take photographs, but we shouldn't try to distract anyone working in there. When it came to my turn, I poked my head inside. It was very murky, and all I could really make out were two people in white forensic overalls, some lumps of broken concrete slab and bare steel columns that had been stripped of their protection by the force of the blast. There were few visual reference points to grasp, although I sensed there was a large space in there in the darkness. I took a few photographs, though I was sure that my puny flash unit didn't have the throw to be able to light the entire scene.

After we'd all had a go, we were then led back down the corridor and we took another turn towards an area in front of us that was also lit by temporary electrics. Our man stopped and raised his arm to gesture towards a doorway. It was the emergency command centre, he said. I looked inside and it was crammed full of people in overalls and hardhats poring over building plans. Half the people seemed to be talking on the telephone. There must have been a hundred or more people inside a very small space. No one batted an eyelid when we appeared at the doorway; they just kept their heads down and carried on with whatever it was that they were doing.

We were keen to get in there and have a look around. Our guide initially said it was out of the question, but, again, when pressed, he relented and said we could have a look around for a couple of minutes, as long as we didn't try to talk to anyone. We accepted the condition and wandered in. He stayed true to his word, however, and just as I was looking over people's shoulders and starting to get a handle on what the different groups of people might be doing, he came in and ordered us to leave immediately. We slowly gravitated back towards the doorway in a slovenly manner that seemed to make him anxious, but we complied eventually.

Once out of the room, he appeared to be relieved that none of us had got away. He turned and gestured for us to follow him back to the outside world. As soon as he turned his back, I did a big side-step and disappeared back into the emergency centre. I was sure that I'd buy myself a few minutes at least to ask some questions, but just as I was about to interrogate three guys who appeared to be looking at wiring diagrams, I noticed the large figure of the handler filling the doorway. He looked angry and hurt. I held my hands up and walked towards him.

It was a good day's work but, although I had some very decent stuff to report back on, I knew I was missing a knockout story to put a cherry on the cake. There was less than 24 hours to go, as I had to get back and file a story in time for that week's issue. It was getting towards the end of the day now and there were no press conferences scheduled for later, so I thought I'd make my way back to the hotel and get some dinner from somewhere, as it didn't have a restaurant. I could go back to the WTC later in the evening perhaps.

For some unknown reason it popped into my head that a trip to the Empire State Building might be in order. I could get some good shots of the towers from the top and, besides, it was something that I'd always wanted to do since childhood. I acted on the inspiration and hailed a cab.

I arrived and took my place in the queue for the lift to the top. I was marvelling at the art deco beauty of the granite- and marble-clad lobby when a police officer asked me if he could inspect my rucksack. He was surprised to find a builder's hard hat in there. I had brought it in the hope that I could wear it and mingle with the engineers and rescue workers at the scene, thus gaining access to the crater site. Unfortunately, American and British hard hats are of distinctively different designs, and I decided not to risk it. The cop was suspicious, and he asked me to step out of the line. I was escorted towards a man in plain clothes sitting behind a desk on an imposing marble platform. He questioned me, and I explained who I was and presented my expired press card. I don't think he noticed as he was more interested in finding out why I had the hard hat. I explained it was purely for safety reasons, as I was covering the World Trade Center story. They eventually let me proceed, although I got the impression that my explanation wasn't entirely believed.

I got the cherry on the cake the next day. There was a press conference at the Marriott in the morning, just a couple of hours before I had to leave and check in for the flight home. I secured an interview with the chief engineer of the twin towers after the event. He told me that he had been stuck in a lift between two floors over seventy storeys up when the bomb severed the power supply. He was stuck in there with a dozen or more people and smoke started to fill the lift. He realised that they were at risk of suffocation and needed to get out quickly. The walls of the lift were made from dense plasterboard, and he said he fished out his car key and started to use it to saw a hole that they could crawl through. The key fob had a tiny light built into it, and he used this so he could see what he was doing. They succeeded in escaping just in time and that car key, for a Volkswagen, saved their lives.

It was a great human-interest story and it was mission accomplished, I felt. As the plane climbed out of New York, I settled back and felt overwhelmed by a sense of comfort and satisfaction. I opened a newspaper that I'd bought at the airport and started reading the coverage of the bombing, to see if there was anything I'd missed. One story grabbed my attention. It quoted US officials naming the suspected mastermind behind the attack as one Osama bin Laden.

SECOND BASE

When the call came at around 13.50 on 11 September 2001, I was at my desk in the office in the middle of my irregular ritual of scrawling out late-payment cheques, silently cursing a credit card company. Sitting next to me was my new boss Alastair, who had just slammed down the phone. I turned my head towards him to see what was up. He said his girlfriend had just got a call from a friend in the States telling her that an aircraft had crashed into one of the twin towers of the World Trade Center. We stared wide-eyed at each other for a second, then both turned to our computer screens to start finding out more.

I couldn't see anything on the Press Association news wire, but when I refreshed the screen I saw a one-liner that had just come in headed '1 US PLANE'. Eyewitnesses had reported seeing a 'small jetliner' crash into the south tower of the World Trade Center, and there had apparently been an explosion.

President George W. Bush later remarked that his first reaction on hearing the news was to think, 'That's one hell of a bad pilot', and that's more or less what I was thinking at the time: that it was a terrible accident. But those words 'small jetliner' leapt out at me, because they hinted at something more than just a wayward executive jet clipping the corner of one of the towers, which was the consensus scenario among those around me at this early stage.

There was no TV in the office. My request to buy one had been turned down by the publisher a few weeks earlier. At the time I was working as the news editor on an Internet start-up venture with EMAP, one of Europe's largest publishing groups. The ambitious plan was to create an online hub for the construction industry across the globe and to monopolise this new market. The publisher was new to the business and I explained to him that every news desk has a TV and we needed one, but he turned me down on the grounds of cost. I was absolutely bloody furious about it, and his already low credibility rating with me dropped close to zero.

The operation was being funded to the tune of around £10 million and there wasn't a shortage of cash. I was spending something like £250,000 on news content; but the bulk of the money seemed to be going on the inflated salaries of the directors and general managers, whose jobs appeared to consist largely of chairing numerous interminable meetings. Yet the purchase of a small TV was deemed to be an unjust extravagance. It was for these kinds of reasons that, among the journalists, it was said that EMAP stood for Every Manager's A Prick. Too many people had been sniggering at that and a decision was made somewhere to try to revise history by claiming that it stood for Every Meeting's A Party. The TV debacle (and others) proved to me that the former was nearer to the truth.

Anyway, the fact remained that we were in the dark while something deeply ominous was occurring. The simple solution would have been to have wandered into one of the magazine offices on one of the four floors above us, but I'd have been taking my life in my hands. We were part of a new, separate division called EMAP Digital, which had been set up to lever the magazine brands online and to fast-track Internet-related projects. That meant that the print teams had no real say in how their brands were used by the new online upstarts. Each side despised the other, leading to a state of cold war in the building, and I was on the losing side. The dotcom bubble had started to deflate a few months previously and we all secretly knew that the traditionalists were going to win out eventually, even if this was never spoken of.

News of the crash had spread around the office in seconds, and everyone was checking websites for more information. Then the shocker came. I checked the PA feed and there was another one-line story saying that a second aircraft had crashed into the other tower. I told Alastair, and a look of incredulity spread across his face.

'Terrorists,' was all I could say. It seemed to me to be the only logical explanation, although there was nothing on the wires yet to suggest that. It was an instinctive response.

After that, it was all hands to the pump. In the absence of a TV, we all started to search the Net for streaming video feeds and live pictures – and everyone in the world with an Internet connection was doing the same, it appeared. All the major news sites had crashed. Nothing but error messages saying 'page cannot be displayed' appeared, causing the welling up of the deepest stomach-clamping frustration. The Internet let us down spectacularly just when we needed it, and this eroded much of the remaining professional faith I'd had in the medium.

There followed around ten minutes of a news blackout with text-only one-liners coming in over the wires and nothing else: no BBC, CNN or any pictures at all. Despite all the latest equipment and the fastest network connections that anyone could wish for, we were completely cut off inside the modern offices of a major publishing company in central London. It was hugely ironic and deeply embarrassing, humiliating even. Going elsewhere in the building to find out what was going on would be an admission of defeat: I wanted the Internet to work, goddammit.

Finally, the CNN website came back up with an emergency page, and around 30 of us gathered around a single computer monitor where one of the marketing guys had managed to connect to a decent-quality video stream. At last, there they were: two towering infernos this time, although the images were fuzzy and jerky at full-screen resolution. We all stood staring in shocked silence, and there was no collective destruction revelry this time around.

'Who could have done this?' one of the girls in the office finally wondered out loud.

'Osama bin Laden,' I replied, and became aware that all heads had turned towards me.

'Who's he?' she asked.

'He's, er, a Saudi billionaire who leads a terrorist group that supports the Palestinians,' was just about all I could dredge up by way of a quick soundbite.

'The Palestinians! I knew it!' she said, and wandered off, mumbling angrily to herself. I was momentarily puzzled by the ferocity of her response, until I remembered she was Jewish.

A Palestinian group, the Popular Democratic Front for the Liberation of Palestine (PDFLP), claimed responsibility for the attacks later in the day, and then quickly retracted it. But I knew this had to be the work of bin Laden, and, sure enough, he was officially declared the prime suspect a few hours later. He'd been a passing interest of mine since the 1993 WTC bombing and I'd always lingered to read articles about him, as I was fascinated by his riches-to-rags story and the motivations for his supreme single-mindedness. I knew bin Laden had moved from Sudan to Afghanistan, and that his family were involved in the construction business. The Americans had launched a cruise missile attack against him in Afghanistan after the bombings of two of their embassies in east Africa in 1998, but they'd missed him by a couple of hours – these kinds of facts now started to pop into my head.

Whilst I was arguing that this was probably the biggest news story in history, and someone else was sticking doggedly to his line that it didn't eclipse the death of Princess Diana, the south tower of the World Trade Center collapsed. Alastair shouted the news across the office, and we watched blurry images being beamed from a helicopter showing a huge dust cloud spreading out over the city.

It was completely unexpected. Unlike in 1993 – and probably because of 1993 – I hadn't really thought about the possibility of the towers collapsing until a couple of minutes beforehand, when I overheard two of the directors discussing what might happen. The managing director was adamant that they wouldn't topple; the chief technical officer wasn't so sure and was talking about the 1968 Ronan Point tower block collapse in London as a case in point.

It was the first time in my career that the news was moving too quickly for effective human comprehension, and I think this was the cause of the infamous 'shock period' which gripped the profession that afternoon, bringing newsrooms to a momentary standstill as everyone pondered the same questions: 'Just what the hell is going on here and what will be the consequences?'

I could almost feel my brain throbbing from the strain of trying to assemble the big picture using each little snippet of news coming in over the wires: fighters scrambled, hundreds of airliners still airborne, President whisked to secret location, hijacked airliner searching out Air Force One, suspected car bomb explodes outside the US State Department building in Washington DC (not true, it later transpired), more suspected truck bombs, plane crashes into Pentagon, another plane crashes into a field in Pennsylvania, all US Navy ships ordered to sea, DEFCON 2 declared, US airspace closed, UK airspace closed, 50,000 people possibly dead – all in quick succession, though not necessarily in that order.

The remainder of the afternoon was spent working flat out to update the news on the websites and discussing special coverage in the days to follow. All I wanted, though, was to get home to watch the day's events in high resolution. Home was definitely where I wanted to be – it was like a beacon, an odd all-pervading longing that I couldn't shake off.

Perhaps this was a hangover from growing up during the Cold War in the 1980s, when nuclear annihilation was a very real and constant possibility. We were young kids, and we'd often discuss in the playground what we'd do if the sirens wailed the three-minute warning. We all knew we had to look away, resisting the temptation to stare directly at the flashes, in order to avoid being blinded, but we also knew that the Royal Small Arms Factory was just a few miles away and that it was bound to be high up on the Soviets' target list. It was where Barnes Wallis's dam-busting bouncing bomb had been developed during the Second World War. We'd walk to school most mornings accompanied by the distant sound of heavy-calibre machine guns being tested.

We were doomed by our close proximity to that place, we agreed: there would be no hope of escape from the massive fireball. We'd debate whether it would be feasible to run home and arrive in time to be with the family when the attack came. I lived literally at the bottom of the road, but it was nearly a mile long. I estimated that it'd be touch and go as to whether I could make it home in time, even at full pelt without my schoolbag, but that was my plan, with or without functioning eyeballs.

I left the office for a breather and paused to spark up a cigarette. I heard a whining noise and looked up to see an aircraft flying low overhead. I watched it for a while and noticed that several other people waiting at bus stops were doing the same. There were no indications of panic; just people looking for any signs that something was not quite right. It occurred to me that, at the height of the crisis a few hours earlier, there had been very little concern that targets in the UK might also be hit. Sure, buildings in Canary Wharf in London's Docklands, home to Europe's second-highest skyscraper, were evacuated (voluntarily by the tenants, the owner of the development was quick to point out), but no one thought it was under serious threat. I knew people who were working there at the time, but I didn't see that there were any grounds for calling them and telling them to get out.

SECOND BASE

Out in public, there was a palpable air of gloom rather than panic. As I walked towards the Tube station at the end of a long day, I started regretting not seeing the family as much as I could have done and I seriously wondered about an abrupt change of career. I don't know why, but many of my friends were thinking along the same lines. There was a similar downbeat public air on the train, more pronounced than usual – rows and rows of unsmiling faces interspersed with evening newspaper front pages splashed with large blue and orange images of those moments of impact.

Perhaps it was the unconscious expression of a population who'd been forced to face the fact that their high hopes for a more peaceful future at the start of the new millennium had now been cruelly dashed. It was certainly a time of tribulation that caused feelings of great confusion. It was on the way home from work that I decided that I would quit my job in favour of investigating this new terrorist phenomenon.

I was glued to the full coverage on the TV for the rest of the evening. As well as the two planes that we'd seen crash into the World Trade Center, another two aircraft had been hijacked. One had crashed into the Pentagon killing 125 people in the building and the 59 passengers and crew on the plane, while the other had crashed in a field in Pennsylvania. This had clearly been a major, carefully orchestrated series of attacks that had left the world's greatest superpower looking vulnerable and exposed.

One of the few moments of levity, for me anyway, was the sight of Yasser Arafat donating blood for the rescue effort inside his emergency bunker, in a feverish 'Honestly – nothing to do with me. No cruise missiles, please, Mr President' kind of fashion. Perhaps he was worried that the retracted PDFLP statement would put him in the frame when the predicted US backlash came. Many people were half-expecting bin Laden's adopted home country, Afghanistan, to be wiped off the map in a nuclear strike. Thankfully, the British Prime Minister Tony Blair was reportedly urging the Americans in private to hold off from making any rash decisions.

The Foreign Secretary, Robin Cook, issued a statement saying something like 'history changed today', and that resonated with the feelings I had. The most poignant news of the day was reports that some people trapped under the rubble were using mobile phones to call for rescue and to speak to their families for the last time.

Speakers at a rally staged by militant Islamists outside Finsbury Park mosque in north London that evening, who no doubt included followers of the radical cleric Abu Hamza, were reportedly cracking gags and belly-laughing about yuppies flying out of windows. They were very much the exception: the public mood degenerated into the People's Depression over the couple of days that followed. I think everyone knew that there would be major ramifications as a result of those unprecedented events, and we were now entering dark and uncharted territory.

I trudged on at work in the days that followed, but I'd really lost all interest in what I was doing. It seemed to me like I was wasting my time and talents by, basically, feeding words into a computerised monster with an insatiable appetite. It was like having to constantly shovel coal into a steam-engine boiler, and I was flagging. I wanted the operation to be the best of its type, and it was, but the high-maintenance nature of the dreadful digital beast that I'd created became starkly apparent to me. To my colleagues, it was business as usual, but it seemed to me that the strength of gravity had doubled overnight. I was doing menial tasks for inflated wages, as I saw it, and there was no getting away from it.

When I was a reporter, this would have been a time of high excitement: foreign trips in the offing, a busy atmosphere on the news desk, discussions about coverage and tactics to keep the competition at bay. I was cut off from all of that as a digital new media person. I deeply craved the excitement and adrenalin rush of being at the centre of great journalistic endeavours, but there I was, trapped in an office that was as quiet as a public reference library and sticking to the clockwork schedule of machine-feeding and listening to Internet-bollocks in meetings.

Funding was now drying up for our online venture and we were probably heading for redundancy anyhow, I figured. I had taken on the job knowing that it would probably end on a sour note, but I judged that there'd be a couple of years of plain sailing at least. All sane people who were caught up in the dotcom boom knew in their hearts that it wouldn't last for long, if they were absolutely honest with themselves. There had already been a round of heavy cuts and the managers were in the habit of talking in hushed voices and holding increasingly frequent secret meetings.

SECOND BASE

The day after the hijackings, the US government claimed there had been no intelligence to suggest that the country was about to be attacked, although this turned out to be false in the weeks and months that followed. Bush came in for a lot of media flak for flying around the US in Air Force One in the aftermath of the attacks instead of returning straight away to Washington, and he was lampooned in newspapers on both sides of the Atlantic as an imbecilic coward on the run. Bush's political strategist Karl Rove claimed that the Secret Service believed that the terrorists had had access to special presidential communications codes and they were seeking out Air Force One on the day, although that was widely derided in the media as a cover story.

On 13 September, the blame was officially pinned on al-Qaeda by the White House, and the FBI released a list of 18 hijackers, which was revised to 19 in a matter of hours. There were many big questions being asked about the attacks in the days that followed, and top of everyone's list seemed to be: was Flight 93, the plane that crashed in a field near Pittsburgh, shot down?

The official FBI line was that no firm evidence had surfaced to suggest this, which seemed like an odd thing to say. It made it sound like the Air Force wasn't telling the public everything it knew. The passenger lists for the doomed flights were also released that day and the numbers didn't tally, because it appeared that the passenger lists didn't contain the names of the hijackers. Debris from Flight 93 had been found eight miles away from the crash site, which would suggest a mid-air break-up. This formed the kernel of a thought in my mind that maybe there was a cover-up here. That would make perfect sense, in a perverted way. No government was going to readily admit to blasting 45 innocent citizens into freefalling meat chunks.

The FBI announced that the black box flight recorders from this plane had been recovered on 13 September, and it was suggested that a bomb might have detonated on board, although this was retracted days later. There was a disquieting secrecy and lack of clarity about the American government's responses to questions posed, which I attributed to the bent of politicians and their servants towards blame evasion. Others were less charitable and sensed that the spin doctors were trying to divert attention away from something altogether more sinister. People suspected that the truth was being deliberately concealed, and theories soon started to emerge.

The basic facts were being revealed too slowly, and each morsel of information left me wanting much more. I was becoming hooked, especially when the FBI broke the news that some of the hijackers had received flight training in the US. I made a mental note that it might be well worth taking a closer look at the world of US flight schools and investigating allegations of Central Intelligence Agency 'Air America' type links with some of them.

On 14 September, Congress granted Bush carte blanche to take military action against the aggressors, and it was clear that anything could happen from now on in. Nuking bin Laden seemed to be on the agenda as an outside bet, but I was sure that sanity would prevail. Besides, they first had to locate this phantom menace.

In August 1998, bin Laden had easily evaded an attack involving 75 cruise missiles, having been tipped off about the attack hours earlier by Pakistan's intelligence service, the ISI. Another opportunity was missed in 2000, when he was caught on the camera of an armed Predator drone as he was walking across a road towards a mosque. The images showed that his bodyguards had sealed off all the roads surrounding the mosque to form a protective cordon around their leader, but the target was lost while officials in various departments argued over whether to open fire on him. He melted away once more.

Faced with a lack of knowledge about his exact whereabouts, it was hard to see how a quick and dirty operation could be launched against him now, unless an order was given to lay down a chain of multi-megaton 'city-busters' in southern Afghanistan in blunderbuss fashion, in the hope that he'd be caught in an atomic fireball somewhere along the line. Doing something like that would be madness. The fact that there hadn't been a conventional cruise missile attack against bin Laden in the early days after the 11 September attacks to me seemed to speak volumes about the presumed paucity of US intelligence in the area.

Bush announced the start of the 'war on terrorism' nine days after the attacks on New York and Washington, telling us all that, 'Either you are with us, or you are with the terrorists.' This angered me, as well as many others, because a foreign leader was effectively demanding that I pledge allegiance to him. With Bush, it was too much to stomach, though there followed a period of weeks during which I noticed that people were reluctant to criticise the President.

Friends who had once been forthcoming about his shortcomings felt uncomfortable talking about the situation, in case any dissent was construed as sympathy for al-Qaeda. I was actually warned to keep quiet when I was expressing views on the audaciousness of the 11 September attacks in the office. Bush had imposed a form of enforced censorship on us from afar. He also used the speech to issue an ultimatum to the Taliban and demanded that they hand over al-Qaeda leaders hiding in Afghanistan.

The waters were getting dirtier by the hour when it was reported that bin Laden had agreed to stand trial for the 11 September attacks. Islamic leaders had apparently brokered a deal with him and the Taliban leader Mullah Omar, which would have seen bin Laden held under house arrest in Peshawar before defending himself before an international tribunal. It seemed like just a delaying tactic, but Pakistan president General Pervez Musharraf scuppered the plan by saying that he couldn't guarantee the safety of the al-Qaeda leader.

After a frenetic couple of news weeks, the crescendo of news and work started to ease, as the US started gearing up for a war in Afghanistan. The Taliban were dragging their feet, and it gradually became apparent that they weren't going to hand over bin Laden, so conflict seemed to be inevitable. The headlines were dominated by facts that were slowly emerging from the investigation into 11 September, which largely focused on the movements of the hijackers in the US prior to the hijackings. There was also feverish speculation over whether a nation state was in cahoots with bin Laden, because many commentators felt that such an operation was something too big to be masterminded by a man living in a cave in Afghanistan.

Then, three days after White House Chief of Staff Andy Card had warned about the dangers posed by terrorists armed with biological weapons, the anthrax letters hit.

The first case of infection appeared in Florida on 4 October, and the letters continued to be received until 19 October. Five people died and there were eleven infections in total. Although the letters appeared to be written by a Muslim extremist, there were many puzzling anomalies. For a start, the targets that were chosen – Democratic politicians and media organisations – appeared to have been deliberately selected to galvanise opposition to al-Qaeda. Various theories were put forward, including one that the letters were part of a secret US military exercise that had gone wrong. Other suggestions were that they were parting letters from the 11 September hijackers or other fundamentalist terrorists, or that they had been sent by a lone domestic nutter.

As war loomed, obvious signs of censorship were creeping into the news coverage. The untrained eye wouldn't have noticed anything unusual, but I was seeing too many stories based on spin-doctor briefings and official rhetoric instead of facts and genuine insights. For example, there were quotes from unnamed sources theorising that Saddam Hussein must have been involved in the planning of the attacks. By and large, the mainstream media had bought into the official version of events.

I was becoming increasingly frustrated, as I knew I could do far better than the lame stuff I was reading. I was trying to work out when I should hand in my resignation, but I was wary of giving up the day job too hastily and throwing away a guaranteed monthly income. So, I decided to do both jobs at the same time and see what happened. I first needed to test the theory that I could come up with stories and sell enough of them to make a living as an independent journalist covering terrorism. I knew this meant the end of any spare time: coming home from work and continuing long into the early hours of the following morning, then getting up and going into the office after too little sleep. But I was driven to do it.

The only story in town at the time was the location of bin Laden, so I decided to have a crack at that one first. It was as good a place to start as any.

I'd already noodled my way around the Net looking for background on him for the day job, and I was aware that his father owned a major construction company in Saudi Arabia. I hadn't appreciated just exactly how large the group was, however. It seemed to have had a hand in every major construction project in the kingdom and had very close ties to the ruling royal family. But I could see that this was going to be a dead-end line of enquiry. Osama hadn't worked for the company for years, and the family had disowned him when he was stripped of his Saudi citizenship and his bank accounts were frozen in 1994. He was the black sheep of the family.

I took advantage of lulls during the day to do some more research, using the Internet to plunge into a strange new world of Arabic,

Islamic customs and Koranic verses. It was very confusing at first, and clearly I was going to have to put myself through a crash course in Islam if I was to make significant headway.

I started to feel a little more urgency when bin Laden's first video statement was broadcast on Al-Jazeera late on Sunday, 7 October, after the first US and UK air strikes were launched against Afghanistan. Dressed in a camouflage jacket against a background of what looked like a cave with grey rock formations, he claimed that the 11 September attacks were a punishment from God. The US was launching a 'war on Islam', and every Muslim must prepare for the fight ahead.

This first bin Laden video statement post-11 September received saturation media coverage of the kind that any Western political leader would kill for. The spin doctors had tried putting the frighteners on the media by claiming that they'd be aiding the terrorists by broadcasting it. Intelligence analysts suspected that there were secret messages contained in these addresses, and there was all sorts of speculation about the possible hidden meanings in the kind of watch he was wearing, the position of his hands, how he handled the microphone, the patterns on his camouflage jacket, finger tremors and even suggestive eye movements. Nothing stood up to serious examination, however, and the video was broadcast across the globe.

Though it might have seemed completely crazy, I decided to attempt to trace the location of bin Laden by using high-tech methods to elicit leads from tribes of people who lived in near palaeolithic conditions in a hostile and impossibly mountainous environment. I figured that there might be a chance of an early breakthrough if I talked to ex-pat Afghanis who spoke English and who might have received recent news and information from relatives inside the country.

Researching stories using email and web sources can compress the time it takes to find leads by factors of 100 to 1,000 compared to traditional methods, so it seemed that I could cover a vast amount of ground this way, learning on the job and zigzagging towards promising targets. I started the ball rolling in what would be a big experiment.

I needn't have worried about the feasibility of this project, however, because it took me less than one hour to locate al-Qaeda's mastermind.

Before the end of my lunch break, I'd homed in on a website that was full of pictures of village life in Afghanistan. I sensed that I'd arrived somewhere significant, because many of the images showed black-turbaned and armed Taliban guarding access to a road. I starting feeling a 'eureka moment' coming on when I saw a picture gallery entitled 'Ben Ladin's Home'.

The images started to load, and the first thing I saw was a concrete box structure set into the side of a mountain, with a long horizontal slit along the second storey – which could be for a machine-gun nest, I thought – then there were shots taken inside tunnels and storage areas that looked like they were inside the bunker structure. One of the captions said that this was where bin Laden hid to escape from the Russians during the Afghan–Soviet war during the 1980s. The site appeared to be commemorating the scene of a famous event.

I'd recently read an interview that the journalist Robert Fisk had conducted with bin Laden when he was in Sudan in 1996 and recalled that he'd said that on one occasion the Russians had come within a whisker of capturing him in Afghanistan:

> Once I was only 30 metres from the Russians, and they were trying to capture me. I was under bombardment, but I was so peaceful in my heart that I fell asleep. This experience has been written about in our earliest books.

There seemed to be a strong possibility that the pictures I was looking at might be of that very place. Could bin Laden have returned there to evade the Americans? A strong tingling throb in the gut told me that I needed to contact the website operator, which would have to be done carefully. A sudden email demanding that he disclose what he knew about the world's most wanted man would very likely spook him into silence.

The website owner and my would-be source was a Pashtun, a people numbering 15 million who live largely in a network of tribal groups occupying a vast area either side of the border between Afghanistan and Pakistan, though he was now living in the US. The Pashtuns have a reputation for preferring a stricter form of Islam than most, although each group has its own idiosyncrasies, leading to a mind-bogglingly complex web of diplomatic relations between tribal elders. I knew that the Taliban leadership was largely comprised of Pashtuns, and realised I would have to tread very carefully here.

A bit of surfing quickly unearthed some very curious background information. There are claims that the Pashtuns may be descendants of one of the ten 'lost tribes of Israel' – the Tribe of Benjamin – that disappeared from the Middle East in 772 BCE after the Assyrian occupation, as some of their tribal customs are remarkably similar to Jewish rituals: circumcision of male infants, strict dietary rules and so on.

I was flabbergasted at the irony of this: the Taliban a lost tribe of Israel? It was too much to take. Then I came across a message in an Afghan discussion forum that brought a smile to my face, where a Pashtun explained that, whilst there might be some truth in this, the people should at least be accorded credit for realising the error of their ways by converting to Islam many centuries ago.

My initial approach to my source was to say that I was a journalist writing a general piece about life for ordinary Afghans living in Paktia province and ask a few vague and inoffensive questions about the place. Sure enough, I got an encouraging response, and he sounded like a very switched-on and likeable guy. He recalled making the arduous ten-hour trip to Kabul across the mountains on unpaved tracks and roads after his last visit to his home village and was keen to tell me that Western media coverage was focusing too much on the negative aspects of the country and that most women in Paktia didn't wear the *burka*. 'Sincere, simple and honest' is the way he described his people. He even sent me a link to a recording of the local music, to give me more of a flavour of the place. I played one of them, and the shrieking of the singer and the distorted high-pitched wail of fiddles had the same effect as hearing fingernails scraping across a blackboard, but I told him that it was wonderful to hear the sound of his beautiful homeland. The scenery was spectacular, and I'm not one to be disrespectful about local customs; I'm sure my music would have seemed weird and tuneless to him.

After we had exchanged such niceties, I decided to get down to business. The first of his pictures showed what looked like a group of Taliban guards at the entrance to the concrete structure, which appeared to be connected to a series of tunnels, so I thought I'd start with this.

He told me that he made the trip only last year, so the photographs were fairly recent.

ND: What were the Taliban like?

P: Taliban were very friendly. That's why I went back to Afghanistan after 20 years, as I was able to see my homeland after so long. I think if the Northern Alliance comes back then I am afraid I will never go back.

   If I did, they will kill me, or put nails in my head, or cut my tongue. That's what they do. They massacred 4,000 Taliban a few years ago, not to mention rape, ethnic cleansing and many other things.

ND: Do you know what those tunnels were used for?

P: Oh, yeah, those caves. They were made during the Russian invasion.

ND: What was it like inside?

P: I went into one tunnel and it was not very long, but long enough, I guess, a little less than one kilometre, or maybe 500m. I don't know exactly, it was too dark and I was afraid of the weapons around me.

   Just beside the tunnel was a weapon depot, where you can see the bags used in the war, and beside the depot was a hospital. This depot and hospital helped the Afghan people a lot during the Russian invasion.

I followed up with some questions about bin Laden's connections to the place, but when I asked if I could use his pictures with my article, he started to clam up.

He said he knew nothing of bin Laden and that I could use the pictures only if what I wrote was 'pro-Afghanistan'.

'My brother told me that America attacked those depots, tunnels and the hospital a few days ago,' he added.

That was just about all he could tell me.

The pictures alone were a unique selling point, because, as far as I could make out, they were the only recent pictures of one of these fabled Afghan Mujahideen mountain tunnel complexes. I knew from the cuttings that that area south of Kabul was full of tunnels that had been built using heavy construction equipment procured by bin Laden.

But better was to come. As I was lashing together an article, on 19 October a report came over the wires saying that an American geologist, Professor Jack Shroder of the University of Nebraska at Omaha, had studied the rock formations in the background of the bin Laden video statement and had positively identified the location as . . . Paktia. He'd worked inside Afghanistan during the late '70s as part of a project to produce the first atlas of the country but had been expelled in a row over spying. Professor Shroder said that the sandstone formations seen behind bin Laden were unique to the region, and he'd recognised the location immediately.

There was no doubt in his mind. He recalled how he was watching a TV news report about the video: 'I turned to my wife and told her "I know where he is",' he said. I sent him an email and asked if he had any pictures that I could use, but he said that the State Department and the FBI had asked him not to release any. I pored over the video and the bunker images from the website time and time again to make sure in my own mind that they matched, and there was no doubt about it. The colour of the rock, the size of the beds and the inclination of the strata looked the same.

This unexpected apparent confirmation now made my own story and the pictures I had found very hot property, although I felt a little aggrieved that Professor Shroder had stolen a bit of my thunder. I now had a positive location for bin Laden at the time that he must have recorded the video statement that was broadcast on Al-Jazeera on the day of the launch of American and British air strikes against Afghanistan, although it felt wrong that it had taken so little time to complete the task. I was suspicious that I'd made a monumental error somewhere along the way, and I sifted carefully through my notes and the source materials several times. Eventually I concluded that it was indeed a watertight world exclusive.

I took my time writing the story, as I wanted to do justice to it. And then, as I was polishing the copy a couple of days later, a BBC Monitoring report added another layer to the story. Three Russian-made Taliban helicopter gunships had taken off from Paktia and landed just over the border in Pakistan. Though it is impossible to confirm that bin Laden was among them, it looked like some very important people were on the move . . .

I'd been mulling over which paper I should sell the story to and who I should contact first, and it was a difficult task. There was a huge range of possibilities and therein lies one of the main skills of a freelance journalist: matching the right story with the right paper. But you have to dig even deeper than that and identify which person working on a particular title is likely to be the most responsive.

I eventually opted for the *Daily Mirror* and phoned the news desk on my mobile whilst I was out of the office having a cigarette. I got through and explained the basics of the story. The news editor, Conor Hanna, said he was certainly interested, and he asked me to email the details to him. I was back in the office five minutes later, and I sent him the copy I'd prepared the night before, along with the images, using a Web-based email account.

The subject line read: 'INSIDE BIN LADEN'S MOUNTAIN HIDEOUT – EXCLUSIVE PICTURES'. I went with an angle declaring that when an allied search-and-destroy mission finally catches up with bin Laden, then the setting for the final shoot-out may look like this.

He called me back a few minutes later.

'This is very interesting,' he said, slowly, with gravity, and I proceeded to reel off the background to the story.

'So, you're telling me that this guy just walked into a bin Laden base and wandered about?' was his slightly incredulous summation. It did seem unlikely, on the face of it, to be fair.

'Well, yes, exactly,' I responded, before going on to explain that the contact was a member of a Pashtun tribe, the locals were Taliban-friendly and giving him some more detailed background. I explained the email correspondence we'd been exchanging, and he seemed satisfied after this. He said that the story was a front-page contender, and he'd set the wheels in motion. I was off to a dream start. Conor was keen that I should stay in touch and alert him to any similar stories that might come my way. 'Keep 'em coming,' he said.

The news broke on 30 October 2001, the day before publication, that the US had started round-the-clock bombing of a suspected bin Laden tunnel complex in Paktia in a week-long operation aimed at collapsing one side of a mountain and blocking all the entrances. It sounded like the same place, even though they'd raided it once already. The tunnels were guarded and stocked with weapons, so this was not a derelict and deserted installation from the Soviet era; it was being used, now.

It was an odd coincidence and I started to wonder whether the attacks had anything to do with my email exchanges. I was well aware that the joint US/UK Project Echelon eavesdropping operation, based at Menwith Hill in Yorkshire, is capable of monitoring and analysing all electronic communications throughout the world. All UK communications are supposedly piped directly into that place for analysis. Batteries of supercomputers scan for certain patterns of key words and other criteria, according to constantly updated dictionaries of suspects and suspicious characteristics. It seemed possible that my email conversations about 'bin Laden', 'bombs', and 'secret tunnels' had set off the alarm bells somewhere. I'll never know but surely the combined efforts of the West's intelligence agencies must mean that they were several steps ahead of me. If not, then we're in deep trouble, I thought. They shouldn't be spying on journalists to draw up target lists when they've got budgets running into the billions and more spy satellites than you can shake a Kalashnikov at.

Lunchtimes now took on a new meaning, which centred less on eating and more on firing off salvos of email queries and lists of questions. The time difference meant that contacts in the States would receive them first thing in the morning, and I'd harvest quotes from the replies that would be waiting for me when I got home in the evening to start on my second job.

I was scouring through vast amounts of background material and getting up to speed on all aspects of the terrorism business. It was a tough subject to get a grip on because it's so vast, but I was enjoying a lot of interesting reading. One of the first things that got me excited was the discovery that the FBI knew all about the planning for the 1993 WTC truck bombing – and the agency allowed the attack to happen. It was a monumental cock-up, to say the very least.

I could hardly believe what I was reading. Ten men were brought to trial for plotting to bomb landmark structures in New York City, and it was revealed that the bomb-maker within the al-Qaeda cell, a former Egyptian army lieutenant-colonel called Emad Salem, had been paid $1 million to infiltrate a group of Muslim extremists and become an FBI informant. The group, including the Egyptian cleric Omar Abdel Rahman, had been planning to bomb the United Nations, the FBI's New York headquarters, plus a number of bridges and tunnels.

Later, during a second trial of four people, it emerged that the FBI knew that an attack on the World Trade Center was being prepared. On tapes played in court, Salem and an FBI agent named John Anticev discussed how they were going to replace the explosives with some harmless powder before the attack took place. However, the plan was called off by an unnamed FBI supervisor, for reasons that have never been made clear. The bungle, if it can be called that, led to the deaths of six innocent people, hundreds of injuries and around half a billion dollars' worth of damage.

The root of the confusion seems to have involved a state of rivalry that existed between the Washington and New York offices of the FBI. I listened to a tape recording of a telephone conversation between the bomber and his FBI handler in which they were arguing over the price of building the bomb. Salem was upset that his expenses claim for the bomb materials appeared to be being questioned, and he considered making an official complaint about the whole affair to FBI headquarters in Washington.

'Everything was submitted with a receipt and now it is questionable,' he complains.

'No, it's not questionable, it's like a bit out of [the] ordinary,' replies agent Anticev.

Salem retorts: 'I don't think it was, if that's what you think, it's fine, but I don't think that, because we had already started building the bomb which went off in the World Trade Center. It was built . . . by supervision from the Bureau and the DA, and we was all informed about it and we know that the bomb started to be built. By whom? By your confidential informant. What a wonderful great case!'

Anticev talked him out of making a complaint. Another FBI agent, named as Nancy Floyd, said the FBI's New York office would 'get their butts chewed' if Salem contacted Washington.

It sounded completely farcical, although the consequences could have been much more horrific. The full scope of the plans for that day was not revealed until 1998, when documents found on the computer of an al-Qaeda operative, Ramzi Yousef, came to light.

He'd fled to Pakistan after the 1993 bombing, travelling on an Iraqi passport, and he was eventually captured in 1995 and extradited to the US, where he was sentenced to 240 years in solitary confinement. During the trial, it emerged that the full plan had been to fell one of the twin towers on to the other, thereby causing both of them to collapse. The bomb also contained cyanide. The terrorists hoped to kill 250,000 people in the cloud of poisonous gas that would envelop the city. Luckily, however, the bomb lacked the power needed to cause such fearsome damage, but it was powerful enough to incinerate the cyanide. I was stunned when I discovered this, because it meant that I'd been at the scene of probably the first attempt by terrorists to attack the US with a genuine weapon of mass destruction (WMD) all those years earlier. I replayed all those events in my head for a moment, just to see if I had had any inkling of such a situation.

The one thing was that there had been a faint whiff of sulphurous bleach about the place, but not the smell of bitter almonds that is said to characterise cyanide. I wasn't sick afterwards, as far as I can recall. Perhaps what I actually detected was decontamination chemicals.

ANTHRAX FAXES

My success with the *Mirror* had proved a point: it looked like it could be entirely feasible to cut myself adrift and operate successfully as an independent. Being unencumbered by silly corporate nonsense was an added attraction. I had been a freelance operator before joining the company, but the difference this time was that I'd be selling to national newspapers, rather than magazines. It's a far more daunting prospect. Pitching to the news desks of daily papers is not something to be done lightly; amateurs can get chewed up and spat out if they are not very careful.

Despite my growing confidence, however, I decided to err on the side of caution and opted to continue to receive the regular pay packets while continuing with my terrorism freelancing experiment, for a few months at least – long enough for me to get a few more exclusives under my belt and feel a bit more comfortable about going solo.

The tunnels story made me wonder what else was out there on the Internet waiting for me to find. I knew I'd have to be quick about it, as it was likely that incriminating material was being deleted at a rate of knots now that al-Qaeda was in the full glare of the media spotlight. I knew that some prominent Palestinian militants made vigorous efforts to get mentions of their names removed from websites wherever possible, to minimise the amount of open-source intelligence available to the authorities in the West, and it seemed safe to assume that al-Qaeda would be doing likewise.

Sure enough, I was getting a fair few error messages while chasing promising leads. The militants, prior to 11 September, had been quite liberal about promoting their message, although I noticed the volume appeared to decrease markedly around June.

From the sites that were still available I learned that the chief goal of bin Laden and his supporters appeared to be nothing less than ensuring that the entire world was governed according to Koranic *sharia* law, under which the church and the state are as one. Sharia law derives from a strict fundamentalist interpretation of the Koran and the teachings of the Prophet Mohammed. Sharia courts are known for imposing draconian punishments for certain crimes, like amputating the hands of people found guilty of theft. The Taliban in Afghanistan, who were now coming under ground assault from the US-led Coalition and their Northern Alliance allies, were lauded by bin Laden as the guardians of the only truly Islamic nation on earth because of their strict adherence to the Islamic code of law.

I had to marvel at their sheer naked ambition: converting the world's population to Islam. Why stop there? What about outer space? These were facetious thoughts, I assumed, but I nearly fell off my chair when I read about a group of Russian Muslims that had already drawn up plans for the first mosque on the moon.

The ideal location had already been selected: Malapert Mountain, 122 kilometres from the moon's south pole. It is over 5,000 metres high and enjoys near constant exposure to sunlight. Considerable thought had been given to methods of calculating the direction to Mecca from settlements further out in the asteroid belt and as far away as Saturn. But NASA had also marked it out as an ideal spot for a commercial space port.

Al-Qaeda and associated groups were concentrating on world domination first, however, and making powerful arguments about championing the cause of the ordinary Muslim. One of the issues they highlighted was oil. According to one pre-11 September pamphlet produced by an al-Qaeda-affiliated group, the US had 'robbed all Muslims' of precisely $36.96 trillion by exploiting oil interests in the Middle East. It went on to give a long and detailed breakdown of its calculations, claiming that this is why America is responsible for the crushing poverty that many Muslims endure.

By challenging the might of the US, it was no wonder that bin Laden was starting to be seen as a saviour figure in many parts of the globe. He'd also now proved in spectacular fashion that he could match rhetoric with decisive action. However, no one in the UK or elsewhere in the West was about to express the view that maybe he had a genuine gripe. Bin Laden was now public enemy number one, as was anybody believed to be supporting or harbouring him. I think it's fair to say that, as far as the vast majority of people were concerned, there was little sympathy for the Taliban and a general feeling the US had every right to do what it pleased in retaliation for 11 September.

There were therefore few Western objections to the war that had started in Afghanistan: no demonstrations in the streets, no clamour for negotiations at the United Nations – just an impatience to see the action get under way. There was a positive frisson about this new war, which was heightened by more than a soupçon of public curiosity about whether improved technology would mean that we'd see better battlefield images on the TV news than had been possible during the 1991 Gulf War.

I'd hesitate to call it another lucky strike, because I was actively seeking out al-Qaeda-related material. 'A bloody good find' is the way one editor described it, and I liked that. It was a Web discussion group with virtually nothing on it at first glance, even though there were 92 group members listed. Nothing much in the way of discussion was happening there, but it had the word 'Qaeda' in the group title, and I felt that it was worth stopping by to have a nose around for a while.

There were just a few messages in Arabic, which may as well have been written in code, as I had no quick means of translating them at this stage. I was just about to move on to other things, but then I clicked on to the latest message to check it, just for the sake of thoroughness. There was a short Arabic message there with an attachment that looked like a copy of a fax, judging by the jagged edges of the characters. It was in Arabic also, although there were four English words at the top of the page that immediately prompted my mental alarm bells to start clanging loudly: 'Secret Army for Justice'.

I desperately wanted to know what that fax said now, as I had a very strong inkling that it was important. I needed the services of a translator, although this was going to cost money, and I wondered for a moment whether it would be wise to part with hard-earned cash on the basis of little more than a hunch. This was bound to be a situation that would arise again in the future, and it could easily turn into a costly business if I couldn't recover my expenses. The other alternative would be to learn Arabic, but I just didn't have the time to spare, unless it could be done whilst I was asleep, and it didn't look like a language that was easy to learn.

After spending a lot of time scanning lists of translation services, I eventually settled for a company that said it worked for media organisations. It didn't sound like it was a huge operation so I hoped that the rates would be more reasonable than the larger outfits. Security was also an issue, as I didn't want to give away a huge story to an unscrupulous operator who would then take it to a newspaper himself. There was no way of knowing in advance, so it would be a gamble.

I opted to take the plunge and phoned the guy, Mohamed, and explained what I wanted. No problem at all, he said. Just email the site address and he'd reply with the results later in the day or first thing in the morning at the very latest. I sought some reassurance about confidentiality, and he told me that everything would be undertaken in complete secrecy. He'd worked for many media companies, and he knew the score. Then he demanded that I send him a cheque right away to cover the two hours of work that he estimated the job would take, based on my description, which made me a little suspicious. It was the first time I'd dealt with him, after all.

I kept my side of the bargain and posted a cheque to him, and then got on with other things, although it was difficult to concentrate. My mind kept drifting back to the fax, as I pondered what it might say. It appeared to be a statement of some kind, and I was itching to know the details. Then, towards the end of the day, I got a phone call.

'I thought I'd better ring you and warn you,' said Mohamed.

'You were right: it is out of the ordinary. It's a statement claiming responsibility for the 11 September attacks and the anthrax letters.'

Bull's-eye! This was far better than I'd hoped for; this was wild. He also made some interesting observations about the writing that only a native speaker could pick up on. It was perfect classical Arabic with no mistakes, and the way one word was written indicated that the author was an Egyptian. One character with two dots above it was only used in Egypt. Other grammatical indicators suggested that it had later been edited by a Jordanian or a Palestinian.

I was feeling jubilant and was already making mental plans to sell the story while I was still making notes on the phone, but what was it doing on a publicly accessible website, albeit in an obscure patch of the cyber-realm? The quality of the writing indicated that it wasn't some amateurish hoax or the work of a crank. Mohamed said the accompanying message explained that it was 'a release waiting for approval'.

'It looks very genuine to me,' he added.

Perhaps, for whatever reason, that approval had not been forthcoming and someone had simply forgotten to delete it, or perhaps that person no longer had access to a computer.

The person who posted it had signed off with the slogan: 'Death to America, death to Israel!' The logo at the top of the page might have some significance, Mohamed thought. It was a shield and sword design, and he felt that the direction in which the sword was pointing might have some covert meaning. The initials of the group, SAJ, in Arabic, translated as 'the continued cooing of the dove', and might be another clue to follow.

I thanked him very much, and he pre-empted my next query by reiterating that he would treat this matter as being in the strictest confidence. I needn't worry about him nicking the story.

It seemed that I was now handling a very hot potato. I started reading it carefully, over and over again, scouring every line to see what else I could derive from the body of the statement. It was a strange feeling of power: having a blockbuster piece of information on al-Qaeda sitting on my desk (face down), while life continued as normal all around me – the usual office chit-chat and everyone tip-tapping away, all unaware that their colleague was preparing to unleash a major exclusive on an unsuspecting world. I was flushed with a secret kind of pride.

I say al-Qaeda, but the statement claimed that the Secret Army was not directly connected with bin Laden's organisation, although this left open the possibility of indirect links of some kind. The full translation read:

THE FIRST COMMUNIQUÉ ISSUED BY THE SECRET ARMY FOR JUSTICE

The Secret Army for Justice declares its responsibility for the spread of anthrax in the United States of America. We are issuing this communiqué now that we have decided to address the whole world and inform it of the objectives of the Secret Army after the government of the United States has misunderstood the clear message sent to it on 11 September. It now seems that the US is still determined to use the same tactics which made it a hated entity plunged in a mentality of arrogance and hegemony.

The Secret Army declares its responsibility for the operation and continues its march on the road of the heroic martyrdom operation in New York, Washington and Pennsylvania. The Army announces in honour, glory and joy the death of the martyrs of Cell 15, headed by the leader brother Muhammad Atta, who sacrificed themselves after they had sacrificed time and money for the pride of the nation. May God bless the souls of the martyrs and open for them the doors of heaven.

Let it be known that the Secret Army for Justice is not affiliated with al-Qaeda and does not receive any direct instructions or support from Osama bin Laden. The Army works independently of al-Qaeda, uses different methods and tactics, and has specific objectives.

The Secret Army is a group of cells established around the world and aimed at directing painful strikes against the United States as a punishment for its support for Zionism in its violation and denials of the rights of the Palestinian people on their land. The operatives of the Secret Army shall not end until the US, which kills and tortures Palestinians via the Israelis, changes its stand. The spread of the anthrax operation and the operation of the Cell 15 brothers on 11 September are the beginning of more painful and wider operations in which the Secret Army shall preserve its right to use new weapons and tactics.

On the first anniversary of the uprising of the Palestinian people, in which an unarmed people face American planes and tanks, the Palestinian people have lost 750 martyrs and 2 billion dollars while the United States has lost 7,000 dead and 120 billion dollars, and the battle goes on.

God is the greatest. Praise be to him.

There were two possibilities as I saw it: this was an aborted attempt by al-Qaeda to deflect blame away from bin Laden and the organisation, or it was a disinformation effort by an intelligence agency that was never put into practice. In any case, this was the only written admission of responsibility for 11 September to emerge so far, and it had a concrete news value, whatever the motivations of the writer.

The claim that the US hadn't understood the message of 11 September was certainly redolent of al-Qaeda's recent phraseology, as was the warning about new weapons and tactics. In summary, al-Qaeda's message was that 11 September was a final reminder to America that it must withdraw from the Middle East or face more serious consequences. This theme has been maintained in even the most recent messages, such as the video that appeared on the Net in May 2004, showing the beheading of the US civilian Nick Berg in Iraq. This horrible act was supposedly carried out by the leader of the terror network's forces in Iraq, Abu Musab al-Zarqawi, to serve as a warning: get out and stay out. The message was reinforced by the kidnapping and subsequent beheading of another American, Paul Johnson, in Saudi Arabia one month later.

The Palestinian stuff was consistent too, but this was usually accompanied by a warning that US troops should be immediately extricated from the 'land of the two mosques': Saudi Arabia. Maybe its absence was due to the influence of the Jordanian/Palestinian editor. The name of the group was entirely new to me, but, again, consistent in style with the wide variety of names and monikers used by al-Qaeda.

These included: the Islamic Army, the Islamic Salvation Foundation, the Group for the Preservation of the Holy Sites, the Islamic Army for the Liberation of the Holy Places, and the World Islamic Front for Jihad against Jews and Crusaders. As far as I could see, al-Qaeda leaders rarely referred to the network as al-Qaeda. I also knew that bin Laden himself was seldom referred to by his real name; he was usually called 'Abu Abdullah' or 'the Sheikh'.

I was very concerned about lending credence to a hoax or an obvious piece of disinformation. Not only would it be professionally disastrous but it would also be completely unethical. It appeared to pass muster, however, although there were unresolved questions, certainly, and some of those questions would probably never be resolved.

Writing up the copy took some time, as I wanted to make sure that it was as accurate as possible, and I needed to carry out further background checks. I checked the website where the statement had appeared, but it had disappeared. This was odd, but from a professional standpoint it was good because it would foil attempts by other journalists to follow up on the story after publication. After a couple of nights of writing, fine-tuning and polishing, I was happy with my handiwork. I called Mohamed to go over his observations once again, just to make sure I had it all right, which I did, and I was ready for launch.

I'd already decided that I'd take it to the *Daily Mirror* first, to anchor the relationship I'd already struck up with the news editor, and, besides, they paid well. I phoned Conor and pitched the story to him. He was more than interested and asked me to fax over all the material. I duly obliged and within 30 minutes a reporter, Wayne Francis, phoned me.

'Conor's passed the anthrax story on to me. He's says it's a special.'

'Yes, it is,' I told him, and proceeded to run through the basics with him.

'You know we'll have to go to the cops with this, don't you?' he said.

I was momentarily puzzled as to why he was warning me about this. I guessed it was a final check to make sure that it wasn't an elaborate hoax.

'That's fine. Go ahead,' I said.

I eagerly made my way to the newsagent on 7 November, bought the paper and leafed through it outside the shop. There it was, splashed over a full page under a gigantic 250-point headline: 'WE DID IT'. There were quotes from the Anti-Terrorist Squad and the FBI that said that they were looking into the matter. I went back into the shop to buy four more copies for the cuttings file, probably grinning like a loon as I did so. I resisted the urge to tell the owner that it was my work. Seeing your material in print, well, there's no other buzz like it. It's always a massive ego and confidence boost. Potentially millions of people would be pouring over the story and shaking their heads in disbelief at what I had uncovered.

The only blot on the landscape was the fact that I didn't get a byline, which was annoying but unsurprising. The British red tops rarely, if ever, credit reporters who are not on the payroll. It's a situation that's peculiar to the UK, it seems. American newspapers always give credit where it's due, and staffers have been sacked for using freelance copy without acknowledgement. It was irritating to see others benefiting from my work, but there was nothing I could do. I'd have to be satisfied with the money as it's the way the system works.

I emailed news of my success to a number of contacts later in the day, suggesting that they might want to follow it up. It was a futile exercise in a way, because I knew it was a dead end: there were no obvious ways of taking the story forward. An editor at the *Sunday Times* congratulated me, although he questioned the authenticity of the statement. It was a fair point and he explained that the use of the term 'Cell 15' just didn't look right to him.

This preyed on my mind, and I resolved to consult an expert to get an informed opinion. I needed to develop more contacts in this kind of area anyway, so it would be a useful exercise. I'd already put out some preliminary feelers, and I now turned to a promising source I'd been cultivating to see if he could shed some more light on the subject. His knowledge of international terrorism was awesome – miles ahead of me – and he was connected to the intelligence community, although I didn't bother enquiring as to how exactly. They never tell you.

He was working as a consultant, and I gathered from others that I'd spoken to that he was a world expert on computer hacking and a leading authority on how terrorist groups use the Internet to communicate. A fascinating conversation ensued. He knew about the Secret Army, which he confirmed was an al-Qaeda cell, but there was more to it.

'Roger' told me: 'It doesn't look as if the Secret Army had anything to do with the attacks; it's just that they're trying to use events to get their own name in the game.'

The Secret Army was an al-Qaeda cell based in Syria, he believed, which had been rendered virtually impotent by a crackdown on militant Islamists by the Syrian government some years previously. President Assad had become concerned that his power was being undermined by the growing influence of groups such as Islamic Jihad, and he ordered a wide-ranging and brutal purge.

'It's unlikely that there would be a real group functioning as such. People in the West commonly miss the fact that these groups are foremost at war with their own governments first.'

He also suggested that there might be a connection with Israel;

that an element in that country's intelligence service might have put it out to prompt the US to put pressure on Syria.

'In many ways, it looks like the Israelis trying to pump up action against Syria. You'll note that the "war on terror" has managed to identify a number of targets of no real threat in the region other than to the Israelis.'

He gave me much food for thought and left me with the general impression that groups such as al-Qaeda were more sophisticated than we in the West gave them credit for. Indeed, the prevailing view in the media at the time, which resonated with the public at large, was that al-Qaeda and the Taliban were mostly quasi-Stone Age people to whom a mobile phone would seem like electric trickery. I'd also seen a number of comments claiming that they were a bunch of illiterates who'd congregated around bin Laden because he was the only one who'd had some business training and knew how to do basic arithmetic.

Some of my other spookish contacts also espoused these views, and this really did shock me. It was dumb racism of the 'ragheads' variety, which too many Americans seemed to subscribe to, and I found it sickening that these views were also held among supposedly well-educated intelligence operatives. Any intelligent person knew that these claims simply couldn't be true. You couldn't organise something like 11 September by drawing pictures with sticks in the dirt of a cave floor.

Towards the end of 2001, it was becoming nigh on impossible to sell al-Qaeda stories. Coalition and Northern Alliance forces had started a massive assault on Tora Bora in Afghanistan at the start of December. The Taliban had withdrawn from all the major cities, and it was now looking like this would be the militants' last stand. It was clear that my newspaper contacts believed that it would be game over in a matter of days, or hours even.

One wire report said that bin Laden had been seen riding a white horse and leading the troops on the front line. Women and children, presumably the families of the al-Qaeda leaders, had been clearly visible through binoculars. The kids were playing, seemingly unconcerned about the bombs raining down from American B-52s. I phoned one newspaper to pitch a story, but the news editor wasn't interested. All eyes were on Tora Bora, and I could tell from the excitement in his voice that he expected to hear news of the death of bin Laden any time now, with complete victory for the West and a quick end to the al-Qaeda menace.

Indeed, bin Laden supporters were talking about the battle on a website discussion board that an intelligence contact had flagged up to me. One guy, who was suspected of being a mid-ranking operative based in Pakistan, was fielding questions from people who were getting all teary-eyed about bin Laden's predicament. According to a translation I got, he said that even if he was killed, it wouldn't matter a jot. A 'new Emir' would take over and, we shouldn't forget, tens of thousands of operatives who had been trained in the camps in Afghanistan were spread out all over the world – veterans of the Soviet–Afghan war and the new generation of al-Qaeda fighters. It would just be a minor propaganda victory for the West, he explained in a very matter-of-fact way.

Then I got a breathless call from a reporter on a Sunday newspaper who said he was desperate to get hold of satellite images of Tora Bora. Could I procure any from my contacts? I said I'd get straight on to it, although I felt that the chances of getting hold of anything were pretty slim. A company called Space Imaging was the first port of call, as it had recently begun operating the first civilian spy satellite and was starting to sell high-resolution images to whoever wanted them.

I contacted the press office, but I was told that the Pentagon had bought the rights to all images of Afghanistan for the foreseeable future, which effectively blocked al-Qaeda and the media from spying on US military activity in the country. The press office did, however, offer me other, older images of al-Qaeda facilities in the country, but it was no good: it was Tora Bora or nothing. Gary was very helpful and he did suggest that I might be interested in an image showing a suspected terrorist training camp in Iraq. This did sound like something that I might want to take a look at further down the line, but not at the moment. He emailed it to me and it sat in my in-box, unopened, while I tried to crack the matter at hand.

I tried various other obvious sources of satellite imagery, but to no avail. In desperation, I tried some intelligence contacts to see if I could get something slipped to me, as it were, and I had some success this way. One guy said he'd got a very friendly contact in Moscow who was able to re-task a satellite to peer at any location of my choosing. This was more like it. It was a sexy thought: I loved the idea having a military spacecraft fire its thrusters and change orbit to fly over a target on my command. The $3,000 price tag was certainly on the high side, but when I considered the effort that would be involved and the risk the Russian contact would be taking, it seemed more reasonable. The downside was that it would take a minimum of two weeks to get the images to me. This was no good for the newspaper, as it was going to press in three days.

The Battle of Tora Bora was over in a few days, and a large number of al-Qaeda and Taliban operatives had managed to slip over the border into Pakistan, although the Pakistani army was supposed to have sealed the border to stop this happening. There were strong suspicions that the ISI intelligence agency had helped the fugitives to flee to safety. The big question was: bin Laden, was he among them? Initially, the US was putting out signals that suggested that they thought they'd got him. There had been a few patches of the earth that had been subject to such an intense pounding by US military ordnance that it might take weeks or months to sift through the wreckage at the site and carry out DNA analyses on bodies and body parts found there. Then again, it was possible that his remains had been completely incinerated and they might never know for sure.

The US exuded confidence, but whether this was a ruse to distract media attention from the possibility that he'd vanished over the border with his compatriots or not, it was impossible to tell. And so began a phoney war over whether bin Laden was alive or dead. Half the media erred on the side of the military; the other half suspected that he'd managed to escape, though the effect of this limbo-like state meant that the entire media backed away from publishing any stories about him. Any newspaper that had been reporting sightings of him or messages attributed to him would see its reputation comprehensively trashed if it was later proved that he had been killed at Tora Bora.

I suspected that he'd escaped and was keeping a low profile, making best use of the confusion. It seemed inconceivable to me, if the terrorists were escaping, that bin Laden wouldn't be somewhere near the front of the queue. All al-Qaeda operatives had to swear allegiance to him and he was deeply loved by all of them as a father figure. His bodyguards would surely have hustled him out of the danger area at the first opportunity, whether he liked it or not.

Many journalists I spoke to were convinced that he was dead and that his terrorist network had been effectively eliminated at Tora

Bora. It was time to move on to other things. That was very frustrating for me, as I knew that the threat hadn't diminished, although, to be fair, there were few terrorism experts on news desks. I knew that, by its very nature, the al-Qaeda network was self-repairing, like self-sealing rubber. You only had to look at the Islamist rebels in Chechnya, who posed as great a threat as they ever did to Russia, despite their top commanders being snuffed out on a regular basis.

The plot thickened when another bin Laden video was released on 26 December 2001. This time he looked a little flustered and upset in the video, and he was much more animated. More to the point, there was a brown cloth hanging in the background, which looked like it was designed to conceal any clues as to his whereabouts. It seemed that he might have learned a lesson from the first video, when the rock formations had betrayed his location as being Paktia province, where the base I'd discovered was located. Had he still been hiding there and recorded this latest video when the US bombed the bejesus out of the place two months earlier? I still found it hard to believe that I might have pinned him down to within a few metres. Maybe the cloth backdrop was obscuring the bomb damage. It could have all been mere coincidence, of course.

I was starting to realise that the Internet was a great tool for gathering intelligence, and I was learning that a journalist was best placed to use the information to the greatest effect. I was also learning that you had to go off-piste to find the knockout stuff. Scrolling through endless Google results was a mug's game: any idiot could do it, and I had quickly discovered that you could waste many hours in the vain hope of stumbling across something decent. To make headway with Google, you at least needed to know the advanced search methods used by programmers.

Search engines can only cover a very tiny portion of the Net, only the very obvious pages that people want to be discovered. They don't tend to index material on website discussion forums, for example, which is a huge omission. I was much more interested in the sites that weren't meant to be discovered, where the site owners had gone to pains to make sure that they weren't logged. This underground has been called the Invisible Web, and it has been estimated that search engines only cover around 0.002 per cent of the totality of what's available online, at best.

It was a surprise to discover that the leaders of al-Qaeda were Internet pioneers. Before Western newspapers started reporting on these new magical things called email and the Internet, Islamic militants based in Pakistan had been using them since the early 1990s to communicate and to distribute manuals and tactical guides. A former CIA spy who operated in Pakistan at the time told me, 'Al-Qaeda documentation has been floating around in a fairly significant way from at least 1995, in all likelihood since 1993–4, perhaps even sooner in the Middle East and the subcontinent.

'Indeed, the *Encyclopaedia of the Afghan Jihad* – the first major work – which started to appear in Pakistan around 1992 to '93 was probably in part gathered via the Internet even at that early date. The manuals thank the computer technicians who made the publication possible, and I suspect that they were quite conscious then of the possibilities that the Internet and email offered.'

The use of this technology also had its downside for the militants, it seemed. Just after bin Laden's flight from Tora Bora, I came across a website that was plastered with images of bin Laden and Kalashnikov rifles. It sported a logo that consisted of the silhouette of a man on a prancing horse holding a rifle aloft. I suspected that it was an al-Qaeda site, and I asked Mohamed the translator if he'd take a look at it, even though I knew it was going to cost me.

He confirmed that it did appear to be the terror network's official site. It was titled al-Neda, which translated as 'The Call'. He soon got back to me with a rundown of the site's contents, which consisted of the text of speeches by bin Laden and Mullah Omar, a few eulogies dedicated to noted Islamic scholars and a 'clarification about the withdrawal from Kandahar'. What caught my eye, however, was a piece entitled 'Warning on Security of Information'. I ordered a translation of this, and it turned out to be very illuminating. It was my first confirmed al-Qaeda communications intercept.

The 1,400-word tract appeared to be suggesting that middle-ranking members had been inadvertently leaking information about the plans of al-Qaeda and the Taliban, and that they had been picked up and used by the Americans. The publisher of the statement was credited as the Centre for Islamic Research and Studies, which has previously issued statements attributed to bin Laden, his deputy Ayman al-Zawahiri and Taliban supreme leader Mullah Mohammed Omar. It said that it had already issued a warning one month previously, but that had not been heeded. Arabic emotions don't translate well, but the writer was clearly miffed, though he was trying to remain polite at the same time. It looked like Internet gossips were being fingered.

Part of it read:

> It is pivotal to continue, as we always warned during this war, and refrain from the spread of rumours that could damage and impede the jihad and the Mujahideen. We should caution against this matter, which constitutes a higher risk than the espionage of the enemy against us. By this we mean the relaxing of our guard regarding the security of information in respect to jihad and the provision of data to the enemy on a golden plate.
>
> When we start to appreciate the value associated with the gathering of data by the enemy, we can then grasp the importance of the information we hold and the benefits to the enemy in case it is revealed by mistake.
>
> Some Muslims have behaved in a way that causes pain to our hearts. They hurry to publish any piece of information they receive about the Mujahideen. This information could be so dangerous as to risk the lives of many and it endangers the Mujahideen. Some may say they have only transmitted the news to people they trust. And those trusted people may transmit the same news to others they trust, until it falls in the hands of the enemy.
>
> We beg Muslims not to think that publishing news about the Mujahideen is a media scoop that should be recorded as soon as possible and in any manner. War is not for propaganda gains. It is to defeat the enemy. Will Muslims allow the Mujahideen to lead the information war as they have allowed them to lead in the military war?

I asked Roger about it and he said that it demonstrated al-Qaeda's 'justified concerns about operational security', because of the speed at which information now moves. 'A casual comment or slip of an operational detail can be picked up in a remote backwater and spread through the network in a bare instant. The world is on alert now, including intelligence and law enforcement agencies in every country.'

I was starting to find the technological struggle between the two sides fascinating, and I thought it might be interesting to explore just how wide the technology gulf was between the militants and the West. If the newspaper reports were to be believed, the skies above Afghanistan were crowded with spy satellites that were scouring every nook and cranny for signs of bin Laden and his entourage. It was said that even goats couldn't move without their hoofprints being logged and recorded by banks of liquid-nitrogen-cooled supercomputers, in case the information might prove to be useful in the future.

As far as classified information goes, the secrets of America's 'black' space programme constituted the very holiest of the holies. Trillions of dollars have been poured into military Unacknowledged Special Access Programs, and, as far as anyone could judge, a lot of that was invested in outer space. No one knows exactly where it was spent, because these projects are supposedly comprised of technology that is at least 30 years in advance of anything that is in the public domain. We still marvel at the awesome sight of the stealth bomber, but that was developed in the 1960s and it's said to be an obsolete jalopy compared to what lies hidden in hangars in the desert wastes of the American hinterland. Those in the know laugh at it.

Whatever is out there, they are America's crown jewels and as such are guarded ferociously. Numerous Congressional investigations have tried to get a handle on how this money has been spent, but to no avail. Officials are empowered by law to lie about them when questioned – even to the President. Rumours are always rife in this area, and there are even claims that the military have progressed as far as developing a space fighter craft that is operated far from prying eyes somewhere in the Arctic Circle. Some have suggested that odd flashes of light seen by astronomers on the surface of the moon, called transient lunar phenomena, might betray the existence of a US military base on the dark side.

On the face of it, it seemed that this would be the most impossible of nuts to crack: the US didn't officially admit that it had an agency operating spy satellites until 1992. Called the National Reconnaissance Office (NRO), it has been referred to as America's Other Space Agency. It is shrouded in the deepest of secrecies and there is very little information in the public domain; it's an agency of the US Department of Defense, although its staff is largely drawn from the CIA.

A cursory Web trawl revealed only one interesting slight security breach: someone unknown had leaked an image of a mission patch for a secret satellite launch in 2000. It featured the image of an owl and four boomerang-shaped objects flying in two overlapping orbits in tandem formations. It also revealed that the NRO had a rather spooky slogan: 'WE OWN THE NIGHT'.

Making enquiries in this area might prove to be dangerous, but I still wanted to know how the spies in the sky were participating in the hunt for bin Laden, and so I started scouting around for a chink in the armour. I needed to find a good angle of attack. I didn't fancy my chances of getting officials to talk, and I didn't want to flag up my interest to them in any case. I needed somebody who was in the know but who was independent of the agency. I racked my brains, and I eventually concluded that perhaps I might have some luck in the sphere of astronomy. Satellites whizzing around the skies couldn't have gone unnoticed, surely, unless they were disguised somehow.

After the collapse of the Soviet Union, America's 'birds' were safely out of reach of any harm. There was no other country in the world with known anti-satellite technology, although I'd read somewhere that Saddam Hussein had been trying to develop such a capability. He'd had scientists working on a plan to launch anti-satellite satellites, which were basically bombs containing glue that would explode near US spacecraft and splatter them with gunk, rendering their cameras useless. If I remember correctly, it was a bit of fantasy that never left the drawing board.

After a little research, I became aware of a group of amateur astronomers who specialised solely in monitoring objects in low-earth orbit. They were spread out across the globe and swapped information via email. I joined the party and lurked for a while to acclimatise to this new world and see what they were getting up to. They had surprisingly sophisticated equipment and were using software to track and identify objects, making predictions about when and where certain objects would be visible. It was an impressive set-up. Often, a member of the group would report seeing an 'unknown flasher', and the rest of the group would consult their laptops and try to identify the object.

As well as operational satellites, it turns out that there's an exotic junkyard up there whirling around at 17,000-odd mph: old spacecraft from the early days of the space race, rocket boosters, discarded space shuttle fuel tanks, all the way down to nuts and bolts, spanners and flecks of paint. It has been estimated that there are some 110,000 large bits and pieces up there. Using their accumulated data, the observers predict when objects will re-enter the earth's atmosphere and even where they might land.

I approached one of the senior members of the group, a Canadian called Ted, and posed a series of questions to him. We spoke on the phone, and when I explained what I was trying to look into, he said he'd be happy to help. He wanted to speak to me in the first instance to reassure himself that I was who I said I was. It was a somewhat sensitive area, and he wanted to make sure I was bona fide, although, not being American, he wasn't that bothered about possible visits from the men in black.

I was in luck. He said there were some indications that all was not well up there, but there was a learning process to go through first. He started by familiarising me with the different types of spacecraft that were being flown and their capabilities. He briefly suggested that there might be more ultra-secret stuff that was lurking in deeper space that he wouldn't feel comfortable speculating on.

The biggest of the known craft are the KeyHole satellites, which are the main optical workhorses. These are monster, bus-sized craft that carry advanced cameras and infrared sensors, and they are estimated to cost around $1 billion apiece. It is thought that there are four of these giants orbiting in pairs between 200 and 600 miles above the earth in polar orbits – vague equivalents to the civilian Hubble Space Telescope. Between them, it is thought they are capable of imaging the entire surface of the planet every day and picking out objects as small as 100 mm wide. There was something ironic about this: one space telescope was probing the outer reaches of the universe while four others were pointing in the opposite direction and secretly probing the activities of earthlings in minute detail.

It's been estimated that there is a fleet of 200 classified spacecraft above us valued at around $100 billion. It's said that at any one time and in any location on earth, it's likely that there will be five US spy satellites above you, silently traversing the sky at Mach 25. The data gathered is relayed back to a widespread network of listening stations. The main node in this network is the US base at RAF

Menwith Hill in Yorkshire, near Harrogate, in the UK. The actual name of the hill on the map is Snod Hill, but I guess that didn't sound groovy enough. In US military-speak, it is simply known as Station F83.

Ted said that a new 18-tonne KeyHole had been blasted into orbit just before the start of the US bombing campaign in Afghanistan, but there were signs that everything was not well with the new craft. Codenamed USA161, it had recently made an unusual series of manoeuvres, which could be a sign that ground controllers were attempting to recover it.

He offered to undertake an analysis of the orbital changes of this class of satellite for me, and, of course, I said I'd be very interested in seeing the results. The following day, he emailed me some spreadsheets, which showed that the KeyHoles have very variable lifespans: between three and seven and a half years. It would be fair to say that there would appear to be issues of reliability here, he said. I must admit, one billion dollars for three years of work seems like a high price.

The KeyHoles operate in conjunction with 15-tonne Lacrosse radar imaging satellites, which can 'see' through cloud cover and even detect underground structures. This was the type of satellite represented on the leaked NRO mission patch.

Ted had also looked at another type of spy satellite known as NOSS, for which no official orbital data had ever been published. Costing an estimated $500 million each, they travel in triangular formation and are able to pinpoint sources of radio transmissions by comparing the minute differences in the timings of the signal received by each satellite.

Ted said that a new NOSS triad had been launched into space in September by a US Air Force Atlas rocket, but only two satellites were visible after launch. This suggested that one of them had failed to deploy. Even worse, one satellite in an existing formation had recently started flashing, indicating that it was out of control and spinning wildly about its axis.

Clearly, the US military and intelligence community were experiencing some major difficulties with their spacecraft just when they needed them for scouring Afghanistan for signs of bin Laden. Another hunch of mine had been confirmed, and, even better, it was backed up by completely independent information based on scientific analysis.

The results of this spying blindness were perhaps best demonstrated on the ground around a month after the start of the US campaign in Afghanistan. Al-Qaeda forces, which were said to include top officials, had evacuated from Kabul in a convoy of at least 1,000 cars and trucks in early November 2001, yet it seems that the US was unaware of the huge traffic jam just outside the capital city. The same thing happened again when members of the Taliban and al-Qaeda escaped from Jalalabad unmolested in a 1,000-strong convoy, which is believed to have included bin Laden, and headed for the mountain fortress of Tora Bora.

The news that, at certain times of the day, bin Laden could probably have a fireworks party or a polo tournament in safety wouldn't have gone down too well during a time of high patriotic fervour in the States. I just got silence when I pitched the story at the American market, and the British papers didn't really care because it was a US-oriented story.

Months later, however, people were forced to pay attention when the president of the US spacecraft-builder Spectrum Astro, Dave Thompson, a man with access to highly classified information, lambasted the NRO and its 'shocking' and 'sorry' decline in a speech delivered at a dinner at the 18th National Space Symposium on 11 April 2002.

He catalogued a string of calamities, which included loss of communications a few days after launch, melting components causing mission failure, failures caused by faulty software, spacecraft that failed to meet basic performance criteria and many projects that failed to take off because of mismanagement.

'Unfortunately, none of this has done anything to make innovative new satellites to fight al-Qaeda, which is our number-one priority today,' said Thompson.

He added that, 'the NRO has suffered a shocking decline in the technical performance of its satellites over the past several years', but said he couldn't describe many more technical disasters, as it would be too revealing.

He did reveal, however, that the agency had demanded changes to the electrical sub-system of a KeyHole satellite. The modifications amounted to little more than an extra light switch, but this minor alteration had cost $200 million. However, the change had caused constant power upsets to the spacecraft's computers once it reached orbit.

It was riveting stuff. He went as far as mocking America's secret space agency: 'They have a public website now and on their website it says "One team revolutionising global reconnaissance". Well, maybe they are one team, but they aren't revolutionising anything at the NRO. They're evolving at about the speed fish evolved into reptiles.'

Other barbs included: 'The average time for the NRO to deploy a new major system to first launch is about ten years. Actually, they're slower than the Air Force and NASA'; and: 'You know the NRO's real slogan should be "Buying Yesterday's Technology at Tomorrow's Prices"'; and 'I say they are a bunch of hypocrites.'

It looked like professional suicide, and it occurred to me that maybe he shouldn't be expecting to fulfil many more government spy satellite orders in the near future. But he obviously felt it was a situation that was impinging on national security, and it was of such gravity that it transcended matters of commerce. He went on to condemn the NRO as a 'rogue agency – arrogant and holier than thou', and he called on President George W. Bush, who also addressed the meeting via a video link, to put a stop to the madness.

Steven Aftergood, who directs the Federation of American Scientists project on government secrecy, told me, 'It is an extraordinarily revealing document [Thompson's speech] . . . It is certainly the most blistering critique of the NRO ever uttered by a knowledgeable insider in a public forum. By far!' It certainly appeared to validate the questions raised by information that Ted and his group of amateur observers had accumulated. And it pointed out yet again that I was on the right track.

NUKEDOM

There was something ironic about a story about the failure of electronic intelligence failing to sell but it didn't dampen my enthusiasm, as I was enough of a pragmatist to know that a 100 per cent strike rate is a completely unrealistic expectation. Even before Dave Thompson's incendiary speech had provided confirmation of my theory, the saga had given me confidence to wade deeper into classified territory and to try to find out if the terrorists had access to weapons of mass destruction. There was ground-breaking work to be done in this area and I was keen to crack on with it.

I'd included some speculation in the bin Laden tunnels copy to the effect that, if he had a nuclear arsenal, it might be concealed underground in such a place. It got chopped from the piece, quite rightly, because there was little evidence for the claim. So, I got quite excited when it was reported at the end of December 2001 that US troops had detected traces of uranium in concrete-lined tunnels in Khost in Afghanistan. Clearly, whatever was there had been spirited away over the border into Pakistan when the Taliban regime collapsed.

Nuclear terrorism therefore seemed like the next logical step: to find out if terrorist groups had access to atomic weapons. Bin Laden certainly wanted them – more than wanted – they were seen as nothing less than essential in prosecuting the global jihad. Before 11 September, he had declared in a speech that it was an Islamic duty to acquire chemical and nuclear weapons: 'It would be a sin for Muslims not to try to possess the weapons that would prevent infidels from inflicting harm on Muslims.'

He was one of the first people to congratulate Pakistan on

successfully detonating the first Islamic doomsday device and there were certainly lots of rumours and speculation about al-Qaeda's efforts in this direction. There were reports of suspect couriers dying from radiation poisoning in Pakistan and other accounts insisted that the trafficking was more extensive than anyone had imagined, as the mules were usually shot dead at the point of delivery, their information dying with them.

I discovered that in March 2000, customs officers in Uzbekistan stopped a lorry destined for Quetta on the Pakistan/Afghanistan border which turned out to be carrying ten lead-lined containers filled with strontium 90: enough to manufacture dozens of radiological dirty bombs. I sensed that there was something to be uncovered here, maybe to accompany a headline along the lines of: 'NUCLEAR SUICIDE BOMBERS POISED TO STRIKE'.

I set about nosing around this area for a while; just reading up on background material, although I knew that I'd probably need some spookish guidance on this one at some point. I put off tapping the spy world for information for now, mainly because you can get distracted by the bewildering spectrum of opinions. There did seem to be a more solid and recent plank of fact in this area that had arisen out of a court case in the States.

A Sudanese ex-associate of bin Laden gave testimony in a New York court in February 2001, where four suspected terrorists were on trial over the bombings of American embassies in Africa in 1998. Jamal Ahmad al-Fadl told how he'd been working from Sudan to obtain nuclear materials since 1993 and that he had been sent on a recent mission to procure a cylinder of enriched uranium from a contact in Khartoum, an ex-minister in the Sudanese government.

Aided by a translator, he told the court:

> Basheer, he told me, 'Are you serious? You want uranium?' I tell him yes. I know people, they very serious, and they want to buy it. And he told me did [I have] the money ready, and I say what they need. They need the information about uranium, they want to know which quality, which the country make it, and after that we going to talk with you about the price. He say I going to give you this information in a paper, and we need $1,500,000, and everything go well we need it outside. We need the money outside of Sudan.

He relayed the information to his superiors, who said they needed to test samples using a machine that was on its way from Kenya. A few days later, he and two colleagues headed for a house in the north of the city to view the goods. The contact produced a large bag and lifted out a cylinder that was two or three feet tall. He said it had writing in English engraved on it, and his bosses looked pleased with what they saw. He left the room while they talked business with the man called Basheer and then departed.

A few days later, al-Fadl was sent to pick up a piece of paper with the words that had been inscribed on the side of the cylinder written on it.

'It's information, I remember it say South Africa and serial number and quality something. It's all in English. So I don't remember all the what in the paper,' he recounted in court.

His superiors looked at the paper and told him to go back and tell Basheer that they wanted to buy the cylinder. They paid al-Fadl $10,000 for his assistance. His involvement ceased at this point, and it's not known whether, as some have suggested, it was real uranium that was a relic of South Africa's nuclear programme, which was abandoned in 1991. It could also have been a fake deal set up by criminals or intelligence agents.

Al-Fadl ended up as a US government witness because he was caught stealing $110,000 from an al-Qaeda front company in Sudan, where bin Laden was residing at the time. He was summoned to a meeting with the al-Qaeda leader at his Khartoum mansion, where he was angrily told that he'd let the side down and could only be forgiven if he paid the money back. Al-Fadl couldn't pay the money back and, as it dawned on him that defrauding bin Laden hadn't been such a bright idea, he panicked. He fled Sudan and approached the US embassy in an undisclosed country. He ended up in the Witness Protection Programme, which paid him a shade under $800,000 for his testimony.

The horrors of nuclear guerrilla war are a lot to take on board, and it was of no comfort to discover that it's not too difficult to assemble an atomic weapon these days, given access to the critical ingredients. A recently declassified US government report from 1967 revealed that two newly graduated physicists were told to try and build a nuclear weapon from scratch, as a secret experiment. The findings revealed that, in the pre-Internet era and without any knowledge of classified work in the area, they came up with a design for a viable implosion device in 'three man-years'.

From the background reading, it seemed to me that the production of a working nuke was less likely than construction of a dirty bomb. For this, you simply enclose a lump of radioactive metal inside a conventional bomb to create fallout, and you could apparently accumulate sufficient material for the radioactive core by bulk buying smoke detectors.

According to documents obtained by a US nuclear think-tank, Iraq was the only country that had tested dirty bombs, in 1987, and with mixed results. The core didn't defragment into fine particles and the fallout didn't spread far beyond the explosion sites. The project was dropped, as it was thought that the yield was too low to cause mass casualties. The only publicised act of nuclear terrorism that has so far taken place occurred in 1995, when Chechen separatists planted a small bomb containing a canister of caesium in a park in Moscow. It failed to detonate and was later retrieved by bomb disposal experts.

The use of such weapons by terrorist groups seemed ridiculously possible, and I kept thinking that I should hurry and get the story finished before someone beat me to it. Some newspapers had ventured only as far as suggesting that there may be some vague threat from dirty bombs, but no one was suggesting that genuine nukes were a real prospect. It seemed that there was some kind of barrier there – some line in the sand that the media weren't supposed to cross.

My first thought was that perhaps the area was covered by a D Notice, which effectively means a government ban on the media covering areas that may harm national security. The secretive D Notice Committee, although it's no longer called that, is a bogeyman in journalism. Rumours occasionally surface that such and such a story had had 'a D Notice slapped on it'. You'd work in fear that, when you came across that big exclusive that was just a bit too hot to handle, someone would leap out of the shadows and you'd get a D Notice slapped on you like a parking ticket, ensuring you were unfairly robbed of a career-boosting byline.

That was the myth, but the reality was DA (Defence Advisory) Notices and the Defence, Press and Broadcasting Advisory Committee, which was made up of editors as well as senior government defence and intelligence officials. It had been modernised and now issued standing notices covering broad areas, such as revealing details of specific intelligence operations and disclosing details about the UK's nuclear weapons. The secretary of the committee was always on hand to help with the media's interpretation of these ground rules. I scanned through the areas covered by existing notices, but I couldn't see that a story about al-Qaeda's nuclear ambitions would break any of the rules in any way, even vaguely.

This didn't seem to be the reason for the apparent nuke ban, and so I ploughed on, aware that unexpected pitfalls could lie ahead.

As I was getting some copy together, I found a report in one intelligence journal claiming that there was 'no longer a doubt' that al-Qaeda possessed a nuclear arsenal. It quoted unnamed sources as saying that Russian intelligence believed that the group had a handful of small nuclear warheads, whilst the Saudis believed the figure could be nearer 20, but beyond that the rest of the report seemed like a summation of all the old hoary speculation about deals with the Russian mafia.

It was the leading theory: al-Qaeda-linked Islamic separatist groups in Chechnya brokered a deal with a Ukrainian mobster in the mid-1990s to buy 20 miniaturised 'suitcase nukes', which were procured from impoverished technicians at a former Soviet nuclear research facility in Kazakhstan. The asking price was supposedly $30 million each, plus two tons of Afghanistan's finest opium.

Trying to put some names to those kinds of sources would go a long way towards achieving my goal of writing the seminal piece on terror nukes. I needed some spy input, and I knew just where to turn. I had learned from a story I did years back that many top US and UK intelligence specialists swap open-source intelligence material with each other via an email group. I decided to send a message to the group and see who and what would crawl out of the woodwork, even though it meant breaking cover and making myself known to some powerful people who might not agree with me pursuing this particular line of enquiry.

I did it with a sense of trepidation, but I was curious to know what would come back to me. The first reply was from a British ex-agent, who informed me that nuclear bombs small enough to fit inside a suitcase did exist and they weren't an urban myth. They were first developed by the Soviet Union, and specially trained military intelligence agents would secretly bury these near key government and infrastructure sites in major Western cities. They were pre-positioned where they could be detonated remotely, to hamper the enemy's ability to respond to a pre-emptive nuclear attack. Indeed, he told me in amused tones that these weapons of mass destruction circulated around the world in diplomatic luggage from the late 1960s right up to the collapse of the Soviet Union in 1989. Each had a shelf-life of about eight years, and they needed to be retrieved regularly and sent back to a laboratory for refurbishment before being reburied. He added that 'uncertainty lingers' over the number of devices that were supposed to have been transferred to Moscow in 1992 from the Ukraine, Turkistan and the Central Asia military districts of the former Soviet Union.

They were disparagingly known as 'golf-bag nukes' to those in the know, due to the bulky nature of the devices, although more modern versions can apparently be as small as two large hardback dictionaries laid on top of each other. The formal name of the American version is Atomic Demolition Munitions (ADMs). He even sent me a picture of one. It looked like a large green ammunition box with a heavily crimped lid.

As well as being forward deployed in Western cities, these nukes were also buried all along the USSR's border with China, for use as nuclear landmines in the event of a surprise invasion. They were often disguised as rocks, and it seems that records of the bomb sites went missing. After the collapse of the Soviet Union, it's assumed that some of these may have lain forgotten and undisturbed in remote corners of former Soviet republics. In 1997, former Soviet General Alexander Lebed claimed that over 100 of them had disappeared from the army inventory and were presumed to have reached the black market, where they were available for sale to terror groups like al-Qaeda. He died in a car crash shortly after making the allegation.

It was an amazing first response and it was shocking to think that these things could be harvested like potatoes, potentially by anyone travelling along the Chinese border. Then a separate source told me that al-Qaeda had bought nine more nuclear warheads recently during the conflict in Afghanistan, and that was the latest whisper on the subject. I never asked, but I felt that he might have some European connections. I followed up with a few more questions.

'Reliable sources report not only that atomic munitions were sold by the Russian underworld and smuggled into Central Asia during the conflict between the US and the Taliban but also that several Russian nuclear technicians were hired by the Islamic fundamentalists to try and make the weapons operational,' he said.

He believed that the weapons had been recently moved by air out of Afghanistan along well-established drug-trafficking routes, and they were now in Armenia. There had been 'repeated attempts' by the Russian mafia to get radioactive materials for the Taliban over recent years.

'US intelligence services believe that bin Laden had a secret nuclear weapons laboratory and nuclear material cache inside Afghanistan, having seen evidence that the Russian mafia had supplied him with chemical, biological and nuclear components.' He said a fax message intercepted in June 2000 detailed plans for two arms shipments to al-Qaeda disguised as fish from Tanzania. The planes were to land at night in Afghanistan on the pretext of having engine trouble. The shipping cost was listed as $50,000, plus unspecified risk bonuses for the pilots.

So the mid to worst case scenario seemed to be that al-Qaeda had a couple of dozen small nuclear weapons at worst, nine at best, many of which may not be operational, and a hoard of radioactive material to construct their own home-made doomsday devices or dozens of crude dirty bombs. Dozens of nukes just sounded like too many to be credible, and the thought tempered the shock of realising that it seemed likely that bin Laden had some kind of nuclear capability.

I was right to be concerned about the pitfalls of investigating in this area. One correspondent, who may have had UK government connections, emailed me to tell me in no uncertain terms that I should cease work on this story immediately. He even threatened me. He thought that the truth about the nuclear situation would frighten the public and they'd be better off in the dark.

'It's not the kind of thing I want to read on the train in the morning,' he informed me, before claiming that he'd already stopped another reporter in his tracks by 'having a word' with his editor.

The guy could be anyone, I thought, before I started to feel angry at this attempt at censorship without reason. I wasn't going to be cowed, and I expressed my feelings very bluntly in a reply to him.

No one would be surprised to learn about this, I told him; it's what people in general suspect, and the story would have no impact on national security. There were no grounds for stopping me, basically. I was not going to truckle.

Another character from the anti-nuclear camp, who worked in computer security, then jumped in and told everyone on this email list that they shouldn't cooperate with me. I could well be an al-Qaeda spy, he told them, but he obviously wasn't the brightest of the bunch. Jesus, if this is the kind of knee-jerk expert advice that our leaders are relying on, then it's probably best that I defect immediately and get in with the winning side while the moment is right, I thought.

My accuser went on to warn everyone that he'd be very surprised if anyone in the group confirmed, in public or private, that it was a working assumption that bin Laden did have these weapons.

Eh? Was I being dumb, or was he giving me exactly what I wanted?

'Thank you very much,' I said, triumphantly. 'I'll be quoting you on that. That's on-the-record confirmation – better than I expected.'

Others contacted me in private with encouraging words and said that I'd stirred up a real hornets' nest. A source who claimed to be a former Russian GRU military intelligence colonel contacted me through a third party to offer support. He said that al-Qaeda didn't just have the suitcase bombs – a Mossad contact had told him that bin Laden had recently acquired warheads that had been stolen from the Russian military.

'They are not the suitcase-type bombs that people often refer to, but more the warhead-type munitions. These are the payloads of short-range missiles, torpedoes and the like.'

He was a little furtive and didn't want to elaborate. He'd already said enough, he claimed.

Later, in September 2002, there even seemed to be a potential oversupply situation developing when opponents of the Ukrainian president Leonid Kuchma produced a report claiming that 200 of the country's nuclear warheads had vanished. It claimed that 2,400 of the weapons were supposed to have been transported to Russia during the 1990s under an arms control agreement, but only 2,200 have been accounted for. If true, that would seem to validate what I had been told in private.

Kuchma was facing allegations that he had given the go-ahead for illegal shipments of arms to Iraq. The US State Department suspended some aid to Ukraine in the same month, after it said it had authenticated tapes made secretly by the president's former bodyguard on which the veteran leader is recorded approving the sale of a $100 million Kolchuga early-warning radar system to Iraq.

Before this report emerged I had turned to academia to gauge the temperature there and found there was scepticism about al-Qaeda's nuclear capability, even though Defence Secretary Geoff Hoon confirmed to the House of Commons: 'We are certainly aware that he [bin Laden] has some material that could contribute to a nuclear weapon.' All of the scientists I contacted expressed varying degrees of dubiousness. Perhaps the difference of opinion was down to a lack of access to secret information, or maybe they were just more impartial and not pushing agendas, as the politicians might be. Maybe people just didn't want to accept that such a situation might exist.

Professor Paul Rogers, head of the Centre for Peace Studies at the University of Bradford, had calculated that the combined force of the two explosions caused by the impact of the planes and the collapse of the twin towers in New York represented only 60 per cent of the damage that would result from an exploding suitcase nuke. Each has a yield of around 1 kiloton – equivalent to 1,000 tons of TNT. It has been estimated that one ADM could immediately kill 100,000 people if it detonated in a major city centre, with hundreds of thousands dying later from cancer caused by the fallout.

'The effect of the [World Trade Center] plane-fuel explosion and the gravitational forces of collapse of the two towers was about 600 tons of TNT equivalent, so an ADM would destroy a couple of city blocks, or a major bridge, or an airport terminal,' he told me.

He wasn't convinced that al-Qaeda possessed this capability: 'There were unconfirmed reports that one or two Soviet-era tactical nuclear weapons had got to Iran a few years ago. Apart from that, I do not have any evidence that al-Qaeda has access to such weapons.'

A semi-skilled operative could programme the bomb using an in-built timer, given the right codes, or detonation could be triggered with a mobile phone call. The Americans developed these bombs after Russia, for use against dams and other large infrastructure during the Vietnam War, but there are no reports of them ever being used. I just hoped that the US stockpile was safely under lock and key, and not lying around in the tundra in Alaska.

Rose Gottemoeller, senior associate at the Carnegie Endowment for International Peace and assistant energy secretary for non-proliferation in the Clinton administration, told me that she thought it was more likely that bin Laden would have a dirty bomb capability rather than a nuclear one.

She said: 'I believe that the chance that bin Laden controls actual warheads is virtually nil. It is much more likely that he has acquired some nuclear materials, but here the range could be very wide: from depleted uranium or low-level radioactive sources, such as those used in smoke detectors, all the way up to weapons-usable material, i.e. highly enriched uranium or plutonium.

'I think it more likely that he has some kind of lower-level sources than the weapons-grade material, but this cannot be excluded. The origins for the lower-level materials could be very broad, virtually worldwide; weapons-grade material is much more precious, therefore proliferating countries tend to hold onto it.'

She added: 'It is possible such material could have come to him from a former Soviet nuclear facility, not only in Russia but possibly in Kazakhstan, Georgia, Uzbekistan, Ukraine, etc.'

Robert Sherman, director of strategic security at the Federation of American Scientists, said that this was 'more likely than getting a ballistic missile warhead'. Asked whether he thought al-Qaeda may have de facto control of Pakistan's nuclear weapons, as some feared, he added: 'I have suspicions but no hard evidence of that.'

Suspicions that al-Qaeda may be in league with 'Talibanised' elements in Pakistan's military high command were strengthened when it was revealed that two retired nuclear scientists had admitted meeting bin Laden twice in recent years. Sultan Bashiruddin Mahmood and Abdul Majid left their senior positions at the Pakistan Atomic Energy Commission in 1999 to set up a 'relief organisation' in Afghanistan, they claimed.

Despite the conflicting views of various experts, the Bush administration was taking the nuclear threat seriously. On 11 September they had enacted an emergency plan dating from the Cold War and America now had two governments: the real one and a skeleton copy spread across the country in bunkers waiting to leap into action should a terrorist attack decapitate the elected government. Unmarked vans and helicopters were scouring the country with radiation detectors in a desperate bid to protect high-profile sitting ducks like the Super Bowl and the Winter Olympics in Salt Lake City.

I'd obviously hit on something that was quietly boiling away which some in the security community apparently felt the public shouldn't know about. It seems we could expect the same attitude to prevail when astronomers spot a 100-mile wide asteroid on a collision course with earth. We wouldn't be told; we'd have the final 20 seconds of our lives to work it out for ourselves when, distracted by a flickering light in our peripheral vision, we'd look up and notice two suns in the sky.

Just to cap it all, the media went nuclear nuts after bin Laden declared in an interview with Pakistani journalist Hamid Mir on 8 November 2001 – his first since 11 September – at a secret location, believed to be to the north of Kabul: 'I wish to declare that if America used chemical or nuclear weapons against us, then we may retort with chemical and nuclear weapons. We have the weapons as a deterrent.'

He refused to elaborate further and, when asked where he'd got them from, bin Laden snapped: 'Go to the next question.'

I pieced the story together but I couldn't shift it, and I started wondering if mister nasty spook had indeed enacted his threat of censorship. There was just silence and disinterest in what I thought was a fantastic story of a would-be world dominator with real doomsday devices. It looked like there might be some voluntary agreement by editors not to cover 'nuke terror horror' stories.

As I was wondering whether I'd been nobbled, my laptop crashed fatally, after I'd discovered that hackers had got in and could have been checking up on me for months. Also, my rubbish had not been collected – the only house on the street. I was stretching and looking out of the window early one morning when an unmarked van pulled up outside. Two shifty-looking men in green fluorescent jackets got out and returned my rubbish bags to their rightful place in the front garden and drove off again. They must have been going through the bags and had overlooked the fact that the bin men arrive extremely early, thus missing the collection. I had good reason to be paranoid by that stage, as I knew the garbage scam. It had happened before, about four years previously when I was working on a story about possible connections between secret military programmes and a rash of UFO sightings over Scotland. But to be honest, I wasn't that bothered. After the first experience, I'd been going to the trouble of burning all unwanted personal information – even envelopes and reject printer efforts. It is a good practice to get into to avoid problems with criminals and identity theft anyway. If I'd thought of it in time, I'd have started placing rank things in the core of the rubbish, just to make it a task that was just that little bit more unpleasant and even more pointless.

The discovery that hackers had been using me, which I only detected when I decided to buy firewall software to block unwanted connections, was more worrying and made me think that I'd have to invest some time in finding out how to set up watertight, next generation-strength cyber-defences.

There were no signs that I'd leaked anything important. If the security people were looking into my activities, then I had nothing to hide; I wasn't breaking any laws that I knew of. I was careful not to go around asking people to hack into email accounts or anything, because that's certainly illegal, although it wouldn't be difficult to find someone to do it. One contact said he worked with a hacking wizard who could put a picture of Gerry Adams in a dress on Sinn Fein's website, or at least he could if it was legal. He laughed like an asthmatic madman after saying that, however.

Too much work had gone into the nukes story just to let it go, and a few months later I had another shot at flogging it, because it seemed like a waste not to. I decided I might be better off trying an American newspaper, and chastised myself for not thinking about that earlier. I could be forgiven, though, as selling stateside borders on being a sub-economic activity. The pay rates are laughable and vastly lower than they are in the UK – shockingly so. Getting the story out into the public domain and partially covering my costs would be better than nothing, though.

It was a great shame in a way, because the US media was hot for terrorism news, while the UK press was not too concerned at missing out and more inclined to think that it was largely an American problem. This seemed a pretty parochial approach to me. If there was a threat that an American city would be destroyed by a suitcase nuke, then it had already relegated itself down the UK news list by being a foreign story, although this strict filtering failed to account for the consequences that such an event would have in the UK, or anywhere else. I'm sure that if a threat to destroy the World

Trade Center had been issued by al-Qaeda before the event, it wouldn't have made the front pages in the UK, unless it was a particularly slow news day.

I'd made some contacts at the *Washington Times* a few months earlier, so this was the first route I tried. David Jones, the foreign editor, liked the story and it was earmarked for immediate publication.

One of the more frustrating aspects of US journalism is the phenomenon of fact checking. It appears to be a system that's peculiar to the US: someone scours through your copy and you're challenged to back up every factual statement, just short of faxing your notes over to prove that you've talked to who you claim you talked to. It's long been a matter of debate as to whether this is an unnecessary layer of bureaucracy or not. I've been asked to provide company registration numbers for another newspaper before, to prove that companies mentioned in a story actually existed, and I felt a bit affronted by that. It's a layer of production that's not seen as necessary in the UK, as it's assumed that you're a professional and you've done a professional job and covered the basics to start with.

The *Times* was satisfied with what they'd got, however, and I can't remember any major queries arising. A couple of days later, on 28 October 2002, I saw the story on the *Times* website: a long special news feature about al-Qaeda and nuclear weapons. It looked even better when the cutting arrived in the post about ten days later, because it was spread over a full page. I watched on the Internet as the story made its way around the globe, and the piece was eventually used as briefing paper for the Washington DC-based Center for Arms Control and Non-proliferation.

The spook had only delayed the inevitable, and that gave me a nice warm egotistical glow inside.

In the intervening months, the hobby of bird-watching had started to occupy my mind. I thought I'd dig a little deeper into the underground world of cyber-terrorism: if, as seemed increasingly likely from the research I'd been doing, real-deal terrorists were using websites and chat rooms to communicate, then I wanted to find them. Almost immediately, I became intrigued by a discussion on a website about birds and babies. I kept going back to it, for reasons that I wasn't quite sure of at first, but I knew there was something odd about it.

It was meant to be the website of a group dedicated to fighting jihad in Afghanistan, yet there was no discussion about bombs raining down or burning villages being attacked by helicopter gunships, which you'd think would be pretty hot news and not hard to come by during the war that was going on. There was the occasional flurry of jihadism, but otherwise there was much talk about the beautiful wildlife and news of forthcoming weddings and talk about the names of new babies.

These people seemed to be completely oblivious to what was going on around them, and I just felt that it was very odd. I sensed there was something more to this when I was following a discussion there involving a guy, apparently a young student, who was on holiday and travelling along the border between Afghanistan and Pakistan. Every now and then he'd post messages along the lines of: 'I have arrived in Parachinar and the people are warm and welcoming. I saw three eagles soaring high above me today.'

No one appeared to respond directly, yet others in the group appeared to have a strange disjointed rapport with him. Other messages that stood out were those from new parents apparently asking the group for suggestions for naming a baby, but there seemed to be a lot of babies being born during this time of war. The virtual exclusion of any war news suggested to me that there was a deliberate policy not to talk about it and that there might be security reasons for what was obviously guarded talk.

It would have seemed perfectly innocent given just a cursory glance, but it then dawned on me that the various birds could be code words for aircraft. I checked and discovered that bin Laden had been spotted in the village of Parachinar recently. If this student (who had otherwise fallen victim to some dastardly travel agent who had sold him the world's worst package holiday) had described the people as welcoming, that could be coded talk for saying it was a safe area. It seemed like an idea worth pursuing, and I set out to ask Roger, my friendly cyber-terror expert, for some advice.

He told me that my instincts might be correct and advised me not to disturb the group in any way, as it was probably being monitored by Western intelligence agencies. He continued: 'Of all the places in the world to vacation, that border is very near the bottom of my list. The trick is to figure out which parts of the communication are euphemism and which parts could be code.'

Roger wasn't at all surprised; he'd come across this before. Al-Qaeda figures had been known to communicate in this way, but they usually spread discussions across several websites, so anyone seeing these kinds of messages on a site might work out part of the picture but wouldn't be able to piece the whole thing together without knowing which other sites to visit and in what sequence. Apparently it was a very effective system.

'There is good reason to believe that al-Qaeda is using codes. You've seen the traffic, which makes no sense in the context, but we don't quite have a good "mapping" on the meaning of the coding systems yet. It looks like various groups or cell structures use their own codes.'

Could the wandering student be, say, an al-Qaeda/Taliban scout preparing the ground ahead of bin Laden and his entourage? He wouldn't rule this out and said he'd have to do an analysis of all the messages on the site to get an idea of exactly what might be going on, although he believed it was entirely feasible that safe routes of passage through the tribal areas along the Afghanistan–Pakistan border were being organised in this way.

He said trial transcripts show that this technique was used by the cells involved in the failed Millennium Eve plot to bomb Los Angeles airport, when web-based discussion groups were used to communicate with al-Qaeda planners based in Jordan.

'Their communications back with the al-Qaeda core were structured in wedding terminology – probably enough to pass casual examination, unless you knew who was talking,' he said.

'It's worth noting that chapter 13 of the al-Qaeda training manual, which was deleted in the version the US released, specifically discusses secret writing, ciphers and codes.'

They varied in sophistication, to the point where encrypted orders for sleeper agents had been found embedded in Web images and even music files. The message could be compressed into a short string of numbers and placed somewhere in the source code of any kind of picture or MP3 music track. Finding them was far harder than looking for a needle in a haystack.

The codes, which can be just two bytes long, do not affect playback of the file, which can be many megabytes long. Al-Qaeda is suspected of using a 'Boyd Cycle' type codebook, which can reduce targeting and attack orders into a short binary code. A clear order to assassinate a particular head of state in particular circumstances and on a certain date might look like this:

1 111 1100 1 101 0101

Identifying that among all the innocent binary code that makes up a music track is a very tall order indeed and, although codes can be sniffed out with a software detector, you first have to find suspect tracks. I'd heard rumours about this method of hiding messages, called steganography, although it was my understanding that nothing positive had ever shown up on the Web. Roger said this was not the case, so I asked him if he could describe what had been intercepted in this way.

'Real traces have shown up, but they shouldn't be discussed. People are mistaking their competence because they think of these men as living in caves and primitive, which is far from the truth indeed.'

According to Roger, the code-breakers have been concentrating their efforts in the wrong place. Music files provide greater protection against discovery of 'stealthfiles' because MP3 tracks tend to be far larger than image files and this provides a much bigger haystack to hide the needle in. He said law enforcement agencies needed to develop a database of suspicious music files with possible 'cipher signatures'.

It's fairly mind-blowing to think that anyone could be listening to some music downloaded from the Net and be completely unaware that it also contains hidden orders from bin Laden. Roger was painting al-Qaeda commanders as being proficient at communicating and 'hiding in plain view' using cost-effective methods such as free anonymous email accounts and 'throw-away' websites. They were using Western technology to defeat the West, and it seemed that officialdom was struggling to keep up.

Another source corroborated this and said that the 11 September attacks were organised though a website run by Abu Zubaydah, an al-Qaeda fugitive who was thought to be one of the chief planners of the operation. Otherwise known as Mohamedou Ould Slahi, he'd allegedly sponsored the training in Afghanistan of one of the would-be Los Angeles airport bombers. He'd been in close contact with a bin Laden-owned front company, a construction firm, in Sudan.

Investigators had looked at the site earlier in the year and found that the guest book on the site was password-protected. Usually they are left open for visitors to leave inane messages, like, 'Great site, dude'. When they cracked the password, the investigators found 2,300 coded messages and data files. The access logs showed that the site had been operating since May 2000 and there was a surge of traffic in July and August 2001. Visitors had dwindled to zero by 9 September 2001. I checked the site, but it had been deleted, so I asked an intelligence contact if he had a copy and if he'd be kind enough to send it to me.

It was a run-of-the-mill 'pictures of my pony' type of site that said: 'I hope you have nice time during your surfing'. It was utterly nondescript and there were no outward clues as to the horrors that had been plotted there.

My contact said it was a 'novel' and 'resourceful' way of communicating. 'We believe that terrorist instructions were dispatched back and forth through this guest book from cyber cafés, making them tricky to track and decipher,' he said.

'An intensive US investigation strongly suggests he [Zubaydah] played a major role in communications for the 11 September strikes.'

He added that it was becoming clear that the al-Qaeda network is not as loosely knit as once thought; in fact, it appeared to be highly structured.

'For example, the German units specialise in financing the organisation, Spanish and Belgian units provide counterfeit documentation for the terrorists, and the British units are responsible for logistics and recruiting. All of these detached strands are subsequently woven into a tight web of terrorism.'

This was all prime material for a story I put together, entitled 'CODED AL-QAEDA MESSAGES INDICATE NEW ATTACKS'. It wasn't a seller, because I was starting to get ahead of the game, and it wasn't proving to be as economically advantageous as I'd anticipated. I was veering alarmingly off the trodden path and stretching credulity too much for the liking of some, as there was a collective belief in the media that leaned towards the Neanderthal view of the enemy.

One journalist even snapped at me and said: 'Come on! These are people who live in *caves.*'

'Yes, but they are very ambitious,' I replied, sarcastically.

Some took at face value the cavemen propaganda put forward by the media, while others sensed the shadow of something cold and menacing lurking just over the horizon. Measuring the true nature of the threat posed by bin Laden was exercising many great minds at this point: it was a new phenomenon.

A source told me that, while he couldn't disclose classified information, I might care to take a look at a suite of documents produced by a private-sector security and risk management consultancy called Decision Support Systems. The firm worked for major corporations and unnamed 'wealthy individuals'. The documents explored the issues of al-Qaeda's tactics and long-term goals in intricate detail. If they had been produced by a US government agency, they would certainly have been stamped 'secret'.

They were enormous documents, and I spent ages waiting for the printer to churn it all out. I'd clearly have to invest a great deal of time reading, and paper versions would reduce my risk of getting eye cancer. The main report was the smallest of the batch, but it was the most explosive by far. It was the result of a brainstorming session held just after the 11 September attacks between intelligence analysts trying to establish what exactly bin Laden's game plan was.

It concluded that his prime aims were to kick the US out of the Middle East and destroy Western civilisation to pave the way for a new global Islamic dictatorship: Planet Taliban. Chillingly, the report concluded 'that such ambitions are achievable' – if the West plays into bin Laden's hands, which it currently appears to be doing.

Al-Qaeda had set a trap, which the US had walked straight into, the report argued. The organisation could not hope to destroy the US military machine on its home turf, so the 11 September attacks were carried out with the full realisation that American troops would be drawn into the Middle East where they could be engaged in guerrilla warfare and be 'bled to death'. We were in the very early stages of the first phase of al-Qaeda's three-phase battle plan, which could be summed as: ungovernability–control–destruction.

Bin Laden himself clearly seemed to be modelling his tactics on those used by the Assassins during the Crusades in the Middle Ages. The similarities were certainly curious: the Assassins built fortresses in the Syrian mountains; they believed in a rigorous routine of education and physical training; they operated networks of sleeper agents in enemy camps; and they specialised in taking out their enemies using two-man suicide teams armed with daggers. The suicide stabbings were usually carried out while the operatives were under the influence of hashish, believing that their heroic deaths would earn them VIP status in paradise.

They specialised in war by terrorism, and it all sounded remarkably similar, apart from the upgraded weaponry and the dope smoking. That obviously had to be dropped because powerful drug fears and acute paranoia spikes would not be helpful to potential hijackers trying to slip unnoticed through US Customs. Thanks to advances in genetics, marijuana is much stronger in the modern era than it was in the Middle Ages, and the Assassins would probably struggle to get off the safe house sofa these days.

Al-Qaeda believed, like the Assassins, that the strengths of an enemy could be turned into their weaknesses and that patience was a golden virtue. The conflict started many years earlier with the 1993 bombing of the World Trade Center and has slowly evolved over the following years, the report noted; calling it 'controlled escalation'. I read this and realised that, without being aware of it, I'd been quietly following this escalation with interest, even when I was not directly involved in reporting on it.

We were in the first stages of the ungovernability phase of the plan, where US military intervention in Afghanistan, and possibly Iraq, would stir up resentment against the US among grassroots Muslims. The situation held many benefits for bin Laden, as he was personally identified as the chief bogeyman and this provided malcontents with a central figure to rally around. The US had effectively turned him into an icon, and, in propaganda terms, he was now seen as having parity with America and inspiring future generations of terrorists.

The second control phase would probably start with a series of massive terrorist attacks, in the manner of 11 September, which would be designed to spook the US into ramping up its military presence in the region and carrying out reprisal attacks. The document warned that the backlash would convince the wider Arab population that the Great Satan really was hell-bent on destroying Islam, and this unrest would threaten a series of governments of key petroleum-producing states in the region that are already viewed as weak, corrupt and un-Islamic.

Kuwait, Saudi Arabia and the United Arab Emirates would be particularly at risk, and any unwelcome developments would also destabilise nuclear-armed Pakistan. The impoverished states of Jordan, Syria, Lebanon and Egypt would quickly follow.

Bin Laden and his supporters planned to fill the power vacuum. The propaganda wasn't simply aimed at the US; its efforts were also directed at the 'apostate' regimes in the Middle East that it regarded as being propped up by the West, and I knew that bin Laden was rabidly opposed to the Saudi royal family. If this plan should come to pass, he might control the vast majority of the world's proven oil reserves and, by default, hijack the global economy. I thought bin Laden was on record as saying that the price of oil would increase to $125 a barrel if he had his way, which would be devastating to the interests of the West.

At around the time of the hijacking of the world's economy, the panel concluded, a mass-casualty terrorist attack against US troops in the region would occur, and this would prove to be a tipping point for the future of the world. The Americans would be faced with the dilemma of either accepting the demands of al-Qaeda or attempting an all-out invasion of the entire region.

The attack could well be nuclear and it might be targeted at airbases where there would be large troop concentrations. The report noted: 'Al-Qaeda may already control Pakistan's nuclear weapons (command and control for these weapons is human-centric, and thus susceptible to infiltration or subversion), or could acquire control through overthrowing the destabilised government.'

It did not discount biological or radiological attacks, but the analysts erred on the side of nuclear, suspecting that one of the motives behind the anthrax letters may have been to mislead the authorities into preparing for the wrong kind of attack. The feasibility of biological and chemical attacks is also limited by the range of delivery systems available to the terrorists, whereas a suicide bomber carrying a suitcase nuke is an attractive choice as a precision guided weapon.

Nuclear suicide bombers: it had seemed like that might be the conclusion when I first started out on this story, and I had mixed feelings when I saw my suspicions confirmed in print in the report. It put an end to the semantics, I thought, and indeed this was the message the report was sending. We have to assume that it's a possibility that they might have them, and, if they have, they will use them at some point. Maybe they don't have many and they are weapons of last resort to be used sparingly. Then again, they might have a stockpile of the things and innovative and ambitious plans for their deployment, like a simultaneous multi-city strike.

I knew now that we were living in extremely dangerous times, and I was starting to think that maybe the guy who didn't want to read such stories on the train had a point. There were tens of thousands of Afghanistan-trained jihadis spread out around the world, and all of them would clamour to volunteer for such missions. It was a terrifying and apocalyptic forecast of future events, but it was anchored in solid reason and ultra-realism, which made it all the more depressing. Bin Laden's rumoured health problems could lead to an acceleration of his plans and more 'drastic terrorist actions'.

There was more. The analysts believed that this middle 'control' phase of the war would be temporary and that we'd quickly move into the final destruction phase. The panellists judged that America would feel bound to undertake an attempt to regain control of the oilfields and this would be the trigger. Bin Laden would then destroy the oil production system across the Middle East, removing at a stroke all reason for continuing US economic interest in the region. There would be nothing worth fighting for after that, and the world would face the mother of all economic meltdowns as oil supplies dried up, never to be replenished.

The thought of a world deprived of energy conjured up images from the film *Mad Max*. Power generation would be decimated, with not inconsiderable knock-on effects for transportation, manufacturing, especially high-technology products, agriculture and the production of pharmaceuticals. The world as we know it would change completely in a very short space of time and we'd enter a new Dark Age.

The destruction of the oilfields could happen in three ways. The first method is reminiscent of Saddam Hussein's destruction of the oil wells in Kuwait during the 1991 Gulf War. A rolling programme of destruction with hand-placed conventional explosives would be feasible, given that al-Qaeda could call upon the help of many thousands of recruits.

The other options are both nuclear. In a 'limited number of strategic positions' a small nuclear device would expose the Middle East's oil infrastructure to massive radiation exposure, with sand causing fallout on a scale that would be out of proportion to the yield of the device. In addition, hydrostatic shock waves transmitted through pipelines could destroy production and delivery facilities over wide areas. The very worst case scenario would see simultaneous attacks on major oil centres outside the Middle East, including the USA and Central America.

I consulted the academics on this point, and few demurred from the assertion that terrible damage would result, although predicting the scale of that damage with any precision was difficult because it hadn't been tried before. 'If you presume perfect accuracy – that is, hand placement within inches of where intended – there are very few objects that would not be severely damaged by a small nuke,' said Robert Sherman at the Federation of American Scientists. 'I presume that someone with a detailed knowledge of the oilfield could cause a cascading effect with great damage.'

Professor Rogers was more sceptical: 'Portable Atomic Demolition Munitions typically have a yield of one kiloton or less. Such warheads would have a limited effect against an oilfield because well-heads are normally quite dispersed, but could do substantial damage to a refinery or a major pumping facility.'

In fact, the terrorists may not need their own nuclear weapons to achieve this; the document suggests that bin Laden's 'not unthinkable' endgame could be to give the order to fire Scud missiles with WMD payloads at Israel. The retaliation would be sure to be nuclear and targeted on the launch sites that had been deliberately scattered around the Saudi oilfields.

Bin Laden stands by the Scud launcher and says his last cheery goodbyes to his old comrades in the final moments before he is martyred in the white heat of an atomic fireball and finds himself transported into the arms of the beautiful virgins in paradise. He grins widely with the satisfaction of knowing that his mission on earth has been accomplished and he starts to feel himself relaxing as slender fingers start to slowly massage his scalp and slide sensuously down through his long hair.

THE MISSING LINK

In the months that followed the 11 September attacks, theories that the authorities had something to hide about what had happened on that fateful day started to emerge. It was the US administration's apparent reluctance to hold an inquiry into the events that was fuelling the speculation. Some started suggesting that the US government knew more about the attacks than it was willing to admit, and it didn't want these smoking guns to be dredged up in a public inquiry. I found it odd that there wasn't a public inquiry in the UK, as some 60 British citizens perished that day. That's a major incident of mass murder in anybody's books, and if they'd died in a train crash somewhere in Britain, then the setting up of an inquiry would have happened almost automatically.

I was prepared to accept that a kind of institutional hebetude had allowed the terrorists to get through, and Bush appeared to advocate this defence when he set up the Department of Homeland Security to coordinate intelligence gathering. As soon as 11 September happened, however, I thought it would be just a matter of time before JFK-style theories about conspiracies started to emerge; in fact, I expected an explosion of them, because there were so many different angles to look at. All those people who'd spent years studying all the finer aspects of what happened near that grassy knoll now had a much meatier matter to grapple with, at long last.

The first alternative theory that I can recall seeing was from a guy who was seriously trying to argue that the planes which crashed into the twin towers were actually cruise missiles painted to look like airliners and that the real flights had landed at military bases where the passengers . . . well, who knows what happened to them.

It was the first and the worst one, probably ranking with a picture of a pigeon taking to the air with the burning twin towers in the background, which lots of people were trying to argue was a mysterious low-flying fighter plane. Image enhancement technology was deployed to try to reinforce the argument, and blow-ups and comparison images were presented, but it still looked like a startled pigeon to me.

There were legitimate areas of concern on a lot of major issues, like whether Flight 93 had been shot down over Pennsylvania or not. Some people really wanted there to be more, much more, even suggesting that the US government itself had sanctioned the attacks. It was a very grave charge, probably the gravest that could be levelled against an administration. There were frequent mentions of Operation Northwoods: a declassified military plan that was made public three months before the 11 September attacks, after years of rumours about its existence.

It was revealed that on 12 March 1962, the Joint Chiefs of Staff recommended enacting a plan of 'fake terrorism' inside the US, which included hijacking airliners and blowing up unmanned aircraft in mid-air, and blaming it on Cuba. The public outrage caused by the events would have provided the pretext for a full military invasion of Cuba and the removal of Fidel Castro, but President Kennedy rejected the proposal. The top brass were incensed, and they continued to develop other schemes along these lines, including flying U-2 spy planes over the island at low level so that they could be shot down – and even attempting to provoke a war between Cuba and another Latin American country that would require US intervention.

The myriad of 11 September theories being put forward even prompted President Bush to appeal for an end to the speculation. Just two months after the attacks, he told the United Nations General Assembly: 'Let us never tolerate outrageous conspiracy theories concerning the attacks of September the 11th; malicious lies that attempt to shift the blame away from the terrorists themselves, away from the guilty.' It could be seen as a case of the lady protesting too much, but the fact remained that Bush had labelled questioners as, effectively, unpatriotic. Attorney General John Ashcroft went even further and warned that Americans who questioned the official version might face prosecution for treason or 'lending comfort to the enemy'.

Bloody hell, this was starting to have all the hallmarks of *1984*. Many of those sceptics being criticised included the grieving relatives of the victims, who wanted the inquiry that the Bush administration was resisting – presumably they'd all be locked up now. Luckily, they were not alone: 73 per cent of the population thought that the Bush administration was hiding or lying about something relating to 11 September, according to a *CBS News* opinion poll. Even more interesting was that 77 per cent were now following news stories relating to the FBI investigation and how the attacks had been planned and executed.

I was intrigued as to what the relatives of the victims might think about all of this, but I knew I'd have to be especially sensitive when contacting them. I had no wish to compound their grief by intruding with a load of daft questions about silly conspiracy theories. I asked around and gathered the email addresses of some prospective candidates. I took care to compose a sensitive introduction to them. I nearly abandoned the project a couple of times, as I was worried that I might be overstepping the mark, but I eventually hit the send button.

The first to respond was David Potorti, whose brother James perished on the 96th floor of the north tower at the World Trade Center. He worked for Marsh & McLennan, a major financial services company that lost nearly 300 people that day. That floor was the point of impact for Flight 11; there were no phone calls from there afterwards. To my relief and surprise, he was encouraged by the public's distrust of the official story.

'I do support their efforts, and the efforts of many others, in their pursuit of the truth,' said David. 'I don't think of them as conspiracy theorists; rather, I think of them as using plain common sense.

'I genuinely think that the answers will have a direct effect on my safety and the safety of my family.'

That line resonated with me, because the corollary suggested that he felt like he might be in danger at this time.

He said a full and open inquiry was desperately needed to resolve the outstanding issues; and secret hearings at Congressional committees just wouldn't do. David and hundreds of other relatives had joined together to launch a lobbying campaign in Washington DC. It seemed to me that it was a matter of the deepest shame that their government was turning its back on them.

'I unequivocally favour a full, thorough, public, nongovernmental, no-holds-barred investigation into the complete failure of US institutions on 11 September, as well as in the months before and after,' he continued.

'It astonishes me that it has taken this long to even begin talking about an investigation. That the mere need for an investigation can still be questioned makes me tremendously cynical and suspicious of the motivations behind the calls to "put this behind us".

'Determining what went wrong – or what wilfully was allowed to happen – is not a partisan political issue; it is a matter of life and death for everyone on earth. I truly want to spare other innocent victims the pain that my family has suffered. The only way to do this is to take a brave, unflinching look at all of the participants – both inside and outside the US – who may wilfully or unwittingly have played a role in these crimes against humanity.'

No wonder he felt like his life might be in danger, as he was willing to consider the most extreme theory: that senior US officials knew what was being planned and they let it happen, like a modern-day version of Operation Northwoods.

A name eventually evolved for this theory: LIHOP (They Let It Happen On Purpose). It was being fiercely promoted by grassroots Democratic Party activists, extreme right-wingers and New World Order militia types – which was a very strange coalition indeed. Something wasn't right here.

David's sentiments were echoed by Ryan Amundson, who lost his brother Craig in the attack on the Pentagon. He was a US Army multimedia illustration specialist. Ryan was also suspicious and he told me that, with no immediate prospect of a public inquiry, the families were hoping that the media would soon unearth a smoking gun.

'I think the growing level of scepticism can be attributed to a dearth of information and the Bush administration's subsequent road-blocking of a full, fair and public review. That is a recipe for scepticism.

'There are many victims' families who want an investigation, and I think if this could be seen as a victims' rights issue, then maybe a full, fair and public investigation would take place.

'Until then, I must try to figure out what is going on through a plethora of conflicting media reports. If it weren't for investigative reporters, the public would really be in the dark.'

THE MISSING LINK

What follows is my own condensed version of the events of the day of 11 September 2001. I compiled it as an experiment, to get it straight in my own mind just what did actually happen that day, as many lesser-known aspects of the story were buried under the welter of the media coverage on the day and in the weeks immediately after the attacks. Important facts did not emerge until months after the actual events. I've pulled all this information into one piece, without comment or embellishment. I've also added some exclusive information from my own sources, mainly about the al-Qaeda side of the story.

The first sign of trouble occurs at around 6 a.m. George W. Bush wakes up in the Colony Beach and Tennis Resort on Longboat Key, Florida, and prepares for his morning jog. A surface-to-air missile battery has been stationed on the roof of the building. A van occupied by 'men of Middle Eastern descent' arrives at the resort, and the men claim they are there to conduct a 'poolside interview' with the President. They are turned away after being told that they don't have an appointment.

At the same time, day two of operation Vigilant Guardian is beginning at North America Aerospace Defense Command [NORAD], which will stage an imaginary national crisis in US airspace as part of a week-long war-games exercise. The lead al-Qaeda hijackers boarded a flight from Portland to Boston seven minutes ago and all the teams are now moving into position.

Thirty minutes later, an argument breaks out between a member of the public and five men of Middle Eastern descent over a car parking space at Logan Airport in Boston. The man involved in the argument said they mentioned they had a 'big job to do in New York'. The men's car is later found to have been rented by the lead hijacker Mohammed Atta, and it contains a pass allowing the occupants access to restricted areas at the airport

Fifteen minutes later, at least two workers for Odigo, an Internet messaging company with offices two blocks from the World Trade Center in New York, receive messages warning them that the WTC is about to be attacked by terrorists. Under half an hour on and Mohammed Atta and Abdul Aziz al-Omari board American Airlines Flight 11 in Boston, bound for New York.

During security checks, Atta's bags are found to contain airline uniforms that have been reported stolen in Italy. They are checked

TERROR TRACKER

in nonetheless, but they miss his transfer and are not loaded on to the hijacked plane. In total, nine of the nineteen would-be hijackers are selected for special screening before they board their flights. Six have their bags searched for weapons and explosives, and two are found to have irregularities in their identification documents. All are eventually allowed to board. Two of the men, Khalid al-Mihdhar and Nawaf al-Hazmi, are on a terrorist watch list, but they are not selected.

7.59 a.m. – Atta on Flight 11 phones Marwan al-Shehhi on Flight 175 as both planes are about to take off, presumably to confirm that the operation is on. President Bush sits down for his daily intelligence briefing a minute later, which includes a reference to a general heightened risk of terrorist attacks during the summer.

The first hijacking – of Flight 11 – occurs at 8.14 a.m., when radio contact with ground controllers is lost. The plane starts to veer dramatically off course seven minutes later. The controllers in Boston conclude at 8.20 a.m. that it has probably been hijacked.

Flight 77 departs from Dulles International Airport near Washington at 8.20 a.m., after being delayed for ten minutes.

On Flight 11, passenger Daniel Lewin, a former member of the Israeli Defence Forces' Sayeret Matkal special-operations unit, is either shot or stabbed one minute later on by Satam al-Suqami, as four hijackers make their way to the flight deck. Lewin took part in the rescue of 103 hostages at Entebbe Airport in 1976. One of the hijackers appears to have an explosive device with yellow wires attached to it and a noxious substance is sprayed in the first-class cabin to keep passengers out. They have 25 minutes left on this earth.

At 8.35 a.m., President Bush's motorcade leaves for the Emma E. Booker Elementary School in Sarasota, Florida. NORAD is notified of the highjack of Flight 77 five minutes later and the order is given to scramble fighter aircraft, although the officers believe the incident is part of the Vigilant Guardian war-games exercise. United Airlines Flight 175 is hijacked one minute later, at 8.42 a.m., as Flight 93 takes off from Newark International Airport and veers off its set course after just one minute.

The Carlyle Group, a defence company with strong links to the Reagan and Bush administrations, is holding a conference in Washington. Osama bin Laden's brother Shafig is one of the guests of honour. Mahmud Ahmed, director-general of Pakistan's

104

Directorate of Inter-Services Intelligence (ISI), which is credited with creating the Taliban in Afghanistan, is at a breakfast meeting at the Capitol with the chairmen of the House and Senate intelligence committees.

US Defense Secretary Donald Rumsfeld is speaking at the Pentagon about missile defence and terrorism at 8.44 a.m., and he says: 'And let me tell you, I've been around the block a few times. There will be another event.' For emphasis, he repeated: '*There will be another event.*'

According to an intercepted al-Qaeda communication passed to this author, Atta is in phone contact with al-Qaeda operatives on the ground during the final seven to ten minutes of Flight 11. He is giving 'the brothers' a live running commentary on the operation as it is taking place. The ground-based conspirators are recording the call. He tells them that Satam al-Suqami has killed 'a policeman'.

Soon, the vertical silver and black stripes of the World Trade Center's north tower start to fill the windscreen. Atta turns to his colleagues on the flight deck and tells them: 'Allah is the greatest! We'll meet in heaven, if Allah wishes it.

'Allah is the greatest! Allah is the greatest!!'

Contact stops. Flight 11 crashes into the north tower of the WTC at 8.46:40 a.m. with massive loss of life.

CIA director George Tenet is having breakfast with a senator when he is informed of the crash. He tells Senator David Boren: 'You know, this has bin Laden's fingerprints all over it.'

American Airlines Flight 77 from Washington starts veering off course around 8.46 a.m. and the nearest fighter jets are 207 miles away.

Two F-15s take off to find Flight 11 — six minutes after it has crashed. They are sent after Flight 175 instead.

According to an al-Qaeda communications intercept, at this time Osama bin Laden was taking tea with colleagues at a guesthouse in Kandahar, Afghanistan, when the BBC World Service reported the attack on the radio. The room is filled with shouting and cheering. Bin Laden raises a finger to his lips to urge his audience to keep quiet. With the room silent, he raises an arm and holds out two fingers, indicating that news of another attack will soon be forthcoming.

Air Force General Richard Myers, vice-chairman of the Joint

Chiefs of Staff, goes ahead with a meeting at the Pentagon, apparently unaware that there is an emergency.

8.50 a.m. – radio contact is lost with Flight 77.

President Bush is told of the first WTC crash sometime within nine minutes of the event. As his motorcade arrives at the school, a message is broadcast in the south tower of the WTC telling people that it is safe for them to return to their offices. Bush apparently believes that it was an accident, and he carries on with his visit, listening to a story about a pet goat.

At 9 a.m., an odd incident occurs on United Airlines Flight 23 in New York. The captain tells the passengers after boarding that the flight has been cancelled, but three men of Middle Eastern descent argue with the crew and refuse to get off the plane. Security is called, but the men vanish before the guards arrive.

At 9.03 a.m., Flight 175 smashes into the WTC south tower. An estimated total of 2,662 innocent people will eventually perish in New York.

Bin Laden hears the news in Kandahar. He calms his audience again and holds up three fingers.

A New Jersey housewife, who is looking in horror at the two burning towers through a pair of binoculars, spots five men kneeling on the roof of a white van outside her building. They appear to be filming the events and shouting 'cries of joy and mockery'. She phones the FBI, which issues an all-points bulletin for the van. It's owned by a company called Urban Moving Systems.

The F-15s are still 71 miles away. At no point are they ordered to shoot down an aircraft. This is an order which can only be given on the instruction of the President, who is indisposed.

Bush's security detail now decides it's time to evacuate, but he carries on at the school – even after he is informed of the second crash.

9.24 a.m. – NORAD is informed by the Federal Aviation Administration that Flight 77 is heading for Washington and it may have been hijacked. Donald Rumsfeld and his top aides are inside the Pentagon and apparently unaware that they are in any danger.

A 'ground stop' order is issued by the FAA, effectively banning all movements in US airspace. There are 4,452 aircraft in the air.

Three hijackers on Flight 93 stand up and tie red bandanas around their foreheads. At the same time, three F-16 fighters are scrambled to intercept Flight 77, which is 50 miles from Washington and closing in at a speed of 500 mph, while the fighters are 129 miles away and still on the ground.

A brawl between passengers and hijackers breaks out on Flight 93 one minute later. A brief radio transmission of the hijackers' voices is mistakenly attributed by controllers to Delta Airlines Flight 1989. In all, 11 flights would be suspected of being hijacked.

Bush delivers a short speech, at 9.29 a.m., while still at the Booker Elementary School, calling the events at the World Trade Center 'a national tragedy'. Some 200 students, teachers and journalists are invited to join him in a moment of silence.

One minute later, at 9.30 a.m., the hijackers of Flight 77 announce to the passengers that they are about to die, as they are going to crash the plane into the White House. The plane passes over the Pentagon at 7,000 feet, turns sharply and descends, passing close by the White House.

9.35 a.m. – Bush's motorcade leaves the school and heads for Sarasota-Bradenton International Airport. Minutes before, the Secret Service is apparently informed that Air Force One may be a target.

A minute later, Flight 93 turns over Cleveland and steers towards Washington, which is ten minutes away.

A military C-130 transport plane has a close encounter with Flight 77 as it turns over Washington, and the pilot is told to follow the plane.

Watching TV inside the Pentagon, Donald Rumsfeld says: 'Believe me, this isn't over yet. There's going to be another attack, and it could be us.'

In front of the Pentagon, fireman Alan Wallace gets the shock of his life when he looks up and sees an airliner coming straight towards him. It is 25 ft off the ground, approaching at 460 mph and no landing gear is visible. Street lighting columns are bent over as the plane's wings clip them.

He runs for cover and Flight 77 plunges into the Pentagon at 9.37:46 a.m., killing 125 people.

In Afghanistan, bin Laden now holds up four fingers.

Secret Service agents burst into Vice-President Dick Cheney's office in the White House and propel him down the steps leading to the Presidential Emergency Operations Center in the basement.

F-16 pilots over Washington are told by the Secret Service to protect the White House, and a general evacuation of the building begins. The two pilots of Flight 93 are dead, the hijackers have rebuffed a passengers' revolt and are holding them at bay. Two minutes later, the passengers take a vote and decide to try to storm the flight deck. The evacuation of the Capitol building in Washington begins a minute later and political leaders are flown to secret bunkers.

9.53 a.m. – the US National Security Agency intercepts a call from one of bin Laden's operatives in Afghanistan to a phone number in the Republic of Georgia. He says he has heard good news and that another target is about to be hit.

Air Force One takes to the air at around 9.54 a.m., after a delay caused by thorough baggage checks – and without a fighter escort. Bush authorises the shoot-down of any suspect planes and the President's plane takes off and 'rockets' almost straight up for ten minutes, before circling at high altitude as Bush, Cheney and the Secret Service argue over where it should head for.

Fighting breaks out between hijackers and passengers outside the flight deck on Flight 93. The hijackers inside are chanting '*Allah-u-Akbar*! [God is Great]'. Cheney authorises the shoot-down of Flight 93 at around this time. Edward Felt calls the emergency services from the toilet and reports seeing an explosion and white smoke as a group of passengers try to overpower the hijackers. There is a whooshing noise of wind in the background.

One minute later, at 9.59 a.m., the south tower of the WTC collapses, just after an explosion is heard and seen by both firefighters and ordinary bystanders.

10.00 a.m. – it is reported that there is a fire at the State Department building and subsequent reports blame a car bomb. Deputy Secretary of State Richard Armitage goes outside the building to look and reports that the news is false. There are conflicting reports over whether or not fighters were in the skies over Washington at this time.

Bill Wright, flying a small plane three miles away from Flight 93 over Pennsylvania, sees it rock back and forth three or four times. Two F-16s are closely following the plane. One eyewitness on the ground, Linda Shepley, hears a loud bang and sees the plane bank to the side. Only the rushing of wind can be heard on the open phone line to the plane. It starts breaking up and other eyewitnesses say it was flying upside down in the final seconds before impact.

The US government says Flight 93 crashes at 10.03 in a field near the town of Shanksville in Pennsylvania. Some wreckage is found eight miles away. A seismic survey later commissioned by the US Army puts the time at 10.06:05 a.m. If true, then there are three minutes missing from the cockpit flight voice-recorder tape that was played to relatives. A large part of one of the engines is later found over half a mile away from the crash scene.

Three minutes after the crash, a second aircraft – small and white with two rear engines and no visible markings – is spotted flying low in erratic patterns over the crash site. Bush is told of the crash two minutes later, and he asks if Flight 93 was shot down. The answer he received is not on record.

Armed agents are deployed around the White House. Two minutes later, all US military forces go to DEFCON Three: the highest state of alert for 30 years.

10.12 a.m. – CNN reports an explosion at Capitol Hill in Washington, but retracts the news 12 minutes later. Federal buildings begin being evacuated a minute later at 10.13 a.m., starting with the United Nations building in New York.

The section of wall hit by Flight 77 at the Pentagon collapses two minutes later. The WTC north tower collapses 13 minutes after this at 10.28 a.m., after 15,000 people have been safely evacuated. Once again, there are reports of explosions just prior to the collapse of the tower.

Donald Rumsfeld walks into the National Military Command Center in the Pentagon at 10.30 a.m. For nearly an hour officials have been wondering whether he might have been among the dead.

Two minutes later, Cheney calls Bush and warns him of a threat to Air Force One. A fighter escort is at least 40 minutes away and the plane turns towards Louisiana, as it has been decided that Bush cannot return to Washington.

10.42 a.m. – the FAA tells the White House that there are three planes that it cannot account for. Colonel Mark Tillman, pilot of Air Force One, is told of the threat to his plane. An airliner that is out of radio contact with ground controllers is in front of the aircraft and he takes evasive action.

11.00 a.m. – the FAA says that all 923 flights now in the sky over the US are accounted for. Skyscrapers in several cities are evacuated and tourist attractions, such as Disneyland, begin closing. The former supreme commander of NATO forces in Europe, General Wesley Clark, says in a TV interview 30 minutes later: 'Only one group has this kind of ability, and that is Osama bin Laden's.'

Dr Van Romero, an explosives expert and vice-president for research at New Mexico Institute of Mining and Technology, concludes that explosives must have been used to topple the twin towers, as the nature of their collapse was 'too methodical'. He would retract his statement ten days later.

Air Force One touches down at Barksdale Air Force base near Shreveport, Louisiana. At noon, Bush is ferried into the base inside a Humvee armoured personnel carrier, which is guarded by armed outriders. He spends most of the time discussing with Cheney and others where he should travel to next.

12.05 p.m. – CIA director George Tenet tells Rumsfeld about the call made by one of bin Laden's operatives, which was intercepted two hours earlier.

At 12.36 p.m., while inside Barksdale air base, Bush tapes a video statement to be played later to the TV networks. He refers to a 'faceless coward' and vows that 'freedom will be defended'.

At 12.58 p.m., he agrees to fly to Nebraska. New York Mayor Rudolph Giuliani orders the evacuation of Manhattan two minutes later. Bush puts the US military on high alert worldwide in another two minutes. A plan for continuity of government dating from the Cold War era is activated and a 'shadow government' of about 100 officials are flown to secure bunkers well away from the capital city.

German intelligence intercepts a phone call between two followers of bin Laden and a desperate search starts for two more hijacking teams. One of the callers refers to the '30 people travelling for the operation'. The FBI discovers 'knife-like' weapons hidden on three other airliners that had their flights cancelled.

1.24 p.m. – the pilots of Korean Air Flight 85 accidentally issue a hijacking alert as it nears Alaska. Two fighters tail the plane, and the pilots are told that it will be shot down if it flies over populated areas. Evacuations of strategic sites across Alaska begin. The plane lands later in Canada without incident.

The US Navy dispatches aircraft carriers and guided missile destroyers to New York and Washington at 1.44 p.m. and NORAD goes to its highest state of alert. All over the country, fighters and support aircraft are scrambled.

2 p.m. – Fighter pilot Major Daniel Nash returns to base under the impression that an airliner has been shot down over Pennsylvania.

Forty minutes later, the CIA discovers from the airline passenger manifests that three of the hijackers were known al-Qaeda operatives. Rumsfeld begins planning an attack against bin Laden and Saddam Hussein. An aide made notes during the meeting. Quoting Rumsfeld, they read: '. . . best info fast. Judge whether good enough hit S.H. [Saddam Hussein] at same time. Not only UBL. [Osama bin Laden] Go massive. Sweep it all up. Things related and not.'

Air Force One lands at Offutt Air Force Base, headquarters of US Strategic Command, near Omaha, Nebraska, ten minutes later. After another ten minutes, Bush emerges and enters a nuclear blast-proof bunker where he holds a teleconference with Cheney, Rumsfeld, Tenet, Armitage, National Security Advisor Condoleezza Rice, Secretary of Transportation Norman Mineta and members of the National Security Council.

4.00 p.m. – the white Urban Moving Systems van reported to the FBI earlier in the day is spotted near the Giants stadium in New Jersey. Five men in their 20s are taken out of the car at gunpoint and handcuffed. Inside the vehicle is $4,700 in cash and a pair of box-cutting knives.

The driver of the van, Sivan Kurzberg, identifies the group as Israeli nationals. The passengers were his brother Paul, Yaron Shmuel, Oded Ellner and Omer Marmari. They are taken away for questioning and some of the men are later suspected of being members of the Israeli secret intelligence service Mossad, but they are eventually released after weeks of interrogation. No charges are brought against them.

4.10 p.m. – the 47-storey Building Seven at the WTC is reported to be on fire. Bush leaves Nebraska and heads for Washington 13 minutes later. At 5.20 p.m., Building Seven mysteriously collapses. No one is killed.

A young unnamed Middle Eastern man travelling from Amsterdam to Detroit is arrested after his flight is diverted to Toronto. He is carrying a picture of himself in an airline uniform in front of a fake backdrop of the WTC.

Bush arrives back at the White House at 6.54 p.m. Secretary of State Colin Powell arrives back in Washington from a trip to Lima,

Peru, six minutes later. He says he was unable to communicate with his colleagues for the duration of the flight, due to 'communications problems'.

Bush addresses the nation at 8.30 p.m. and chairs a meeting of the National Security Council at 9 p.m. He meets with his senior national security advisers 30 minutes later, in a bunker beneath the grounds of the White House. Cheney's staff, and other White House personnel, are given the anti-anthrax drug Cipro and are told to take it regularly from now on.

11.30 p.m. – the President is preparing to sleep. He writes in his diary: 'The Pearl Harbor of the twenty-first century took place today. We think it's Osama bin Laden.'

One of the chief pieces of 'evidence' cited by those who support the idea of a conspiracy on 11 September was the apparently slow response of the Air Force. There are conflicting reports about flight times and speeds, and the controversy remains to this day. The evidence points to a cock-up, albeit a very embarrassing one, although those with suspicious minds think a 'stand down' order was given to leave the skies deliberately unprotected so the hijackers could carry out the operation without hindrance. No evidence has come to light to back up this 'New Northwoods' theory.

There was a similar paucity of evidence to support the infamous French Theory, which asserted that an airliner hadn't crashed into the Pentagon. Based largely on the lack of visible wreckage, indistinct CCTV footage shot from the car park, and varying eyewitness reports, the advocates of this theory claimed that a military fighter actually crashed into the building. It fired a missile ahead of itself just before impact. Silly bullshit, I thought.

The simple explanation for the anomalies is that there was a series of mini cover-ups to obscure that fact that the mighty Uncle Sam was not just caught with his pants down; he was caught without pants and dressed in women's clothes. I set out to test the conspiracy theories, although I was spoiled for choice as to the entry point for the story, as an online poll conducted by the relatives came up with a bewildering list of over 500 'unanswered questions' about that day.

My first break came in May 2002 as I was chatting to a friend on the phone, Ray Vandy, a fine journalist. He was a trained engineer in his previous life, and he mentioned that he might have a story for me. The first official report about the collapse of the WTC buildings had been published the week before by a team of engineers working for the Federal Emergency Management Agency (FEMA), and Ray said I needed to take a look at what happened to Building Seven. The experts were baffled, as it shouldn't have collapsed.

He called it 'the mystery of the third tower'. The 47-storey high WTC7 caught fire and burned for an 'unprecedented' seven hours before it crumpled and folded in on itself in the space of 40 seconds. Yet it had suffered only minor and superficial damage from flying wreckage.

'As engineers began to probe the wreckage of the buildings around the twin towers, they discovered that there was no obvious explanation for the spectacular demise of WTC7,' said Ray.

'No other major modern building has ever collapsed in the same way. And to even begin to construct a scenario that might explain the disaster, the investigators had to strain credulity to its limits.'

In a nutshell, the building shouldn't have caught fire. Ray was as baffled as the investigators.

I looked up the floor plans of the building and found it had a list of exotic tenants, which included the Secret Service, the Department of Defense and the CIA. The layouts showed that there were vast storerooms in these areas, but there were no clues as to what they contained.

No high-rise steel-framed building had ever collapsed due to the effects of fire, yet three had done so in one day. Ray thought that answers may have been found in those storage areas and that perhaps they contained chemicals that fuelled the fire: riot control equipment or maybe flammable microfilm files was all he could think of, but he thought it unlikely that these kinds of substances alone could fuel a seven-hour fire.

The FEMA team was not allowed on site to inspect the wreckage, and they admitted that the only explanation they could come up with 'has only a low probability of occurrence'. In other words, their scenario was highly unlikely to be the truth. They suggested that burning wreckage from the collapse of the north tower started fires on six floors of WTC7 and some had managed to smash right through the building and set light to fuel that had been leaking from a standby diesel generator. This cooked the building's two main 2.5 m deep load-bearing girders until they softened and eventually buckled.

That would have been extraordinary bad luck and should have been dealt with by the sprinkler system, but that had malfunctioned. Also, WTC Building Six stood between WTC7 and the north tower, and it did not burn and collapse.

He was heavily hinting that something was very wrong here and pointed to the two different types of smoke that were seen coming from the building. Black smoke was billowing from the upper floors, while only a small volume of white smoke was emanating from the lower floors, where the girders were supposed to be roasting at a temperature of a 1,000 degrees plus. This was where the CIA, Secret Service and the DoD had their storerooms.

'It could have been just records, microfilms and computer tapes, all highly flammable and stored in un-sprinklered storage areas. But these would have been expected to burn out in a lot less than seven hours,' said Ray.

He added: 'So what did burn hot enough and long enough to soften steel up to 2.5m thick? We may never know. But until we do, the fate of WTC7 will haunt the engineering community and cast a long shadow over similar high-rise developments around the world.'

Ray wasn't his real name; he suggested that I use this pseudonym because he didn't want to be directly associated with the article and attract unwarranted attention to himself. It was a good 'in' to the story, but it needed a lot more work; getting to know what was in those secret warehouses was the key and that would be very difficult.

Checking out a wilder explanation from another source would have been an equally arduous task. This source maintained that such secret facilities would have been protected by a self-destruct system: a series of explosive thermite charges would have been placed around the offices ready to be detonated to destroy the contents of the offices and storerooms in an emergency, to stop files and equipment falling into the wrong hands. It sounded vaguely plausible, and he was a trusted contact. I started sketching out an article on all this, when I received an important email which led me to move on to a new, major story.

There was no message, just a link to a Web page. After just a couple of seconds of looking at what appeared on the screen, a 'Bingo!' feeling flushed through me and a wide smile started to spread. The first image was a black and white photograph of a group of people gathered near a large whiteboard and behind a tabletop model of the Pentagon and the surrounding buildings; smoke was rising from the Pentagon. The next image was a close-up shot of the centre of the building, and there was a model of a wrecked aircraft there, complete with miniature smoke and flames.

The link was to an article in a US Army newspaper that gave details of an emergency planning exercise that had been held 11 months prior to 11 September. The Pentagon Mass-Casualty Exercise (MASCAL) simulated a passenger plane crashing into the building and representatives of Pentagon Emergency Management Team, military police, Army medics and the local Arlington Fire Department practised how they'd deal with such an event in a conference room inside the Pentagon. It was estimated that such a crash would result in 341 victims.

The report read like an account of the events of 11 September: 'The fire and smoke from the downed aircraft billows from the courtyard. Defense Protective Services Police seal the crash site. Army medics, nurses and doctors scramble to organise aid . . . the Fire Department chief dispatches his equipment.' The only major difference was that the imaginary plane ended up in the centre courtyard of the building, while the real plane ploughed into one side of it and disintegrated.

The Bush administration's insistence that there were no prior indications that terrorists planned to crash planes into buildings appeared to be false. For those with suspicious minds, the Pentagon exercise might have looked like a rehearsal for what was coming, and the Bush-sceptical *Daily Mirror* didn't need much persuading. It ran a full-page story on 24 May 2002 under the headline: 'PENTAGON CHIEFS PLANNED FOR JET ATTACK'.

The guy who organised the exercise, Don Abbott of Command Emergency Response Training, was also involved in another similar and curious planning incident. He was the founder of a company called FieldSoft, which produced emergency-response software systems that were designed to coordinate the efforts of incident commanders. One of the systems, called FDonScene was endorsed by the Texas Fire Chiefs Association in 1998, while George W. Bush was state governor.

It was at the centre of another strange 11 September coincidence. A few days before the attacks, the company gave a 90-minute demonstration of the software's capabilities to representatives of the emergency services in New York. It was then used on the day to manage the evacuation of people to New Jersey and to coordinate the activities of police units, ambulances, firefighters and federal agencies, as well as to help manage the evacuation of victims to the Atlantic Highlands Ferry Port.

To my amazement, the Pentagon wasn't the only agency planning for a plane crashing into its building. The National Reconnaissance Office (NRO), America's spy satellite operator, had planned to run an exercise on the morning of 11 September that would have simulated a small corporate jet suffering from a mechanical failure crashing into one of the agency's four towers at its headquarters in Virginia. The exercise was organised by a CIA officer called John Fulton, who was also serving as the head of the NRO's strategic war-gaming division.

The NRO was based about four miles from Washington Dulles International Airport, from where American Airlines Flight 77 took off – 50 minutes before the exercise was due to begin – before it was hijacked and crashed into the Pentagon. The agency cancelled the exercise as soon as the real world events began, and a spokesman later described the situation as 'just an incredible coincidence'.

This was all starting to stink like rotten fish guts on a hot summer day. Some observers were starting to suggest that all these exercises indicated that the US government knew what was coming and was taking steps to ensure that casualties would be minimised, yet the administration was doggedly sticking to its line that it had had absolutely no idea about what had been in the offing.

This 'out of the blue' defence was metaphorically torpedoed and destroyed by a NORAD document that soon came my way. It was a PowerPoint presentation detailing a major military exercise, called Amalgam Virgo 01, that had taken place between 1 and 2 June 2001. The first slide was titled: 'Scenario: Counter Terrorism', and subtitled: 'Combined (Joint) Training for Unconventional Threat'.

I sat up straight when my eyes settled on the montage of images on the first slide: a mug shot of Osama bin Laden, surrounded by photos of fighter aircraft, one firing a missile; unmanned drone aircraft; and an orange-coloured ship. One of the main mission goals was listed as 'Train Like We're Going To Fight'.

It took me a while to figure it out completely and realise the full significance of this discovery, as the document was full of unfamiliar military jargon, acronyms and charts crammed with numbers and abbreviations. The gist of the introduction was that the exercise was aimed at practising responses to a missile attack on the American mainland by a terrorist group or a rogue state.

Next to another picture of bin Laden, labelling him 'the world's most dangerous terrorist', was a quote from the *Washington Times,* dated 29 May 2000. 'Defense Secretary William S. Cohen yesterday warned the United States faces a "quite real" threat of a terrorist nuclear, chemical or biological weapon attack on national soil within ten years.'

One of the first charts showed a cruise missile being launched from a ship and an explosion in a high-rise building as dawn broke over the Florida resort of Panama City Beach. One of the exercises appeared to be a 'homeland defense' mission, where various types of sea, land and air assets would practise stopping the missile reaching the city, or 'manned or unmanned air-breathing vehicles approaching North America', as the document put it.

As I read on, the full storyline for the main exercise became clear: a ship operated by terrorists in the Gulf of Mexico had started launching a dozen cruise missiles, or Unmanned Aerial Vehicles (UAVs), and they were heading for targets spread out along the eastern seaboard. The launches would be spread over a 12-hour period, and the military had to destroy the missiles before they hit their targets. The exercise was to be carried out jointly by the US and Canadian armed forces.

Cruise missiles are commonly thought of as being a proprietary US product, but one of the slides illustrated the scale of the potential threat by pointing out that there were some 75,000 cruise missiles and UAVs in existence, owned by 75 different countries. The cheapest type of robotic aircraft that could be weaponised cost just $83,613, it pointed out, and the market was 'ready to explode'.

Another slide showed a map and a variety of multicoloured trails plotting the tracks of aircraft and UAVs as they approached the coast from the Gulf of Mexico. I was perusing these and looking up what each different colour meant on the key on the left of the screen, which explained what each type of mock attack was. I looked up the green flight path, and it was simply labelled 'SUICIDE'. The title at the top of the screen suggested that these were tracks plotted from a similar exercise that had been held in the same area a few months earlier.

I knew right away the significance of this: the US military had practised intercepting an aircraft that was going to crash-dive into an American city. If there were no clues that terrorists planned such attacks before 11 September, then why was the US military repeatedly practising for just such a scenario? The CIA had known about the risks since January 1995, when police in the Philippines busted an al-Qaeda cell in Manila and found documents describing a plan called Operation Bojinka. It proposed blowing up 11 US airliners in mid-air en route to America from Asia and hijacking and crashing a twelfth aircraft into the CIA's headquarters in Virginia. Another plan they were working on involved hijacking several airliners and crashing them into landmark buildings in the US. The targets listed were the Sears Tower in Chicago, the Pentagon, the Washington Capitol building, the White House, the Transamerica Tower in San Francisco and the World Trade Center in New York City.

There was more to come in the NORAD 2001 document: the penultimate page showed that a 'hijack scenario' was also part of the exercise. It showed a picture of an America West Airlines passenger airliner and a map of the US depicting the plane deviating from its flight plan somewhere over the Oregon–Nevada border and heading cross-country for Washington DC. The picture on the right-hand side was of the Capitol building, which indicated that this was its intended target.

There was no doubt in my mind now that the US military at least was very much aware of the potential threat of terrorists flying hijacked airliners into prominent buildings. It seemed inconceivable that this hadn't been communicated to political leaders who, after all, had to approve spending on these massive and costly war games.

One line in the document mentioned that light aircraft charted from a company called Phoenix Air would play the role of 'surrogate UAVs'. I looked up the company and saw that it operated a flight training school, which of course made me wonder whether any of the 11 September hijackers had trained there – or maybe a hijacker or two had actually participated in the Amalgam Virgo exercise. That would be deeply ironic and would make for a dynamite story.

I scoured through the cuttings, but there was nothing to link them with Phoenix Air and nothing to suggest any wrongdoing on behalf of the training school. However, when I looked at their reported movements during the months leading up to 11 September, I discovered that seven of the hijackers, including Mohammed Atta, were living in and around Fort Lauderdale in Florida at the time.

That in itself was quite astonishing: while the terrorists were making their final preparations for 11 September, the US military was rehearsing its response to just such an attack in the same geographical area. The terrorists could easily have taken a short car ride to observe what was going on – and perhaps that was the very reason why they had gathered there.

After delving into the finer details of the events surrounding 11 September, it was obvious that there was a missing link somewhere in the months leading up to the operation. The CIA claimed that it had warned the FBI of the danger posed by one of the terrorists in 'early 2000'. The FBI disputed this and said it had received a warning from the CIA about Khalid al-Mihdhar and Nawaf al-Hazmi only on 23 August 2001 – too late for the agency to be able to track them down in time.

This was probably the main incongruity in the whole saga, and I felt that the key to unlocking the reasons for the intelligence failures might well be found here. The FBI's defence was simply 'Sorry, we just had no idea', even though one of its agents, Kenneth Williams, had sent a memo to FBI HQ in July 2001 reporting that a suspicious number of supporters of Osama bin Laden were undertaking flight training at an aviation school in Phoenix, Arizona. He recommended that all flight schools in the US should be investigated to get to the bottom of the phenomenon, but it was apparently ignored by the top brass. It came to be known as 'the Phoenix Memo'.

I thought I'd try to get to the bottom of this by asking some of my intelligence contacts to see if they could shine some light into this black hole. I struck gold with my first email to a European source, and I was pretty shocked by how explicit and detailed his explanation was, although it made perfect sense. I asked him how he'd arrived at this conclusion, and he said it was a hot topic of discussion among military intelligence officers in Europe: I could take it or leave it.

'The authorities knew something was going to happen that day but had the threat details wrong,' he explained. 'They were anticipating the planes would be hijacked and flown to Los Angeles and they were participating in a sting operation.'

According to what he'd been told, FBI agents were on board the airliners that slammed into the Pentagon and the south tower of the World Trade Center, and Flight 93, which crashed in Pennsylvania.

FBI supervisors apparently decided not to place a team on the plane that hit the north tower, in order to avoid arousing the suspicions of the hijackers' presumed leader, Mohammed Atta.

The Bureau did not intend to stop the hijackings, because it was planning to arrest the terrorists en masse in a spectacular 'roll-up' in Los Angeles, he said. However, the FBI was operating on outdated intelligence that indicated that the hijackers planned to take hostages and demand the release of al-Qaeda prisoners. These included Sheikh Omar Abdel Rahman and his followers, who were jailed for the 1993 World Trade Center bombing and for plotting to attack bridges, tunnels, the United Nations building and the FBI office in New York City.

'The American public has been misled into thinking that the intelligence community was oblivious to the possibility of a pending terrorist attack, while in fact they were very aware that a big attack was in the making.

'They were tracking some of the people involved in the attack, in particular Khalid al-Mihdhar and Nawaf al-Hazmi – two leaders of the terrorist operation. Those terrorists bought their tickets in their own names without any difficulty, even though their names were already flagged on the intelligence community's suspect list.'

If the story was to be believed, FBI agents *were* following al-Mihdhar and al-Hazmi, contrary to the official line that they couldn't be found in time, and 11 September was the direct result of a botched sting operation.

I tried to verify this with a lawyer who was involved in preparing a lawsuit on behalf of the relatives of 11 September, and I received a reply saying that she'd 'heard something along those lines'. Ryan Amundson, who lost his brother in the Pentagon attack, was more forthcoming.

'The theory that the FBI was involved in a sting operation makes a lot of sense, a lot more sense than some of the theories being thrown around, and more sense than the official line. It would certainly explain why there is so much resistance to a full investigation.

'I'm partial to your theory that 9/11 may have been a sting operation gone out of control, which would explain why all the names of the hijackers were known so soon after, and why they had not been arrested or investigated after so many red flags, and possibly why they were let in the country in the first place. But it still wouldn't explain why there were no fighters scrambled. Any ideas?'

It wasn't on my list of questions, and, from what I'd read, I'd need to cultivate a few highly placed whistleblowers in NORAD and the US Air Force and obtain classified documents to get close to any sort of an answer. That would take some doing and if it did turn out to be just the result of confusion on the day, then I could have wasted a lot of time for nothing. I just didn't have the feeling that I'd be successful here, though the events of that day continue to interest me, as facts and allegations about what really happened still continue to emerge on a regular basis.

BAGHDAD OLYMPIAD

Back in February 2002 I was stuck in a rut in my new job as the Web Monkey on one of the weekly magazines. I had the title of Internet editor, but it was just a name. The needs of the magazine came first and I'd now have to jump to the tune of my new masters, who made it clear that there were no plans to spend a single penny on further investment in the website. I felt like a prisoner, although I'd volunteered for it in the belief that everyone would be professional about things and let bygones be bygones. I was now furious with myself that I'd blundered my way into this position.

The desk I was given was at a safe distance from the news desk, and I had my back to everyone else, although I was assured that this was due to lack of office space. What drove me up the wall, however, was the fact that I was second on the phone loop to the office secretary, which meant that whenever she was busy or away from her desk, I had to field the incoming phone calls. The constant interruptions amounted to something akin to Chinese water torture, and maybe that was the idea: I wasn't sure. I planned to resign in a few days anyway, but, by a strange quirk of fate, the phone system prompted me to take flight sooner than I had expected. In the end, I was extremely grateful that I was second on the loop.

I answered yet another bloody phone call for the umpteenth time that day, but this one was different. I was to be glad I took it because the caller asked if I'd like to bid for the construction contract for the new Olympic stadium in Baghdad. I was flummoxed; I'd never heard of such a project and I was mystified as to why he was asking a magazine journalist rather than a building contractor. In any case, it was beginning to look increasingly likely that the US was building up to an invasion of Iraq with the intention of removing Saddam Hussein from power and it was no time to be launching a bid to host the Olympic Games. That was just plain crazy. I started to suspect that this was an elaborate joke of some kind, or maybe the next phase of a plan to drive me over the edge of insanity.

I asked if he could give me more details and the caller explained that he was the manager of a Jordanian export company that had been tasked by the Iraqi government with procuring bids from foreign companies for the construction of an Olympic stadium in Baghdad.

It seemed that he was phoning around and working through a list of British companies, and he'd mistaken the magazine as being a construction firm. He claimed that the project had United Nations approval, although I wasn't entirely convinced. I asked how many companies I'd be up against and for some more background on his company.

'There will be many contractors bidding, but I can't tell you now how many have made bids, because the tender period is still open,' he said.

'We concentrate on the Iraqi market and we participate in Iraqi government tenders based on United Nations approval,' he added.

He finished up by asking if I would like to bid for the project. If so, he could fax me the tender documents and the technical specification for the stadium.

'Yes, I would like to consider bidding,' I replied quietly, deliberately failing to correct his misconception, and I was promptly added to the list of bidders. I was now officially in the running to become the main contractor in charge of building the Saddam Olympic Stadium in Baghdad. I briefly toyed with the idea of actually submitting a low-price bid to make sure I undercut the competition and secured the contract, but I thought that might be taking things a little too far. Besides, I might be arrested for sanctions-busting or lending comfort to the enemy, or something. There'd have to be a very strong public interest defence in going forward with that idea, and I was struggling to come up with one.

It was a freak phone call, and I was obviously on to something big now. I waited eagerly for the fax machine to start whirring, and, sure enough, 20 minutes later, I could see it slowly spitting out what looked like a large document. It took a while and a queue of impatient people had formed by the time it finished. One of the features writers, a nice guy with whom I got on, gathered up all the pages and brought them over to me. He beamed a wide smile at me as he handed the sheaf of papers over, in a kind of 'up to his old tricks again' way – he'd obviously sneaked a peek at the contents.

After the covering letter from the Jordanian company, the next thing I saw was a summary of the project. 'The Ministry of Education has the pleasure to invite you for submitting an offer regarding the construction of a modern Olympic stadium, which specifications [sic] according to the attached list.'

There was a list of ten conditions that bidders like myself had to comply with: my company had to provide a certificate showing 'its financial attitude and good reputation'; my price should include a two-year maintenance period and cover the costs of transporting materials to Baghdad from the port of Umm Qasr; and payments made to me would be denominated in euros.

The specification called for a two-tier stadium with a capacity of between 80,000 and 100,000 spectators, and was to be built on a site in Baghdad that covered 1.25 million square metres. Only 33 per cent of the seats would be covered by a roof, otherwise it called for a structure that would meet all international sporting regulations, including all the facilities that a modern athlete could wish for. The documents had obviously been translated from the original Arabic, and the English was a little shaky and even amusing at times: 'The general design of the stadium should be of modern type to give a more nice view to the construction.'

The main document was titled: 'Technical Brief Report: Olympic Stadium – Baghdad', and it revealed that the stadium was only part of a larger master plan. It was to be the centrepiece of a multi-billion-dollar 'Olympic Sports City'. That, of course, begged the question of how the Iraqi government, which was bound by economic sanctions and had US and UK military aircraft patrolling the northern and southern 'no-fly zones', was going to pay for it. How could it be justified when thousands of people were dying due to the effects of sanctions?

The answer was simply that this was a meaningless question when one of history's greatest egomaniacs/mass murderers was governing the country. It was a fantasy playground for Saddam and his two psychopathic sons, who were terrorising the population and murdering their own citizens at will as a sporting pastime. The issuing of the document, which could only have been approved by Saddam, was either an act of defiance by a dictator after his country had been branded as being part of an 'axis of evil' (with Iran and North Korea) by President Bush in his state of the union address on 29 January 2002, or, more likely, it was an act born of pure self-delusion.

The stadium specification also called for the creation of a special VIP viewing platform, 'separated by other parts by transparent partitions'. No doubt those would have to be bullet-proof, although the exact design of this area would be up to the contractor. It didn't take a great leap of the imagination to conclude that this would have to provide the best there was in terms of luxury and comfort. While the public seats were to be made of plastic, Saddam and his entourage in the first-class seats needed 'very good-quality' seating.

Ironically, the technical codes used for designing the superstructure were largely British and American, and it was to be reinforced to withstand powerful earthquakes. There was a scrappy suggested outline plan of the stadium in the document, showing an oval structure surrounded by extensive landscaped gardens and a smaller practice arena to one side. It struck me as looking suspiciously like the design of Arsenal Football Club's proposed new stadium at Ashburton Grove in London. Maybe Saddam, like bin Laden, was a fan of the team.

I also scanned the document to see if I could pick up any indications that this was some kind of ruse to mask the construction of a facility that might have a military use. And there was a possibility in this regard. A series of underground reservoirs were to be located under the stadium, which needed to be large enough to hold enough water for a day's worth of normal consumption plus firefighting. It occurred to me that, should work on the complex be abandoned at an early stage, due to, say, an American-led invasion, there would a series of ready-made bunkers to hand.

If Iraq was going to make a bid to host the Games, then it was just in time, as the International Olympic Committee (IOC) was due to formally call for bids to host the 2012 Games in a few months' time. I phoned the press office of the British Olympic Association, which had relocated to Salt Lake City for the Winter Olympics, and a press officer was surprised to hear the news, but he said he couldn't think of any reason why Iraq couldn't bid for the Games. It was an unlikely prospect in his book, but there were no technical reasons to bar it, he said.

'It's my understanding that there's nothing to prevent Iraq from bidding. It's a matter for each individual country's organising committee.' I did try to contact the Iraq Olympic Committee for comment, but there was no response to either phone calls or emails.

The UK Export Credit Guarantees Department (ECGD), which, in essence, provides insurance to British companies against commercial and political risks that result in non-payment on overseas projects, said it did not provide cover for Iraq. 'No cover at all is available for projects in Iraq. There's a trade embargo on Iraq and ECGD abides by that,' a press officer told me. However, she didn't think that there were any legal reasons why a UK firm couldn't participate, as unlikely as that was, if the project was not military related. She referred me to the Department of Trade and Industry (DTI) for a definitive answer. The DTI would only say that the government advises British nationals not to attempt to travel to Iraq.

The sad irony of the situation was that Iraq was better placed to land the 2012 Games than Britain. We didn't even have a national stadium at the time, as the demolition of the old Wembley Stadium was under way to make room for a new Sir Norman Foster-designed replacement. The site's owners and their banks, however, were locked in a disagreement with the government over spiralling costs and whether the new structure should cater for athletics or not.

The project was stalled, and the situation had prompted the British triple Olympic gold medal-winner and IOC member Matthew Pinsent to state publicly that the UK was incapable of mounting a serious bid. He thought the UK's best hope now was the 2016 Games, not 2012.

If Saddam was gunning for the 2012 Games, he'd be going head-to-head with the USA, which was poised to mount a strong challenge. New York, Washington DC, San Francisco and Dallas had already been shortlisted as potential host cities. Israel was also pondering a bid, although its plans were very nebulous and protecting the competitors and spectators from Palestinian suicide bombers would be an enormous undertaking. It seemed inconceivable that Israel could be selected when there was no prospect of a resolution to that problem in sight.

Indeed, during a visit to the country in the previous year, former IOC president Juan Antonio Samaranch said: 'It can happen if you have peace. Without peace it's impossible.' Israel had spent some $1.3 million on studying the feasibility of hosting the Games in Tel

Aviv. Some observers expressed hopes that hosting the 2012 Olympics would be an ideal way of celebrating a peace agreement between the two warring factions. This would have a strong emotional selling point, as it would commemorate the 40th anniversary of the murder of 11 Israeli officials and athletes by Palestinian gunmen during the 1972 Munich Olympics.

Relations between Iraq and fellow evil axis neighbour Iran had been improving rapidly over the past year. Some had suggested that a joint bid couldn't be discounted. Iran's sporting infrastructure was well developed: it had no less than six 100,000-seater-plus stadiums – just one less than the USA. Iraq's only large stadium was the 50,000-seater al-Sha'ab national football stadium in Baghdad.

An Iran–Iraq bid could have been sold as the first Arabian Olympic Games: an act of reconciliation to commemorate the deaths of the one million people who were killed during the 1980–8 war between the two countries, as well as marking an end to centuries-old rivalries between Sunni and Shi'a Muslims. As no Muslim state has yet hosted a Games, a pan-Arab Olympic bid would constitute a challenge to the IOC to prove that it's not anti-Muslim. It has been very much a Western affair so far: 20 of the 24 modern Summer Games and 17 of the 19 Winter Games have been held in Europe or the Americas.

While Greece, the birthplace of Western civilisation and the venue for the 2004 Games, was seen as a romantic choice, a Mesopotamian Games celebrating the emergence of organised human society and the world's first cities would hold similar emotional appeal. The Arab world, backed with cash from Saudi Arabia, had been making great strides in trying to boost their sporting prowess. Saudi Crown Prince Abdallah bin Abd al-Aziz al-Saud had announced that the first Muslim 'Olympic' Games would be held in Saudi Arabia in 2005, following the first Muslim Equestrian Championship in 2003. He also announced that the second and third Islamic Games will be hosted by Iran in 2009 and Syria in 2013. The message was clear: include Muslims or we will go it alone.

Iraq's gruesome human rights record didn't appear to be an obstacle to it being a host country. The 2008 Games were to be held in the People's Republic of China, which wasn't exactly renowned as a paragon of freedom and virtue. The risk of imminent war also didn't appear to be a major obstacle. The World Cup soccer finals were due to take place in Seoul, just a few kilometres from the 'Demilitarised Zone' (DMZ) between South Korea and North Korea, another 'evil axis' power. A state of war still existed between the two countries and one million troops from either side were stationed in the DMZ, including 50,000 US troops, in a permanent state of readiness.

As I was looking through the league tables of the world's major sports areas, I realised that I'd inadvertently embarked on a virtual tour of the so-called axis of evil. It seemed that the less democratic the government, the bigger the stadia were. Astonishingly, impoverished North Korea was top of the table in the world stadium league by a long way, the daddy being the 150,000 all-seater May Day Stadium in the capital Pyongyang. It had seen little in the way of sporting action, however, as it was largely devoted to staging huge celebrations of the life and supposed great wisdom of the country's Dear Leader, Kim Jong-Il.

The Baghdad Olympics story was a sitting duck and the story eventually ran in *The Independent*, the *Washington Times* and the *Jerusalem Post* in early March 2002, although I'm still waiting for a cheque from the *Post*, and it circulated far and wide on the Web. *The Independent* had been asking around the British construction industry and it had discovered that, despite all the moral and legal barriers, 'a couple' of major UK contractors were interested in bidding.

I checked with the representative of the Jordanian company that had sparked all this off, and he told me that the Iraqi Education Ministry had been bombarded with enquiries. The deadline for submitting bids was likely to be extended to accommodate all the latecomers. Things were getting too hot, and I dropped out of the race for the stadium to leave the big boys to fight it out between themselves.

Buoyed by the success with the story, I finally quit the day job, at the end of March.

My mind wandered back to the satellite picture I'd been sent of a possible terror training camp in Baghdad while trying to find images of Tora Bora, and this seemed like the most obvious story to tackle next, assuming there was a story there.

The file was massive, and my laptop chugged away, struggling to cope with it. It took several minutes for the image to open and display

Recent al-Qaeda propaganda includes a rap video entitled
'Dirty Kuffar', which features British bin Laden supporters.
Pictured here is 'Sheikh Terra'.

Others members of the 'Soul Salah Crew' performing in the rap video.

A screenshot from a recent video produced by al-Qaeda in Saudi
Arabia, in which an operative warns (in English) of a forthcoming
11 September-style attack on the US.

A Saudi al-Qaeda militant reads his will to the camera.

Osama bin Laden features prominently in al-Qaeda videos
produced since the US-led invasion of Iraq, which
have become increasingly sophisticated.

One recent video included brief footage of bin Laden on
the move at night and surrounded by bodyguards.

A shot of an al-Qaeda operative training in
the use of shoulder-launched missiles.

A Mujahideen fighter delivers a warning on video.

Two al-Qaeda operatives pictured at a meeting apparently held prior to launching guerrilla warfare operations in Saudi Arabia.

A Saudi militant displays his weapon.

Abu Hamza in a still taken from one of his videotapes.

James Ujaama, former associate of Abu Hamza turned FBI supergrass, speaking at a meeting alongside Hamza.

Hamza and Ujaama pictured together.

A masked British gunman encourages the viewer to perform jihad on one of the Hamza videos.

A second British jihadi seen on the same tape.

Abu Hamza and fellow speakers filmed at a 'jihad conference' in 2000.

Scene from the meeting on the Hamza Tapes
where 'Brother Atta' is called for.

Hamza extolling the virtues of jihad.

on the screen. It was a raw unprocessed 'strip' that had been taken as the Ikonos satellite passed over the Iraqi capital on 25 April 2000. What I saw was a river, the Tigris, snaking through a chequerboard pattern of fields. There were no buildings immediately obvious and I needed to zoom in to find them, which was a painful experience. I half-expected to see smoke coming out of the computer at any time, as it took ages to render the image each time I magnified a section of the picture. It took maybe half an hour before I was down to a level where individual structures were apparent.

I wasn't really sure what I should be looking for, but the email contained a link to a story that had been broken by the *New York Times* in November 2001. A defector had claimed that thousands of terrorists had been trained at a secret facility at a place called Salman Pak (also known as al-Salman), some 40 km south-east of Baghdad, which also apparently housed factories that were covertly producing chemical and biological weapons.

The defector, Sabah Khodada, was an ex-army captain who claimed that he had been stationed at the facility for six months. He said that thousands of operatives from Islamic terrorist groups underwent hijacking training alongside Saddam's Fedayeen militia, which was commanded by his son Qusay. It was a secret facility covering 20 square kilometres that was surrounded by weapons factories disguised as farms.

It was quite a story, though I was well aware that information from defectors is usually the most unreliable form of intelligence, as they have a strong tendency to tell their new hosts exactly what they want to hear. He had also alleged that the 11 September hijackers 'must' have been trained at the camp, and that set my alarm bells ringing, as it seemed like a step too far. I hadn't come across links between al-Qaeda and Iraq during my investigations into 11 September.

Large numbers of 'Arabs', some with 'long beards', were training when he was there, although they were not allowed to mix with the Iraqi Fedayeen trainees. The groups were separated from each other by a high wall. Hijacking practice was carried out on an old airliner, a double-decker bus and a train. The training was directed by an Iraqi known only as 'The Ghost', who was putting 700 people at a time through their paces. Khodada had drawn a map for the FBI, who then checked this against a satellite image of the place. They appeared to match and this lent credence to his story.

It was an intriguing story all right, so I thought I'd give it a go. Contacting the guy was going to be tricky, I figured. I called the press office of the main Iraqi opposition group, the Iraqi National Congress, which was based in London. They must know him, I thought, and I hoped they would help me to get an interview with him. His story hadn't been covered in the UK as yet, so it was time to get my skates on.

I left a message and got a call the next day from someone on my mobile phone. He knew Khodada and 'Ahmed' said he'd be happy to talk about him, but I ought to take a look at an annotated image of the Salman Pak site first, which he'd send by email, so I could familiarise myself. I checked this source out on the Web and there were several reports that Saddam had ordered his assassination, so this is why I've called him Ahmed.

The email came through with a satellite image, which was a copy of the one I'd received earlier, except key areas were outlined in yellow and identified. There were 25 captions on the image that picked out key features: a group of buildings was marked as 'VX nerve gas production'; three long industrial buildings were called 'biological weapons factory A, B and C'; and there was an 'urban warfare and explosives area'. The outline of an airliner was clearly visible, and I checked this against my original. It was the same: I could even see a green stripe running along the fuselage. The bus and the train were also there.

There was also, apparently, an underground prison on the site. I checked and it seemed that this might have something to do with a long-running story, a myth some said, that Saddam still held a group of Kuwaiti prisoners who were taken as hostages when Iraq withdrew from Kuwait City during the 1991 Gulf War. It seemed that he was still holding these people as human bargaining chips, if the story was to be believed. There was no form of information about the names of those who'd been incarcerated, or the exact number.

Salman Pak was heavily bombed during the 1991 Gulf War, as it was suspected of producing botulinum – the most toxic chemical known to science – and it was thought that concentrated anthrax slurry was produced there in vast quantities. Other agents developed there included 'gas gangrene', cancer-causing aflatoxins and ricin. If the defector was right, production had since resumed.

Armed with a list of questions and a full understanding of the allegations being made, I phoned Ahmed. I started by asking about the Kuwaiti prisoners. He dismissed this as a minor aspect of the story.

'It's part of the story, but it's a big complex that contains everything. It contains biological facilities; it contains training facilities, plus the Kuwaitis.'

He claimed that 80 prisoners had been taken, and they'd been moved from prison to prison until they were finally taken to an underground facility at Salman Pak. They'd apparently been kept there since 1995, as it was a very secure location. He said United Nations weapons inspectors had twice visited the camp and unknowingly parked their vehicles on top of cells in which the Kuwaitis were being held.

The camp had been built in the mid-1980s for conducting research into chemical and biological weapons. It used to be called the Technical Research Establishment and was headed by Dr Ahmed Murtada, who'd since been promoted to minister of transportation and communications.

I asked him if he'd run through what was shown in the images. He said the camp was divided into two: one section for the Fedayeen militia and the other for visiting Arabs. A high fence divided the two zones to prevent the trainees from mixing. On any one day, 700 people would be training in the Fedayeen section. The Arabs trained in groups of between five and ten, and the course lasted three months, on average.

I asked: 'Why are they kept separate, the Iraqis and the non-Iraqis?'

He replied: 'It's very obvious. First of all they don't want anybody to recognise the Arabs in that camp, because the Arabs will do activities outside Iraq . . .'

He said the camp was run by the Iraqi intelligence service and the Arabs were bussed in from Baghdad every day. The old airliner that was allegedly used for hijacking training was a Russian Tupolev 154, and it was completely shot through with bullet holes, as all training is undertaken using live ammunition. I asked if there were any markings on it that would indicate which airline it used to belong to, but he didn't know. The bus and the train were mainly used by the Fedaydeen, he said.

He was adamant that Iraq provided training, funding and shelter for terrorist groups throughout the region – including al-Qaeda. He said most of the foreigners came from Saudi Arabia, the UAE, Egypt, Yemen and Somalia.

It had been going on since 1996, he added. To prove his point, he said that it was known that the notorious Palestinian guerrilla leader Abu Nidal, who was wanted for a string of terrorist attacks carried out in 20 countries, mostly during the 1980s, was living in a house just outside Baghdad.

According to Ahmed, experiments resumed after UN weapons inspectors left Iraq in 1998. He pointed out the locations of bunkers on the satellite image where he said chemical weapons experiments were being conducted at the moment. There were also three biological weapons factories on the site, and he said that there was a German national and a Canadian working in them. I asked him what he knew about them, as this was news to me, and a possible news angle, if I could identify them.

'All we know about the German guy is that he's been there in Iraq for more than six years, and he's staying in the al-Rashid Hotel [in Baghdad]. And two people are responsible for dealing with him. One of them is the minister of communications and transportation, who I mentioned [earlier], and the other guy is the minister of higher education. And he was also working in the past on the Iraqi chemical programme.'

I asked: 'OK, so he's living there right now?'

'They are there.'

'OK. What about the Canadian?'

'All we know is that he used to work in the past on the Iraqi missile programme, the long-range programme.'

Ahmed said he was working on coming up with names for the two, although it seemed odd that he knew their nationalities and not their identities. He said he'd let me know when they'd got to the bottom of it.

Salman Pak wasn't the only centre of its type; he said there was another chemical and biological weapons site close to Baghdad, near a prison called Abu Ghraib, which became notorious in early 2004 as the site of American abuse of Iraqi prisoners.

Our conversation ended with him promising to get in touch with Khodada and ask him to call me. He had rattled it all off like a man wanting to unburden himself, and there was a lot to take on board. I knew he was highly involved in setting up an opposition intelligence network inside Iraq, and I guessed that he'd been working closely with the Americans at this point, as they were fine-tuning their invasion plans.

A second defector had also emerged days before the interview with Khodada was broadcast on the PBS television network in November 2001. The London *Observer* published a story about Salman Pak, which included an interview with an anonymous former colonel in the intelligence service who claimed to have been in charge of the site, and that apparently corroborated the story. Although it hinged on the testimony of two defectors, especially the terrorist training claims, the place did have a murky history. Experts in the field thought that the notion that the production of chemical and biological weapons had resumed there was very feasible.

I spoke to Professor Paul Rogers of Bradford University, a leading authority on the subject, and I asked whether the Iraqis could be mass-producing VX nerve gas at Salman Pak. He said: 'I would have thought so. I'd be very surprised if they weren't. Obviously, since the [UN] inspectors have been gone now for three and a half years, there is an absolute presumption that the Iraqis have gone back to trying to develop a reasonably competent biological, and possibly chemical, capability.

'One's guess is that they will have some kind of capability for anthrax and botulinum, and maybe some other things, and they will maybe have found some way to actually deliver them, if at all possible.'

Paul said that the Iraqi military had experimented with dispersal systems and were known to have converted fighter aircraft to spray biological agents under remote control. They were developing a cruise missile capability on the cheap, and they planned to pack aircraft with explosives and chemical agents and fly them into long-range targets by remote control.

He pointed out that, when the Iraqis started to retreat from Kuwait during the 1991 Gulf War, battlefield chemical weapons were distributed to regional commanders with prior authorisation to use them if they received news that Baghdad was under attack. This was regarded by many in security circles as being the real reason why the US stopped short of invading Iraq during Desert Storm, he added.

The link between prisons and chemical weapons facilities didn't appear to be too outlandish a suggestion either. The Iraq Communist Party had recently reported that 15 political prisoners were killed 'by chemical gas' inside a newly constructed concrete chamber at a military compound in the town of Falluja. The leadership claimed that at least 3,000 political prisoners had been exterminated over the previous two years during a 'prison clean-up' campaign overseen by Saddam's son Qusay. There were reports of Fedayeen gangs roaming Baghdad at night murdering prostitutes. Apparently on Qusay's orders, they were beheaded and their bodies left in the street as a warning to the rest of the community.

All in all, the story was sitting up a bit too perfectly for my liking, but it would be completely legitimate to report on this. The phrase 'weapons of mass destruction' was starting to be heard regularly, and Iraq was hot news. I don't know why, I think it was to open a new selling channel, but this time I plumped for the *Sunday Express*. The news editor turned it down initially, but he rang back a few days later and said he was interested in running it. It was run in April alongside the satellite image, under the headline: 'SADDAM HIDES HIS CHEMICAL WEAPONS HERE'.

War speculation was at fever pitch and the armchair generals had already started mapping out the course of the coming conflict with Iraq. I wondered what the response would be if the Iraqis did use chemical weapons to defend Baghdad this time. There were mutterings about the use of 'overwhelming force' and that appeared to mean only one thing. By a stroke of good fortune, I already had the official American battle plans for dealing with this scenario sitting on my hard drive, although I didn't realise it at first.

Sensitive information does crop up on websites from time to time, and some of the most productive sources are trade association or think-tank websites. These organisations often receive briefings from military officials and you can sometimes find copies of the presentations which have been given squirrelled away on their websites. These are usually unclassified summaries of secret military plans that have been delivered in private at a conference, and the organisation has placed a copy on their Web server, not knowing that it's then going to be indexed by search engines and become visible.

I'd been developing contacts in the underground hacker community, and I was making friends with groups of 'ethical hackers', who were hunting down websites used by terrorist groups and passing information on to the law enforcement authorities or forcing the sites offline. There were both legitimate and illegal ways of doing that, although the term hacker simply means someone who knows a lot of tricks and shortcuts when using a computer. On the darker side were crackers, who did potentially illegal things like breaking into people's email accounts.

I was getting known for having these useful contacts, but I was a bit taken aback one day when a newspaper editor called and asked if I knew anyone who could break into the email accounts of the wife of a famous politician. It was out of my territory and I said I'd ask around, but I didn't. He gave me the two email addresses that he wanted cracked, but there was no way that I was getting involved in hairy stuff like that. I gave it a couple of days and phoned to tell him that I couldn't do it. It would have been immoral in the first place, illegal in the second, and I could probably go to prison for even appearing to consider the suggestion.

It was a bit of a revelation that there were these groups of cyber-vigilantes out there who were applying their skills in an online anti-jihad. As I got to know them, I also got to know the techniques and the software they used. I was starting to develop some skills in this direction myself, and I could, for example, scan sites and detect hidden directories easily enough by now. I'd rather someone else did it, though, because it can be a tedious business.

There were whole teams of people working more or less full time chasing these sites around the world and gathering up incriminating files and documents along the way. This is what I was interested in tapping into. There would be efficiency savings for me, as I'd only be covering the same ground under my own steam.

There were skirmishes taking place all over the Net and it was a completely unreported war. The online al-Qaeda supporters were no slouches either, and it was rumoured that bin Laden had obtained, via Russia for $2 million, a package developed by the US military that was the last word in hacking software. Called PROMIS, it was allegedly designed for use by military commanders who needed to cut through bureaucracy and locate crucial information quickly. It automatically hacked its way through the military's own databases and was able to sidestep all security measures and fetch the most secret types of intelligence. It was only a rumour, but it was clearly a serious issue for the US if it was true.

My latest find hadn't required such fancy tricks. I'd saved a document that looked quite interesting, one I'd found on the server of the nuclear policy think-tank The Nautilus Institute, which was a copy of a military presentation. It was badly photocopied and it didn't lend itself to much examination, except I saw that it was about 'theater missile defence' on the Korean peninsula. I took a look at it again and realised that it could also be a blueprint for the plan that would swing into action should Iraq resist the US invasion with unconventional weapons.

It described a plan drawn up in 1998 to blitz North Korea with tactical nuclear weapons should the country launch a surprise attack on South Korea. It envisioned the start of a surprise invasion beginning with 'mass synchronised launches' of Scud missiles armed with chemical warheads at key military facilities and, perhaps, major population centres in South Korea and Japan.

Recognising the difficulties encountered when trying to locate Scud launchers during the 1991 Gulf War, the Korea paper concluded that targeting the infrastructure used to support the launch vehicles is 'the Achilles Heel' [sic]. It stated that attacking launch sites is a waste of time, because the mobile launchers can be back on the move within two minutes of firing. In a campaign against North Korea, it instead advocated the destruction of roads, tunnels, bridges, caves and underground 'transload' areas where Scud launchers were reloaded and serviced.

It also officially confirmed that, despite the 'hundreds of sorties' carried out against Iraqi Scud launchers during the 1991 Gulf War, there were no confirmed kills. 'What we saw . . . as recently as Desert Storm, [is] that despite advances in our weapons systems, the launcher remains the most difficult target to hit,' said the document. It considered the success of the Allied bombing campaign against infrastructure supporting Nazi V1 and V2 missile launchers during the Second World War as the model for the new attack strategy.

Heavily censored, under a section titled 'Scud B Chemical Delivery', were detailed estimates of the number of 'leakers' that would need to get through Patriot anti-missile defences 'in order to have a reasonable probability of contaminating an airbase'. US forces would have just a few minutes to respond to warnings broadcast automatically by computers to commanders based in Osan, South Korea. Retaliation would come from the air – nuclear 'bunker-busting' bombs – which would be supported by a sustained bombardment using 'Deep Strike' semi-ballistic missiles carrying multiple warheads.

A second, unrelated document there revealed that the US Air Force went on to rehearse the plan by dropping replica bombs in mock attacks on targets in Florida — where else? The state had recently played the role of a surrogate Korean peninsula in a ten-day-long military exercise, which simulated nuclear strikes against underground missile sites mounted by aircraft operating from the Seymour Johnson Air Force Base in North Carolina.

F-15E fighter-bombers of the 4th Fighter Wing practised dropping dummy 2,000 lb nuclear bombs on the Avon Park Bombing Range in Florida. The dummies were replicas of the new B61-11 earth-penetrating nuclear gravity bomb. Each has the explosive power of 340,000 tons of TNT.

In the document, Wing Commander Randall K. Bigum describes the mission: 'It tested our war fighting ability. We simulated fighting a war in Korea . . . This included [North Korean] chemical attacks to protect against using full chemical gear. [sic] This simulated a decision by the National Command Authority about considering nuclear weapons. We identified aircraft, crews, and [weapon] loaders to load up tactical nuclear weapons onto our aircraft. It required us to fly those airplanes down to a range in Florida and drop a concrete bilvet [dummy bomb].'

The final phase of the Korea plan, as spelled out in the main presentation document, was simply and ominously described as 'Systematic Destruction'. It was clear that this plan could be equally applicable to Iraq should it use unconventional weapons in response to a US invasion. American forces were already trained and prepared for a doomsday scenario in the Middle East, which was now looming large on the horizon.

AL-QAEDA EXPOSED

A hacker contact emailed me to say I ought to take a look at a peculiar website that he'd found. I'd better be quick, he said, as he had the feeling that the site wasn't going to be around for much longer. If there were any doubts that bin Laden supporters meant action, then this would go a long way to dispelling those thoughts, as there was a copy of al-Qaeda's manual for cell leaders on the site.

It didn't have any content, apart from a series of links to some very large files. It looked like a 'dead-letter drop' site, where material is made available only for as long as it takes the intended recipient(s) to download it, after which it is deleted. A spy in the past would have, say, placed a message inside the inspection cover of a street lamp and marked it with a piece of chalk to indicate to his handler that the box was ready for emptying – this was the cyber version.

I downloaded all the material, but I couldn't make head nor tail of it all; I just got file corrupted errors every time I tried to open one of the documents. I went back to my source to ask him what I needed to do next, and he told me that I would need file-splitting software. Apparently, the manual was so large that it had been split into smaller files, and I would need a specialist programme that would join them together and unpack the contents. I'd never have guessed unless he told me, and I suppose it was an added layer of security for the site's operators, whoever they were. It was a throwaway, free website, and there were no ownership details available.

I followed the instructions for decoding the files and pressed the button to see what would happen. Two PDF files labelled 1st and

2nd appeared. I opened the first one and was confronted by a cover page in Arabic, while I watched the counter at the bottom of the page rising past 100, 200, 300 . . . before it finally settled around the 750-page mark. Clearly, there was a lot of work ahead.

I started quickly skipping through the large blocks of Arabic and there were occasional abbreviations in roman – TNT, RDX, PETN, C3 – and a range of names of chemicals. There were lots of diagrams in some of the sections, showing, for example, men on motorbikes firing weapons, trigonometry tables for calculating kill distances, and wiring diagrams. I then went back to the beginning and started to make a list of all the English words in the document. This would give me a preliminary idea of what each section contained, although it was already obvious that it was a military manual of some kind. I proceeded to plough through every page of the documents, noting the words and page numbers of any particularly interesting bits. Getting the whole thing translated from Arabic was out of the question, but getting a few of the most suspicious pages done would be within my budgetary limits.

The list revealed that the manual was split up into many different sections and it seemed to cover the entire spectrum of technical knowledge that a would-be jihadi needed: from setting up safe houses, to codes and communications, right through to arms training and manufacturing explosives. The communications guide explained how to use a phone scrambler and even how to hold a video conference using shortwave radios. One long section seemed to be devoted to analyses of the methods used by Western intelligence agencies. I could see references to MI5, MI6, CIA, KGB, France's SDECE and the Israeli security service Shin Bet interspersed through the Arabic.

One section that leapt out at me contained a series of diagrams showing how box-type objects could be arranged and wired up in different configurations. It also contained a list of chemicals and names of various suppliers, and I looked these up. They were all pesticides and fertilisers that became powerful poisons and nerve agents when subjected to heat. They included methyl parathion, known as 'cotton poison', and carbon tetrachloride, which, when heated, breaks down into phosgene, a poison gas used by the Germans in the First World War. My mind drifted back to the World Trade Center in 1993 and the inclusion of sodium cyanide in the truck bomb in an attempt to create a poison gas cloud. What I appeared to be looking at was a progression from that: 'nerve gas mega-bombs' was a phrase that sprang to mind.

There were other innovations there too: diagrams and instructions for building concealed explosive devices inside a crash helmet, a hairbrush and even a wedding cake. The cake was made of cardboard and covered in icing, but filled with powerful C4 military-grade plastic explosive. It was encircled by two wires that were concealed inside the decorative piped icing around the edges, so, when the happy couple cut the cake with a metal knife, it would touch the wires, completing the electrical circuit, and detonate the bomb. The same principle was shown applied to a hairbrush, where two bristles were replaced by wires which would detonate the explosive when they touched. Similarly, the crash helmet bomb would explode when the chinstrap was connected.

The second volume included a long and detailed guide to operating as a sniper in urban environments. The diagrams showed how to set up a position in a park, preferably with marshland or bushes between the shooter and the target to facilitate a quick getaway. It appeared to suggest that snipers should work in pairs, and there was even a guide to judging distances at night by using star constellations.

There was a heavy accent on guerrilla warfare techniques, which made sense. Many of the images and diagrams showed how to plan assassinations and attacks against hospitals, office buildings, railways and roads. A series of plans showed how to carry out shootings on a motorbike and the correct procedures for firing rocket-propelled grenades from the rear of a parked Suzuki van. Images of buildings were included in a section on carrying out surveillance on potential targets, with tips on evading detection by infrared alarm sensors.

After several hours of work, I contacted my translator, Mohamed, to see if he'd have a look at some images I'd made of some of the key pages. No problem, he said, although it would cost me a few hundred pounds. I initially baulked at the cost, but I knew there was a lot of work for him there and I was sure that I could recover the cost in the fee for the story. I tried to convince myself that it was an investment.

He got back to me in less than 24 hours with the results, and they were spectacular. The documents were an updated version of the *Encyclopaedia of the Afghan Jihad*, which I'd heard about but had never seen. This tome, now simply called the *Encyclopaedia of Jihad* (Mawsu'at al-jihad), was split into two volumes: 'Security and Intelligence' and 'Operational Courses'. It was dated October 2002, and it was hot off the presses. The introduction praised a group of young recruits who'd been working to update and collate al-Qaeda's technical know-how into documents that could be disseminated electronically.

As I suspected, he confirmed that the crash helmet, cake and hairbrush sections were bomb plans. The crash helmet plan was entitled 'trapping a helmet', as there's no equivalent to 'booby-trap' in Arabic, he told me. It was everything I suspected it was. The introduction said:

> As part of our contribution to the spread of the culture of jihad, we are pleased to re-write the *Encyclopaedia of Jihad,* which was written by Arab Mujahideen during their jihad against the Soviets in Afghanistan. Armies of the infidels and unbelievers are wreaking havoc in the lives of Muslims. It is the binding duty of everyone, as has been decided by a group of scholars, to salvage the nation from this shameful and painful state.

Another section dealt with what to expect during interrogation or torture if taken prisoner. It described the effects of 'truth drugs' such as Menticide, and it also gave advice on defeating lie detector machines. Under the heading 'Devices Used During Interrogation', it said:

> Lie detectors are nothing more than a myth to trick the accused. To the extent that the accused does not believe in its effectiveness, it will not be effective against him. Different devices are used to measure the person's pulse during questioning, but these devices are no guarantee of success, otherwise all countries would use them.

A little research on the origins of the document revealed that the original Afghan version was 11 volumes long, ran to 7,000 pages and weighed in at 20 kg. It was written on the orders of bin Laden's late mentor, Sheikh Abdullah Azzam, and was used as a handbook for al-Qaeda cell leaders. It looked like I had the first two volumes of the new, more portable version, and there was a note in the introduction which said that more volumes would be ready soon, God willing, and the entire tome would now be subject to continuous revision.

It wasn't the only military manual that was being circulated by al-Qaeda supporters at that time. My friends were alerting me to a wide variety of similar documents that were appearing on other websites. Jihad sites seemed to have been flooded with them, and the big question was: why now?

There was an abundance of military guides that had been purloined from US Army sites, mostly focusing on urban combat and guerrilla warfare techniques, as well as detailed operating manuals for everything from handguns to RPG (Rocket-propelled Grenade) launchers. I also found guides to demolishing bridges, advice on fighting during a conflict involving chemical and biological weapons, and even plans for constructing a nuclear bomb. Whilst this material was appearing on al-Qaeda-affiliated jihad sites, I noticed that it was also cropping up on Palestinian sites, notably on a forum that was said to be operated by the al-Qassam Martyrs' Brigade.

These people were certainly innovative. One page was full of instructions on how to adapt a model remote-controlled aircraft and a camcorder to produce a cut-price Unmanned Aerial Vehicle (UAV) for carrying out surveillance on potential targets. It even showed pictures of two men (their faces judiciously out of shot) with a homemade UAV and images taken during a test flight. It was also explained that the plane could also be packed with explosives and crashed into a target.

I'd read that there was little love lost between al-Qaeda and militant Palestinian groups, so I was a little puzzled by the link. It seemed that there might have been some sort of exchange of technical knowledge taking place, but whys and wherefores were still mysterious. I had one suspect conversation translated, and a Palestinian seemed to be objecting to the blurring of the boundaries between the two sides. The response from his counterpart went along the lines of: 'Why worry? We're all al-Qaeda now as far as the West is concerned.'

Perhaps the most disturbing document I discovered during this period was the *Mujahideen Poisons Handbook*. I had no idea that you could kill a man with three cigarettes, but this book explained how death could be achieved in 12 to 24 hours. Or that you could achieve similar results with a potato. It's probably not wise to elaborate further on this. Unusually, the document was written in pretty good English, even though it appeared on an Arabic jihad site. It raised the possibility that the author might be a young Brit, as the British spelling of 'colour' was used.

The contents were shocking, describing how to manufacture around two dozen different deadly poisons. In most cases, it was a very simple process that could be undertaken at home using commonly available products. The fastest-acting substance appeared to be ricin, which was also probably the easiest to make, and the manual said it would kill within minutes when administered orally. The name was vaguely familiar, but I couldn't remember why this rang a bell. I thought that perhaps I'd seen it mentioned as a chemical that had been tested in Iraq prior to the 1991 Gulf War for use as possible weapon.

The poisons had been tested on rabbits in Afghanistan, according to the document, and there were descriptions of how the animals reacted during the experiments. One said: 'Three ml was given orally to a strong rabbit. It started shrieking immediately. Blood came out from its mouth. It died after 100 seconds. The same dose was given to a small rabbit. It died in 7 seconds.' Another read: 'We took two rabbits, cleared the back of their neck from hairs. One rabbit needs two drops . . . After 26 minutes that rabbit fell down and started crying. After few minutes the rabbit died.'

The introduction was signed Abdul Muntaqim of something called the Organisation for the Preparation of Mujahideen, although the cover credited the author as one Abdel Aziz. Mr Aziz appeared to be the translator, and the introduction to the 19-page document explained that this was a new addition to the *Encyclopaedia of Jihad*. It also gave instructions on how to contact the author via a convoluted route involving an email encryption programme. His email address cropped up in a report by Sweden's National Defence College, which associated it with Algeria's al-Qaeda-affiliated Armed Islamic Group (GIA).

Aziz had some strong advice for would-be terrorists:

> Warning: Be very careful when preparing poisons. It is much, much more dangerous than preparing explosives! I know several Mujahids whose bodies are finished due to poor protection etc. On the positive side, you can be

143

confident that the poisons have actually been tried and tested (successfully, he he!).

He added:

> Don't become an over-paranoid James Bond figure, especially when you haven't done anything illegal even! Don't get carried away with silly movies/books (Bravo Two Zero) or propaganda about 'special forces' such as SAS, Seals etc. They're just a bunch of boys with big egos and good at running long distances. Equally, don't think there is such a thing as a super terrorist. I've been with the likes of Hekmatyar [an Afghan warlord], Black September and associates of Carlos the Jackal, and just like the 'special forces', they're only human.

Other guides and handbooks available for downloading included 'Snipers in History', 'Setting snare bombs', and US Marine Corps manuals on operating a range of anti-tank missile systems. There were more booklets by 'The Bomber', which described techniques for beating detection by scanners at airports when carrying explosives, instructions on forging documents, and 'A Study on the Basics of Ballistics'. There was also a handbook on 'The Art of Kidnapping Americans'.

Now that I'd gathered all of this material, I had to decide what to do with it. One of the main stumbling blocks when operating in this area had been the reluctance of some journalists to take Internet-sourced information seriously. It was perfectly understandable, as the dotcom bust was not that long ago and the Net was seen by many as a competing medium anyway. There was still a kind of common assumption that if information came from a website, then it was invalid, because everyone in the world with an Internet connection must have seen it.

One newspaper contact confided in me, after I'd sent him a story based on the poisons handbook, that there was definite interest in the story, but it had waned when the higher-ups realised that the document was from a website. He explained that if it had arrived in the post anonymously, then the story would probably have been published.

'They're a bit old fashioned like that here,' he whispered.

'I'll print it out and post it to you next time,' I replied.

He laughed, but I was only half-joking. If that was what it would take, I'd do it.

It was true that verifying the authenticity of these kinds of documents was often problematic, mainly because the authors and those distributing them went to great pains to ensure that they remained anonymous and couldn't be traced. That wasn't always the case, because people do make mistakes, but it ensured there was a vicious circle that meant, in effect, that terrorist suspects could go about their business knowing that it was unlikely that they'd be molested by the media.

The site where the encyclopaedia and the poisons handbook were found was also peppered with advertisements for weapons – everything from knives upwards. There were similar ads on other sites as well, and, judging by the dates on the posts, they'd all started popping up at the start of the month. The weapons were being offered at bargain prices: $840 for a Kalashnikov AK-47 automatic assault rifle, which would cost something like $1,500 on the black market in the UK. These were being touted for sale by characters claiming to represent the Organisation for the Preparation of Mujahideen (OPM), which looked like it was a procurement agency for militant Islamic groups, although there was absolutely nothing known about this group, well, nothing in the public domain at least.

All the dealers were operating through anonymous Hotmail accounts. One was known as 'Banshir, the Merchant of Death', and the charming slogan in his online signature was 'I'm the Death Coming from the East'. Some of the ads promised that they could arrange delivery to anywhere in the world, but I stopped short of actually enquiring about ordering a crate of AKs. I was concerned about the legality of doing that, and there were also security concerns. Although I was sure that I could stay anonymous, my hacker friends had taught me that there were some ingenious ways to discern someone's geographical location even when precautions had been taken. There was also the possibility that the site could have been a honey-pot trap set up by one intelligence agency or other.

It was perfectly feasible that the OPM would have taken payment by credit card or bank transfer. It wasn't hard to find the bank account details of terrorist groups. Some Palestinian terrorist/militant groups had their banking details discreetly tucked away inside their websites. The details changed every fortnight or so, presumably to foil tracking by intelligence agencies.

At the time, money could apparently be transferred to Hamas's military wing, the Izzedine al-Qassam Brigades, via 'Ayman Ataya Mansoor. Bank account no: 38924/2/510 Arab bank – Gaza branch – Palestine'. Hezbollah operated accounts in Lebanon and would-be benefactors were told: 'You can use the following account: Byblos Bank Sal Branch: Haret Hreik, or to: Nayef Abdel Hassan Krayem and/or Ali Mohammed El Zein Account No: 78.02.251.133553.0.8 Beirut, Lebanon.' A fellow journalist I'd met online during this time, Jeremy Reynalds, spent a few days looking through terrorist sites for this kind of information, and he came up with a list of over 100 bank accounts, though there was no evidence that the banks knew what these accounts were being used for.

If an AK-47 was out of your price range, the US KBI SA-2000M Sporter machine gun was presented as a cheaper alternative at $399, although it was limited by a ten-round magazine capacity and inferior range. Romanian MK-11 assault rifles were priced at between $400 and $600 apiece, depending on the quantity ordered. Other weapons on offer, without price tags, were Polish-made 96 Beryl and Mini-Beryl sub-machine guns, which can fire over 700 rounds a minute, and Radom Hunter sniper rifles with a range of over 720 metres. Also for sale were Israeli Military Industries' Galil .223 ARM tripod-mounted machine guns and the smaller .308 AR with a folding stock.

Images of the weapons were provided in each case, along with brief technical descriptions of their capabilities. One image displayed a cache of 13 modern pump-action shotguns and Uzi-type sub-machine guns laid out on a table.

One trader, who called himself 'Shamy al-Alqaqaa of the Islamic Media Centre', used the slogan: 'I have brought you the slaughter'. His digital business card included the OPM logo, and his email address was imposed on a picture of an assault rifle lying on a kitchen table.

He said: 'Can we procure weapons? You have heard of the black market on the Internet, so is that true or what?' He then answered the questions by displaying a large image of a handgun and a banner featuring bin Laden and the late Chechen guerrilla leader known as Khattab. 'The Islamic Media Centre is ready to offer to help find any military information and, with the help of God, guidance to success.'

One of the websites concerned had hit the headlines when it carried a statement from al-Qaeda which claimed responsibility for the bombing of the Paradise Hotel in Kenya. A US newspaper reported that security officials believed that the website 'speaks for al-Qaeda'.

A phrase that I kept seeing time and time again in these jihad forums was 'zero hour approaches'. It was another puzzle, and I, and others, took it to mean that another 11 September-style operation was just around the corner. This time, however, it appeared that there would be widespread random shootings and the demolition of bridges across the US, but that just didn't make sense to me. The weapons ads, the manuals and the Palestinian connections suggested that something big was being planned in the Middle East, rather than the West.

I went back through all the material I'd collated, and I found the answer in the *Encyclopaedia of Jihad*, in the map-reading section. There was an exercise in there to illustrate how to use the techniques on the battlefield, and the map that was used as an example was a map of Iraq. Of course! The penny dropped at last, and I metaphorically smacked myself on the forehead. It made perfect sense: a guerrilla war was being planned in Iraq and the zero hour was the start of the US invasion, which was still looking to be a certainty even through protracted wrangling over the legalities was continuing in the United Nations. It was obvious to everyone that President Bush was determined to go to war, come what may.

I put together a story under the headline 'AL-QAEDA PLANS GUERRILLA WAR IN IRAQ' and started the sales process, but there was no interest – either in the UK or the US. It was never said, but I guess that, to non-experts, it seemed like a ridiculous suggestion. As was traditional during times of impending war, most of the papers were getting all jingoistic about our brave boys who were going to smash Saddam's forces and destroy his weapons of mass destruction, and there were the obligatory stories about SAS teams that were apparently already roving around the country. If the papers were to be believed, it was going to be a walkover like it was during the first Gulf War, and ragtag bands of terrorists armed with cheap imitation Kalashnikovs would be no match for the military might of the West; they'd be crushed like maggots.

I tried another angle of attack with another story, based on the encyclopaedia, under the headline 'AL-QAEDA UNVEILS NERVE GAS MEGA-BOMB', and there was some initial interest in this. I was a little surprised, as it had appeared as though al-Qaeda stories had slipped down the list of priorities due to the looming war situation. The article didn't see the light of day, though, because reporters didn't think there was sufficient blue water between it and the original version. I mentioned the guerrilla war angle, but that seemed to be the final nail in the coffin.

One question I was always being asked in the early days was: 'How do you know that these documents are actually being used by terrorist groups?' There was a tendency to believe that Arab kids were sending them around, like some Western students circulated *The Anarchist Cookbook*. It was difficult to answer, at first, because identifying events that had occurred because someone had taken the courses outlined in these documents wouldn't be easy. A quick look at the cuttings provided an answer, however.

An 18-chapter manual called *Military Studies in the Jihad Against the Tyrants* was recovered during a police raid on a suspected al-Qaeda guesthouse in Manchester in May 2000. It said on the cover: 'Do not remove from this house'. The police were looking for a Libyan called Anas al-Liby, who was a chief suspect in the twin bombings of US embassies in Africa in 1998. He had a $5 million price on his head (now $25 million), but he was not at home when the cops called.

Luckily, bin Laden also came to my aid with regards to verification. During a trawl of jihad sites, I came across a message on a militant Islamic website registered in Abu Dhabi entitled: 'An order to the soldiers of God from Sheikh Osama'. I was testing out Arabic to English translation software, in the hope that it could help me to cut my operating costs. The results were choppy, and it was nowhere near being a replacement for a human translator, but it was reasonably fast and it enabled me to cover a lot of ground. The site's name translated as 'The Fortress'.

The headline read: 'The development of our war with the American enemy on the Internet', and it started:

> We inform our Muslim brothers . . . by means of this statement of some new developments concerning the ongoing war between us and the Americans on the Internet frontlines. The developments in this war consist of the entry of new elements in the conflict, with the American enemy represented in force by Jews on the battlefield.

It was apparently lambasting the efforts of Aaron Weisburd, who ran a site called Internet Haganah which was devoted to exposing extreme content on jihad websites and lobbying Internet service providers to shut them down. Clearly, his targets were rattled by his activities and those of his small army of researchers, and there appeared to be concerns at the highest levels. The message urged al-Qaeda supporters to 'teach them a lesson'.

I had become aware of Aaron's site a couple of month's previously, and I was extremely impressed with it. A huge amount of work had been put into it, and the centrepiece was a searchable database of jihad sites, complete with registration details and summaries of their content. He was being blamed for chasing al-Qaeda's official website, al-Neda, around the Internet and getting it taken off the air wherever it re-emerged. The site's operators had resorted to hacking into web servers containing otherwise innocent content and hosting the site in obscure subdirectories, although even these tactics failed to shake him off the scent.

The bin Laden-attributed statement continued:

> In essence, we have information that he and Jewish organisations in America have declared war against our site and other jihad sites. Our battle with the Jews and the crusaders on the Internet is one of the continuing kinds of conflict between us and them, and we are in a jihad against them by all means, on all fronts. Our war with them on the Internet and the other frontlines will continue, with the help of God.
>
> The Jews have entered the Internet battlefield, but they will not change a thing. Even if all countries join the conflict against us in the Internet arena it will not sway us, for, with the permission of God, we will continue with our battle strategy which is dictated by God. We . . . will continue and we will never stop spreading the truth, God willing, and we will not tire until 20 sites become 20,000.

The foot soldiers obviously regarded it as a direct order, as the number of al-Qaeda-affiliated websites started to increase exponentially. Aaron was typically unrepentant about the 'fatwa' against him. He was one of the new kind of online activist that had emerged since 11 September: people who had decided to use their computer knowledge to do everything they could to disrupt al-Qaeda's activities on the Internet.

Officially, the CIA and other law-enforcement agencies would give the impression that the Internet wasn't a great source of information for them. This dismissive attitude, however, was a feint to cover up just how poorly equipped they were to monitor the Net. I discovered just how appalling the situation was when I talked to a contact who'd been involved in developing computer systems for America's National Security Agency (NSA) and Britain's MI6. He was very discreet, although he told me that most of the NSA systems couldn't even display Arabic characters on screen, and there appeared to be no plans to address these kinds of problems. He was incredulous and dreaded to think what the situation was like further down the food chain.

The authorities were, in fact, far from disinterested in the Internet. I soon learned that changes in America's colour-coded terrorism alert system were driven by the nature of messages that appeared on three of the main Arabic jihad sites that people like Aaron monitored. There was a trend, because on two occasions as soon as specific threats emerged on these sites, the alert status moved up to red. Quotes in the media from unnamed sources talking about the current nature of the 'terrorist chatter' they were seeing chimed with the nature of the messages that I and others were also reading at the time. They were conveying the impression that the chatter might have come from tapped telephone calls and spy satellite wizardry, but the truth was much more mundane.

I knew that some of the online counter-terror trackers had become important sources of real-time threat information to law-enforcement agents, and some of them had been assigned handlers. They'd become a kind of informal digital Home Guard. It's impossible to guess at the strength of this hidden army, as they were spread out across the globe and it was a fractious community. They all operated via phoney IDs and email accounts, and there were probably many who did not break cover at all to talk about their activities. They all shared two things in common: they were motivated to see justice done after 11 September and they were computer experts.

They broke down into three broad groups. The non-interventionist school was largely made up of people who believed that active al-Qaeda sites shouldn't be disturbed but quietly harvested for intelligence. The interventionists believed in disrupting the group's communications wherever possible, tracking down sites and getting them taken offline by hosting companies. The third group, the crackers, indulged in illegal 'black hat' hacking techniques to wreck jihad sites and force them off the air. No one was willing to admit to being in the third group, although there was a circle of hacker types called the Q8crackers that had been associated with such incidents. The FBI took the unusual step of issuing a statement warning people that they were risking prosecution by engaging in illegal activities against suspected al-Qaeda websites, so it was a good indication that this was a vibrant area of activity.

The bin Laden message went on to call on Muslims working in the information technology sector in the West to establish a fifth column and wage a campaign of sabotage against Western software products and computer systems:

> We advise Muslim technical experts to make haste and break the monopolisation by American companies of computer programming languages and operating systems. We ought to say that each Muslim IT specialist can contribute by helping to reduce the effectiveness of their operating systems and software. We know that these are difficult demands and that the development and adoption of new technical systems designed for Muslims may take many long years, but this does not prevent us from reminding Muslims of the problem.

It also criticised the Western media for 'distorting facts' about al-Qaeda and claimed that, while America was seeking cooperation from Western allies in the war on terrorism, it continued to carry out economic espionage against 'thousands of European companies', aided by 'American companies like Microsoft'.

There was no doubt in my mind that al-Qaeda was now doing much of its business over the Internet and had done for many years anyway. I took Sir Winston Churchill's advice on perseverance to heart and kept 'buggering on', though the most spectacular confirmation that I was on the right path would come later when anti-terrorist police, Special Branch and MI5 officers raided a flat in north London on 5 January 2003 and discovered a ricin production laboratory. Six men were taken into custody and Tony Blair was moved to make a statement about how the discovery indicated the scale of the threat posed to the West by Islamic terrorist groups. There was blanket media coverage and feverish speculation about how the group had planned to use the poison. Among the items discovered in the apartment were castor beans, from which ricin is extracted, and equipment for processing them.

The set-up sounded very familiar to me: it appeared that they were following the instructions in the *Mujahideen Poisons Handbook* that I'd found earlier. Then, on Sunday 16 February 2003, it was reported that six Hamas operatives were killed in Gaza City while they were working on a remote-controlled model aircraft that was packed with explosives. It sounded like they'd read the same instructions on that jihad website as I had. It exploded prematurely and some reports suggested that the Israeli internal security service Shin Bet may have booby-trapped the device.

Even before these reports came out, my attention had been turning to finding evidence of al-Qaeda activities in the UK. Prior to the ricin raid, the newspapers seemed to be fairly relaxed about terrorism, and there still appeared to be a collective estimation that it was mainly a problem for the Americans. They appeared to be full of confidence that our intelligence services had it well covered. I guess the basic line of thinking was that they'd done a fine job of protecting the country from the IRA for the past three decades, so why worry too much? A few bombs had slipped through the net, but that was perhaps inevitable over such a long timescale. Our defences against terrorism were believed to be robust and world class, and our operatives were obviously battle-hardened.

Editors were also concerned not to be treading on the toes of the Security Service, and reporters would sometimes mutter on the phone about checking to make sure the story wouldn't be disturbing anything. It was kind of sweet: when it came to pulling down corrupt politicians no stone was left unturned, but beasts of Fleet Street turned into pussycats when it came to national security. It's fair to say that the intelligence services were very much admired in the media, who, in turn, were a patriotic bunch, on the whole.

I don't want to get into a long essay on the ethical dilemma of journalists dealing with spooks and bang on about censorship issues. As far as I saw it, the only way to deal with this is on a case-by-case basis. I'd be on to them like a shot if I came across anything that clearly constituted an immediate threat to the security of my country, because it would be my duty as a citizen to save the lives of my fellow countrymen, if it was in my power to do so, of course. That would transcend my professional obligations as a journalist. There's no way any Briton could, in good conscience, stand by knowing that they'd uncovered a detailed plan and targeting information for an impending al-Qaeda suicide-bombing blitz, for example.

I'd yet to come across anything that specific, although some of the leads I was working on came perilously close. I couldn't even get away for a day's recreation without being reminded about my life as a roving terror reporter. I'd taken a drive down to the south coast to get some fresh air and enjoy a change of scenery. As I sat there at Milford on Sea, admiring the view of the Isle of Wight and the sweeping vista across Christchurch Bay on what was a breezy and chilly day, I watched with interest as a Royal Navy frigate or minesweeper made its way out into the bay.

It's not a sight you see every day, and then, as I was thinking of moving on and getting something to eat, a lifeboat rounded the headland and set off in the same direction. It looked like something was up. As the lifeboat became a small orange blob in the distance, three black inflatable boats, with six people in black uniforms in each, came zooming past and went powering off in the same direction, with a large helicopter hovering low and keeping pace with them. There had been reports that terrorists were planning to hijack ships, and I wondered if there was an alert on.

It was quite a scene, although the conditions weren't ideal for inflatable boats. It wasn't that cold, but the wind was annoyingly gusty, making the water choppy, and there was a large swell. The inflatable boats seemed to stall momentarily now and then when they hit a large wave, before leaping on through the large cloud of white spray they'd produced on impact. There was only one explanation for this – the Special Boat Service (SBS), the maritime equivalent of the SAS.

It was either a practice session or a real alert, though I thought that it was more likely to be a drill, because I could see the helicopter hovering way out at sea, where I could just about make out the Navy ship and the lifeboat. The nearest shipping lanes were in and out of nearby Bournemouth to the west, where cross-channel ferries went to Cherbourg in France and back. I couldn't see a ferry, so I guessed that it must have been a rehearsal, perhaps for storming a ship. I seem to be drawn to these kinds of things and it was even more remarkable this time because I'd picked that spot of coast at random from the map while en route. Being witness to a special forces anti-terrorism operation was just a very unexpected and remarkable experience: pure chance.

There could have been a story in what I saw. When I got back home, I checked and there was no mention anywhere of an imminent threat to shipping. The SBS was said to be based at a location near Portsmouth, but that was meant to be a secret. The black boats were coming from the right direction, and I started thinking about writing a story along the lines of 'our brave boys prepare to take on the terrorists', but I decided to let it slide. It was a very comforting thought, though, that the military was quietly preparing for these eventualities away from the public gaze – well, not entirely on this occasion, but I just felt that they didn't need any unnecessary harassment from the media about this. They were just doing their jobs and I was meant to be on a day off from work anyway, so I let it lie.

It did provoke me, however, to test more vigorously the prevailing media attitude that al-Qaeda was largely a US problem. The sight of the SBS in action brought it home to me that the authorities were preparing for terrorist events in our own backyard and my hacking contacts were now frequently throwing up UK links to suspected terrorist activities. The extent and immediacy of the potential threat were moot points, and the natural thing to do was to try and get some measurements on the nature of the threat.

There were some very fiery militant Islamic groups in the UK, though I steered clear of these at first because I suspected that some of them just had rather blusterous leaders who were taking full advantage of the Human Rights Act. I was after something more substantial to grapple with, rather than looking at the technical differences between the right to free speech and incitement to violence. I was browsing through web pages, just soaking up background information and looking for possible angles, when I came across a link to a site called 'Al-Qaeda Exposed'. I clicked on the link and the home page opened with a curious message: 'aL-QAEDA EXPOSED IN SECRET SPY VIDEO FOOTAGE'.

There were various links to video clips on succeeding pages that showed a wide spectrum of material, including footage apparently taken inside jihad training camps in Afghanistan, gruesome scenes of killing in Bosnia and a variety of speeches delivered by radical Islamic figures. I recognised one of them immediately: Abu Hamza al-Masri, a firebrand cleric from the North London Central Mosque in Finsbury Park who was infamous for his hooked hand. He said he'd lost both hands and an eye while trying to diffuse a landmine in Afghanistan, although I'd heard murmurs that hinted at a more sinister explanation, so he attracted my attention. One comedian had dubbed him Abu 'is it the blue wire?' Hamza.

Maybe I'd been wrong to dismiss these kinds of figures, as the website claimed he was an al-Qaeda recruiter, and added that you could judge for yourself by watching the video clips. I did, and there was some very interesting material, like a demonstration outside an embassy where a group of his supporters were holding up placards reading: 'One bullet, One Bush!' and Hamza was leading the chanting of 'al-Jihad! al-Jihad!' Al-Jihad was a group (Egyptian Islamic Jihad) led by bin Laden's deputy, Ayman al-Zawahiri, that merged with al-Qaeda in 1998, so I could see what the website owner was getting at. That wasn't in any way conclusive, however, and I needed to see more than just a few online clips to make any reasonable judgements. The more I absorbed, the more I became curious about the operators of the site and their motivations.

I wasn't sure what to make of it. It all seemed a bit fanciful, and I wondered whether this might be a sick hoax or, even worse, an al-Qaeda supporter sucking in gullible reporters, like a sort of Max Clifford figure for terrorists. That was my main concern, though I fired off an email to the address listed on the site anyway. A day later, on 15 November 2002, a guy who called himself Glen Jenvey contacted me: 'Hi, I'm Glen, the person who put the terror tapes online. I'm glad you're interested in reporting on Hamza and his al-Qaeda circle here in the UK, as something needs to be done.' He asked me for some details about myself; I outlined my credentials and he got back to me within 15 minutes.

He said that the video clips on the website had directly led the

FBI to an al-Qaeda suspect in the US called James Ujaama, who'd been arrested on suspicion of aiding the Taliban. Glen claimed that the FBI office in Seattle (Ujamaa's home city), via the US embassy in London, had requested that the anti-terrorist branch of the Metropolitan Police procure the full-length videotapes from him, and he'd duly obliged some months previously. It was quite a story, and I was impressed that he was apparently responsible for taking a wrongdoer out of circulation. But he insisted that the Ujaama arrest was just part of a wider investigation into the activities of Abu Hamza.

I asked to see copies of the tapes that he'd handed over. Glen said he'd organise it, although it might take a while as they were in the States with a *Seattle Times* reporter. There were many hours of footage on the six tapes and plenty of stories in there for me to follow up on, he assured me. There were also 19 audiotapes with even more damning material that had not seen the light of day yet. They were in the care of an intelligence contact now and might not be recoverable, although he said he'd try.

I'd have to move quickly on this story, because he'd already had the BBC on to him for access to the tapes, but I persuaded him to stall them so that I could get hold of them first, on behalf of the *Sunday Times*. In between emails, I'd been on the phone to my regular contact there on the Insight investigations team and he was very keen on the story.

The big question for me was: who is this guy? What's he doing with militant Islamic videos and how is he connected to the intelligence community? I started probing him on this, and he seemed to be amused. He told me in oblique terms that he'd only just made my acquaintance and all would be revealed when he was certain that I was trustworthy. Fair comment, I thought, and I took it as a provisional hint that he was who he said he was, as a decent intelligence operative wouldn't spill his guts to someone he'd just met. His response gave me an inkling that I was on to something special.

In order to get the initial *Sunday Times* story out just two days later, I had to take him at his word, but after that he slowly started to outline his background to me. Eventually, as part of the validation process and to authenticate the videotapes, he asked his solicitor to obtain a copy of a statement that he'd given to the Anti-Terrorist

Squad. It was almost as good as getting a signed certificate from the police, so I was eager to see it. It would provide valuable verification of his story and seemed like a good pre-emptive move while we were waiting for the tapes to make it back across the Atlantic.

Glen was born in the UK in 1965; his father was from Mauritius and his mother was English. He was placed into care when he was seven years old and was brought up by an English foster mother and a foster father who was an American NCO working for US Strategic Command at Greenham Common air base. He said he became intrigued by militant Islamic groups whilst studying history at college, and he'd visited Iran in the mid-1990s as part of his research into the Iran–Iraq war. Around the time of the attack on the USS *Cole* in Yemen in October 2000, he started to concentrate on al-Qaeda. 'I have some knowledge of Tamil groups and those willing to undertake terrorist attacks and those carrying out suicide attacks. I believed that al-Qaeda may well be using similar methods to those used by the Tamils,' he stated.

The Iran visit and his knowledge of methods used by terrorist groups were two obvious points for further questioning, and I asked him for more details on these. I could almost see the smile on his face when I got an email reply from him saying something along the lines of there were some things that were glossed over in the police statement and there were other things that he could probably never tell me about.

He grew up in an environment where he was in close contact with his father's associates in military and diplomatic circles. While he was at college, a friend of his father's, who was a London-based diplomat, asked him if he'd be interested in videotaping protesters who'd be attending a demonstration to be held outside the embassy. He was paid £100 and it was his first mission as a spy.

Information and contacts in military intelligence circles are often 'kept in the family', and word is spread among close friends and relatives. Soon, he was regularly being asked to do similar tasks by London embassy contacts, and, before long, an official at the US embassy asked if he'd be prepared to travel to Iran to gather information on military facilities there. One of his unique selling points was his brown skin colour, he explained quite matter-of-factly. He could blend into situations where white folk would stick out a mile, and he tended to get a lot of that kind of work.

He said he posed as a Palestinian Liberation Organisation sympathiser and simply made friends along the way as he travelled across the country photographing everything of possible interest to his military intelligence contact. He was an affable chap, and I could imagine him doing this. Glen said he made it as far as the border with Iraq, where he snapped a series of missile bases, before he was detained by the Iranian internal security service, the Mukhabarat. He was pretty hazy on the details and obviously thought twice about whether he should elaborate. He asserted that he had had to bribe a judge to make sure he was swiftly deported. When we met in person a few weeks later, he showed me an Iranian stamp in his passport.

I asked about the Tamils, and he was more forthcoming. He said he'd been approached and asked if he'd be prepared to infiltrate the Liberation Tigers of Tamil Eelam (LTTE), otherwise known as the Tamil Tigers. They were a militant group fighting for independence on the island of Sri Lanka, having achieved notoriety for inventing the concept of suicide bombing. Middle Eastern terrorists groups had simply followed their example in this regard, I was surprised to learn.

His statement about suspecting al-Qaeda was using similar tactics made sense when I looked at the Tigers' rap sheet. Their first suicide attack took place on 5 July 1987 when, in an effort to stop the advance of army troops on the Tamil capital Jaffna, an explosives-laden truck was crashed into an army camp killing 40 people. The suicide operatives mainly belonged to a subsection called the Black Tigers, although the philosophy was quickly integrated into all of its areas of operation. Some 50,000 people had died during the 20-year struggle between the two sides.

On 26 June 2000, a boat filled with explosives was rammed into a merchant vessel by a Black Sea Tigers suicide team, and an eight-hour gun battle with its naval escort ensued. That happened just a few months before the al-Qaeda suicide boat attack on the USS *Cole*. One amazing coincidence leapt out of the list of LTTE terrorist attacks: on 15 October 1997, 18 people were killed when they launched a truck bomb attack against a target in the country's capital, Colombo, called the World Trade Centre. It even had twin towers.

I later talked to one of Glen's intelligence contacts in London who confirmed, off the record, that Glen had indeed infiltrated the

Tigers on his behalf. He was a highly placed official at a London embassy and he corroborated Glen's tale. This, combined with his statement to the Anti-Terrorist Squad and the stamps in his passport, meant that I should take him seriously. He was a spy, no doubt about it. As a freelance operative he had ties with the intelligence services of many different countries.

He managed to get a job as a press officer for the Tigers in their London office in Katherine Road in east London, around the time that former Indian prime minister Rajiv Gandhi was killed by a Tamil Tigers suicide bomber in 1991. Glen laughed as he talked about organising secret meetings between Tigers representatives and sympathetic Tory, Labour and Liberal Democrat MPs.

'No one knew about it, but there were terrorists taking tea inside the House of Commons on a regular basis.' The group is now listed as a proscribed organisation under the Terrorism Act 2000, which came into force on 29 March 2001.

The Tigers were also in routine contact with other militant groups, such as the IRA and the Kurdish PKK, and the press officers would often compare notes with each other. This enabled him to pick up some valuable information on these groups as well.

'Two years before, they'd invited the IRA to be guest speakers at their Paris conference. One of the funniest things I heard was about supporters of the IRA holding a sponsored walk around Buckingham Palace to raise funds,' he said.

Glen said that he learnt that the press operation was actually there to provide signals to give the green light to operations in Sri Lanka. The timings were flagged up with the issuing of a press release containing a coded message. He said he may have played a part in preventing a suicide bomb attack against Prince Charles.

The Prince of Wales was visiting the island on a three-day trip to take part in the celebrations to commemorate the 50th anniversary of the country's independence in 1998. Glen said he knew that there had been discussions about mounting a suicide attack on his motorcade.

'When I asked the LTTE in Katherine Road about the Prince's visit, the head of the London military wing said, "Let's wait and see", in a tone that I took to mean that an attack was in the offing. The Tamil Tigers were asking amongst themselves about what time the Prince would visit certain places, and they were closely monitoring news reports.'

The Tigers' mole warned his boss at the Sri Lankan National Intelligence Bureau, who was in charge of organising Prince Charles's bodyguards during the visit, that something was up, and he sent regular updates to the Sri Lankan embassy in London by fax. Only the high commissioner and the first secretary had access to the embassy's fax room during the operation.

'The suicide bomber who might have been targeting the Prince, a woman called Indra, I think, eventually blew herself up at a military checkpoint near the airport some hours after Prince Charles had left. She was confused about the timing. The London office was being fed wrong information by me during the whole visit.'

He knew the Tigers' phones were bugged, and so he'd sent out plenty of warnings about the plan, and the Prince's security arrangements were being made in Sri Lanka, in any case. He declined to take any personal credit for stopping a potential disaster during the royal visit. The success, he said, was down to 'wrong information and wrong timings, good security and good luck.

'I used to tell the Tigers all sorts of rubbish to get information for a period of two and a half years. Every day, every word and fax message was reported.'

I asked him why he'd started operating on the Internet, as it seemed like a drastic change. He said that it dawned on him that the very same human intelligence techniques that he'd used to monitor and infiltrate terrorist groups in the past could equally be applied in a digital environment. Tracking the content of a website was roughly equivalent to filming a demonstration; joining and infiltrating a group was easier to do online, and getting in on the loop and receiving email and participating in online discussions was nearly as good as bugging the offices of a terrorist group. He was now passing on his experience and training newly recruited intelligence operatives, taking a break away from the frontlines.

We talked frequently by phone and by email, and we got on well. We had a lot in common, not least because we had both haphazardly meandered into the same area of operation. Then he called to say the Hamza videotapes had finally arrived and we could set to work.

THE HAMZA VIDEOS

I got into a political argument with a US editor about my journalistic activities. It was something that I'd managed to avoid up until then. I'd presented my credentials and my cuttings, and everything seemed to be going professionally when he suddenly assaulted me in an email reply. Why was I hassling Muslims and not exposing the IRA or the civilian casualties caused by the Coalition in Afghanistan?

I groaned as I realised that I couldn't let this one slide, and I'd have to craft a lengthy response to his list of allegations and insinuations. I'd hit on a rampant lefty by accident. Still, it was an opportunity I relished, and it felt like the right time to be having a pause to think through the reasons for myself. The instant answer was easy: al-Qaeda had more journalistic sex appeal than all of the others put together. I thought I'd think it through a bit more than that, however, just to make sure I wasn't wasting my life, for as least as long as it took to knock out a letter.

The editor said that I appeared to be unquestioning about the war on terrorism, which I think he'd have preferred me to describe as 'Bush's so-called war on terrorism'. It was a boring conversation that I knew I'd get into sooner or later: a tedious game of semantics, like much of the discussion on the Internet, where there were numerous Jewish sites monitoring news outlets and accusing, say, the BBC of bias, because a report had said 'militant Palestinian groups' instead of 'Palestinian terrorists'. Equally, there were arguments on the other side for calling Israeli soldiers terrorists.

I told him: 'No, I'm not at all unquestioning – far from it. I'm interested in all forms of terrorism, and terrorism that may be sponsored by Western nations is especially interesting. I have indeed investigated the bombing of civilians in Afghanistan. There's a good story to be done about the discovery of traces of possibly weapons-grade uranium found in urine samples taken from people across the country.' I was surprised he didn't know about this, seeing as he had such a deep concern for the people there.

'I've been sniffing around the IRA of late and I've got hold of some Continuity IRA (CIRA) recruitment videos,' I continued. 'I'm interested in the whole arena. You'd have noticed that I typed "war on terrorism" rather than "War on Terrorism". I'll try to follow the house style of whatever publication I'm working for; I'll even write in English Prime, if required. I don't know how you can conclude that I lack any scepticism about this when I've never written about the subject in the round or expounded any personal views at all on that in the pieces you've seen.'

He'd also lambasted me for having the nerve to write for the *Washington Times*, which was completely puzzling.

'The *Washington Times* is just a major American newspaper to me, where I know that a pitch from overseas will get a fair hearing. I'm aware that it leans to the right, but so do most of them, although I'm unaware of the highly sensationalist reputation that you say it has.

'You can't condemn me for being professional, matching stories with the outlets that are most likely to accept them and getting my work circulated among the widest possible audience. You talk about it having a low level of credibility among US journalists. Why would that concern me? It doesn't. Perhaps it might, if I considered US journalists to be the standard-bearers of the profession.'

He had me down as a fiercely pro-Israeli neo-conservative media agent provocateur, based on purely circumstantial evidence. It is funny how people are prone to get all shirty and confrontational when trying to have a remote discussion via digital methods; it's a phenomenon very similar to road rage, I feel. He said he'd take my comments on board and respond at a later date, but he didn't and I was glad of that. I dealt in facts, whereas he seemed to be dealing in prejudice and dogma, which he was trying to hide under a veneer of journalistic credibility. What a fucking waste of time, I thought. No new money outlet there, then.

Probably the silliest thing he had come out with during his tirade was to call Abu Hamza a respected member of the British Muslim community. He was no such thing. It was an odd description for someone who was a terrorist suspect. In Yemen, he was wanted for questioning about the kidnapping of sixteen Western tourists in the country and the deaths of four of them. He'd been in contact with the kidnappers by phone, although he denied any involvement with the group, from the Islamic Army of Aden. The hostages were taken just days after a group of Britons were detained in the country on suspicion of planning terrorist attacks. They included Hamza's son, Mohammed Mustafa Kamel, and his press officer, Sarmad Ahmed. Abu Hamza was detained for questioning by Scotland Yard detectives in the UK and held for several days, although he was eventually released without charge.

It had also emerged that shoe-bomber Richard Reid and the '20th hijacker', Zacarias Moussaoui, had been regular visitors to Finsbury Park mosque. The Bank of England listed him as a 'target relating to terrorism' and he was subject to economic sanctions.

According to his database entry at the bank, his real name was Mustapha Kamel. He was born on 15 April 1958 in an unspecified country, and he'd used a wide range of aliases, including: Abu Hamza, al-Masri, Mostafa Kamel, Mostafa Eaman and Adam Ramsey. Two residential addresses in west London were listed for him: one in Aldbourne Road in Shepherd's Bush and another in Adie Road in Hammersmith. Prior to my initial encounter with Glen, I was vaguely aware that Abu Hamza was a supporter of bin Laden and had made some headlines with some very inflammatory statements about 11 September, but Glen was much further down the road than me at this stage.

According to his police statement, Glen first came across Abu Hamza in November 2000, when he clicked on his website, called Supporters of Sharia, and was appalled at what he saw there. He told the police: 'The website contained material that concerned me, in particular threats to individuals and UK and US interests.' He emailed the military attaché at the US embassy in London, but he received no reply, so he decided to infiltrate the group, using the insights he'd gained during his work on the Tamil Tigers.

Glen and an online acquaintance called Johnathan R. Galt, a renowned anti-terrorism researcher, set about creating an authentic-looking jihad website to back up his cover story, or 'legend', as it's otherwise called. He bought the domain name Islamic-News.co.uk and they started to populate the site with content that had been cut and pasted from real jihad websites, until they ended up with a site that appeared to be operated by a Kashmiri terrorist group that was covertly backed by the Pakistani military.

Glen then transformed into Pervez Khan: a press officer working for the group. When the site was fully functional, he emailed Hamza to introduce himself and phoned him at Finsbury Park mosque on a couple of occasions prior to 11 September 2001.

'He was so pleased with this he decided to put a link to my site from his site. That was his first big mistake,' said Glen.

'He trusted me. We had been emailing each other a lot, and I had been passing the emails to the FBI. We also started to speak on the phone. I started to suggest I could help him recruit people for his jihad. He became very excited by this. He would burble prayers down the phone in an almost demented fashion. I thought he must be a bit mad.'

Pervez told Abu Hamza that his brother was soon going to be launching a recruitment and fundraising drive in the UK for Kashmir. His imaginary sibling wanted to direct people to attend Hamza's meetings at Finsbury Park. Pervez argued that both sides would benefit, as Abu Hamza would get higher attendances for his meetings and demonstrations, while he and his brother would have an enlarged pool of potential new recruits. It would be a practical way of centralising the recruitment of British Mujahideen fighters who'd be ready to fight on a number of different battlefields when required.

It was audacious, to say the least, as he was proposing the creation of Jihad UK.

'After speaking to Abu Hamza, he agreed to send me a number of tapes that would help me plan meetings and study circles, which would help with the recruitment of fighters for both Hamza's and our groups,' said Glen.

'He said he would send me some material to help me win supporters and prepare them for jihad. He said he had some special tapes but that they were somewhere secret, and he did not keep them in the mosque.'

Traffic to the website boomed as Glen, Johnathan and three other members of the group actively promoted the site in online jihadi circles and ensured that it was regularly updated. Details from the site's logs about visitors and their behaviour were passed to various intelligence agencies for processing through their own databases. Glen explained that a visitor's IP (Internet Protocol) address, a unique sequence of numbers that identifies a computer connected to the Internet, could be cross-matched by governments to credit card details or phone records, for example.

After securing the videotapes and audiotapes from Hamza and realising the significance of their contents, he knew he'd hit the jackpot. It then seemed pointless to hope for a second win, when he had no intention of fulfilling his side of the bargain. Hamza would soon realise that his brother was not delivering extra bums on seats, so Glen brought the project to a close after eight months of work – in a typically high-profile way. He decided to junk all the content on Islamic-News and replace it with a page that started with the message: 'We've changed our minds about this whole terrorism thing: Jihad is Crap!'

It declared:

> We have decided to cooperate with the authorities here in Britain and in the USA. Britain must not be used as a base for worldwide Islamist terrorism. The evidence we have of Islamist activities against India regarding Kashmir will be given to the Indian authorities. We will help the Russians battle the evil of the . . . Chechen Mujahideen. We will help the Israelis overcome Arafat and his goons.

He did get abuse and death threats from time to time after that, but it didn't bother him at all. He was still getting the occasional threat from the Tamils. He sent me an example of what he typically receives:

> From: globaljihad@hotmail.com
> To: Glen Jenvey
>
> What do Americans, Europe and Israel know about history Islam and muslims??? When the hundreds of thousands and millions *of* muslims being maimed, killed and their lands resourses looted by Europe and colonial Britain and satan USA and Israel . . . what happened in USA on 9/11/2001 was just little punishment compare to centuries of muslims being killed and millions and millions of muslims died by the

crusaders Zionists alliance (Europe, Russia, USA, Israel) and also muslims killed by muslim dictators and hypocrite traitors supported by the Europe and satan USA . . . muslims are not evil, terrorists or other criminals, they fight for defending the oppressed muslims of Palestine, Iraq, Chechnya, Afghanistan, Kashmir, and other parts of the world . . . who is the real aggressor and terrorists the west or islam? The one who started killing, maiming, widowing, orphaning muslims around the world and the chief aggressors of muslims are Satan USA and its biggest ally Israel and Europe, they killed millions of muslims since 11th century and when ottoman empire collapse by Kemal Attaturk the agent of the Britain then more and more muslims died and then Europe, Russia and Israel supported militarily and politically by USA they colonized muslim lands and killed millions of muslims . . . the muslim mujahideens have the right to take revenge against Europe and satan USA and Israel and the muslim hypocrite traitors and dictators . . . the true faithful muslim mujahideens will fight untill all crusaders zionist forces are driven from all muslim countries . . . if u followers of devil leaders of satan Europe and satan America dont understand our religion (islam) and misunderstanding why muslims are fighting against you then shut your infidel pig holes and prepare to die and burn in hell stop calling islam 'evil religion' and stop calling all muslims 'terrorists' just because they are defending oppressed muslims around the world and just because they are fighting the aggressors.

Infidel pig holes: I liked that. I'll use that somewhere, I thought.

Looking at the videos in detail wasn't a task I was looking forward to. I'd seen some highly disturbing footage contained in jihad videos that you can find sprinkled around these kinds of sites, like beheadings and castrations. These people had a raging thirst for gore and guts, to the extent that one of the slickest jihad sites on the Net, operated from Canada, launched a pay-per-view online 'jihad theatre' to capitalise on the demand.

I've seen some of the sickest things that it's possible for human beings to do to each other – over and over again. At first I thought being exposed to all that unspeakable stuff would give me nightmares, but it didn't. I just became quickly hardened to it, I suppose, and there's a way of mentally 'de-tuning' from the finer details of what you're watching: detaching yourself yet still paying attention. I see shaky video footage of a young Russian soldier crying and pleading for his life, and I know it isn't going to be a merciful ending. I know from experience what's coming next, and I often stop watching at this point, before all the chopping and screeching and blood-letting starts.

I'm sure the neighbours have huddled together at some point and talked about calling the police, due to the Arabic chanting and screaming noises they can just barely hear coming from next door late at night sometimes. It looked like they might be in for more disturbances, though, because I had hours of material on the Hamza videos to go through.

The classic problem presented itself of where to start. I didn't want to spend any more time faffing around than I had to, so I searched for the part that had been used in the trial of Hamza's associate James Ujaama. I found the section and settled down to take notes. Glen said that Ujaama used to run Hamza's website, under the alias of Abu Samaya, and he'd just cut a deal with federal prosecutors in the US to plead guilty to aiding the Taliban in return for a two-year prison sentence and agreeing to testify against Hamza before a federal Grand Jury investigation. He'd originally denied all the charges, until a clip from one of the videos which Glen supplied to the police was shown in the courtroom in Seattle.

Ujaama had been facing a 25-year prison sentence if convicted. He realised he was caught bang to rights on the video, so he sought a plea-bargain deal. The damning evidence on the tapes meant that a defence would be futile. He originally claimed that he'd only been to Afghanistan to deliver laptop computers to a school for girls, but Glen was on standby to testify against him in Seattle. Indeed, his police statement said: 'I am willing to be interviewed by the US authorities in relation to this matter, and, if required, I would be willing to travel to the USA to give evidence in an open court.' He would not be required now, he was told, after Ujaama's U-turn.

Hamza's friend had previously been regarded as an upstanding member of the community. For his community leadership work in Las Vegas, he was given a key to the city. In Washington state, 10 June 1994 was declared James Ujaama Day, and he received a Certificate of Special Congressional Recognition.

The secret Grand Jury proceedings in New York were said to be concentrating on Hamza's alleged involvement in a plan to establish a jihad training camp in the US in 1999, on a small ranch near a town called Bly in Oregon. Ujaama moved to London in the mid-1990s, became friends with Hamza and took over responsibility for running the Supporters of Sharia website. On a trip back home in 1999, he is said to have sent a fax to Hamza in London from Kinko's Copy Center in Washington, Seattle, to propose setting up the training camp in Bly. He was one of a group of militants based at the Dar-us-Salam Mosque in Seattle, but, unfortunately for him, the FBI had an informant in place within his circle at the mosque and he was aware of the fax.

Hamza then sent two of his lieutenants, Oussama Kassir and Haroon Rashid Aswat, from London to New York City. Ujaama then drove the two to the site of the proposed camp. However, Kassir was upset with Ujaama when they finally arrived, as the place didn't have barracks for troops or any other facilities for jihad training. Still, the group had brought 15 automatic weapons with them and they spent some time firing at targets. Kassir has since fled to Sweden, whilst Aswat is believed to have died fighting with al-Qaeda forces in Afghanistan during the conflict between the US and the Taliban.

According to court documents, Ahmed Ressam, an Algerian terrorist who was convicted of trying to bring a bomb into the US from Canada in 1999, told the FBI that Hamza was the London contact of Abu Zubaydah, bin Laden's former chief of operations. Zubaydah was the number three in the al-Qaeda network and in charge of the training camps in Afghanistan. The US authorities also believed that he was one of the chief planners of the 11 September attacks.

In his testimony, Ressam stated that Hamza had also recommended that two Algerians within their circle of contacts be sent to a training camp in Afghanistan in 1998. 'Such recommendations by someone who is known and trusted are required for access to the training camps and for specialised training such as leadership training,' immigration department agent Darrick Smalley said in an affidavit.

Hamza was known as a staunch supporter of bin Laden and the Taliban, who banned television and most sport and recreation. As I was shuttling towards the end of one tape, trying to find the Ujaama clip, I was therefore surprised to see the tail end of a football match that had been recorded from the TV (featuring Arsenal, I think) and an episode of the BBC drama *Casualty*. I wondered what the Taliban would have made of that. It was quite ironic to think that Hamza was a fan of the British emergency services, or maybe he was just watching it for research purposes.

Much more eye opening was another TV programme on the tape, which appeared to date from 1999. It was a documentary in Arabic about how the World Trade Center towers in New York were constructed. It delved into the structural engineering and the construction process at the WTC, as well as the world's other famous twin towers: the Petronas Towers in Malaysia, the world's tallest buildings. It was an odd thing to be watching, although I guess that Hamza's response would be to say that he had a professional interest in this, as he claimed to be a trained engineer. But, given the nature of the contents of the rest of the tape, it looked highly suspicious, to say the very least. It was the kind of thing that the planners of the 11 September attacks would have studied.

On the tape, Ujaama didn't sound like someone who should be showered with keys to cities. He looked odd in some way I couldn't put my finger on. The clip showed him wearing a natty orange woollen skullcap and a burgundy tank top worn over a shirt that was buttoned to the top, sitting with Hamza at a table in front of an audience. Glen thought the clip dated from May 2000 and Ujaama was delivering a speech that would later be heard in the Seattle courtroom. He was reading from a script, and I've reproduced here the verbatim account of the words used on the tape:

> Because it was not long ago that the evil Christians launched a crusade against the Muslims, the Jews, and even other Christians. Today they are back in Egypt and Turkey, and Algeria, and Sudan, Somalia, Iraq – and even in Islamic lands: the holy lands of Mecca and Medina! Today the crusade is against Islam and they are led by the Jews . . . in Israel's long-awaited campaign to destroy Islam and to dominate the world.
>
> So Sheikh Abdullah Azzam [bin Laden's guru] was killed in a car explosion by the kuffar [non-believers] for enjoying the right and leading the Muslims in Pakistan and forbidding the wrong. Sheikh Abdel Rahman [mastermind

behind 1993 WTC bombing] was framed by a paid informant for the kuffar and later sentenced by a Jew to life in a prison. He is currently under heavy guard and in total isolation. This is no proper way for a Muslim sheikh to live out his life, without proper food or medicine or any provisions. Rarely does he even get any visitors.

Sheikh Osama bin Laden was framed and forced into isolation, having to leave his own lands, his family, then used as a scapegoat to arrest many Muslims who speak out against [wrongdoing] in their lands. Sheikh Abu Hamza: arrested in the middle of the night during a police raid on his home. His family, harassed and oppressed, all because he chose to speak out against the evil rulers living in the Muslim lands and their helpers. Today, the government has still not given him back his passport, and they refuse to hand over his personal belongings. Now . . . he has too been pushed to the limit, jailed, convicted in the media and charged with a crime for which they are seeking the death penalty!

There is a pattern with all of the attempts to assassinate, to rid the Islamic *ummah* [nation] of its leaders, to silence our leaders, as you shall soon find out.

Those words 'as you shall soon find out' leapt out at me, as it suggested that this was recorded prior to 11 September, and that he might have been hinting at a major event in the offing. Perhaps it was a veiled reference to 11 September? In any case, the part that sunk him was his admission in the midst of all this invective that he'd been to Afghanistan and prayed with the Mujahideen. In the coverage of his trial, the *Seattle Times* claimed that law-enforcement sources believed that he was accompanied on one trip, at Hamza's direction, by a Briton called Feroz Abassi. Abassi was later captured during fighting between al-Qaeda and American troops in Kandahar and sent to Guantanamo Bay.

What doesn't come across in print very well is the demeanour of Ujaama, who was supposed to be a balanced, helpful type, yet he was practically screaming with outrage at some points on the tape. He was safely incarcerated and ingratiating himself with the FBI, so it seemed strange that Abu Hamza hadn't yet gone the same way.

One of the more curious things that came up was footage of a meeting of the radical north London militant Islamic group al-

Muhajiroun, which was led by a guy called Sheikh Omar Bakri Mohammad. He held views on al-Qaeda and the Taliban that seemed to be virtually indistinguishable from Abu Hamza's. All there was on the tape of this particular meeting were a few shots of people milling around either before or during the meeting, as it looked like the full proceedings had been recorded over.

'Listen carefully to the sound,' Glen said. I turned it up and replayed it many times to make sure it said what we thought it said. In the general background chatter, an unseen voice can be heard calling 'Brother Atta' three times, as if he's trying to attract someone's attention. Mohammed Atta was, of course, one of the lead hijackers on 11 September. Was he at the meeting? There was no way of telling if it was the same person, but it was a feasible assumption, as several of the hijackers were known to have visited north London.

At least five of them stayed at a flat in Cheshire Road, Wood Green, during visits to London in 1999 and 2000, which is one of the least known and understood aspects of the whole story. The flat was home to an Algerian, Mustapha Labsi, who was being detained on suspicion of terrorism, although he denied any wrongdoing. He was suspected of helping to train the 19 hijackers in Afghanistan and providing support facilities for those who visited Britain. FBI agents and Special Branch detectives conducted door-to-door enquiries in the area after the attacks, showing photographs of the hijackers to the neighbours and asking if people recognised any of them. Curiously, the safe house was a short walk away from the flat where the ricin lab was discovered nearly two years later. The case against Labsi was later dropped, though he was re-arrested to face extradition to France, where he is accused of plotting to bomb the G7 summit in Lille in 1996.

The Ujaama section that was on tape included two sections from jihad videos: one that appeared to show recruits training in a camp in Afghanistan and a second that showed dead and injured people in the aftermath of some sort of attack. It may have been Bosnia. The tape cut to the Ujaama speech, then Hamza started talking at the same meeting. I could see him sitting next to Ujaama, almost out of shot, as he railed against the injustices suffered by bin Laden.

Hamza started by talking about the history of the Mujahideen in Afghanistan. After a few minutes of being fascinated every time he waved his famous hooked hand while he was speaking, I could tell that he certainly had a strong stage presence. He was an imposing figure, of course: built like the proverbial brick house, with a scraggy, greying bread and eyes that appeared menacing as he rammed his points home. He exuded certainty: he had a habit of nodding slightly several times after making a statement, as if he was subconsciously re-enforcing his argument.

He claimed that the American CIA hadn't trained the anti-Soviet Mujahideen; that was done by the Pakistani Army. He went on to describe how inexperienced the local Afghans were at fighting, the elementary mistakes they made when trying to operate their weapons and how volunteers flooded into the country from all over the Middle East. He then told a story, which I noted down as 'Hamza's guide to rocket launchers'.

He told the audience that, at first, jihad fighters were killing themselves with grenade launchers, because they didn't know how to use them correctly. They were firing them from the waist, rather than from the shoulder:

> They were not trained, because there was a time when some Mujahideen they fired, used to fire, the RPG, which is a rocket launcher, which you are supposed to put it on your shoulder to shoot. And they didn't know where to put it and they put it in their stomach and when they shoot the fire goes [gestures towards his stomach] and they get killed.
>
> And they continue to use it and it was sacrificing. They thought it was the kind of weapon you shoot it once and you get killed. These people were shooting; they get killed, until someone teach them that you put it on your shoulder so you don't get killed. After that, they put it on the shoulder and come too close to a wall and the fire reflects from the wall and then the whole of their body . . . they were not counting their losses.

The point he was illustrating was that people were willing to die in order to drive the Russians from the country, but they couldn't survive for long without assistance. He continued:

> What can we do? We need somebody more clever than the Afghanis to come and join the war. Where do we go? We go for the Asians. And the Middle East, Saudi Arabia, Egypt. So

we go, 'Hang on, you're Muslims: don't you have something
in your religion that's called jihad?'

The covert American backing for the Afghan jihadists in the 1980s
had been 'the perfect crime' for the US, as they could kill Russians
without getting directly involved in the fighting. But, apparently,
they 'shot themselves in the heads' when people started to realise
that they were being used and that the concept of jihad wasn't taken
seriously by the Americans.

Hamza went on to say that he'd actually met al-Qaeda's dead
spiritual leader, Shiekh Abdullah Azzam, during the Haj in Mecca
in 1987. It was Azzam who developed al-Qaeda's policy that banned
any negotiations with the West. Hamza then urged the audience to
support the Taliban in Afghanistan and its mysterious one-eyed
leader, Mullah Omar.

'You should do another Afghanistan in your own country,' he
advised the audience, before talking about a £3,000 donation that
had been made to the Taliban. He said that they needed money to
buy up land in Afghanistan and build houses there. Five
representatives from the mosque would be travelling between the
UK and Afghanistan to administer the 'housing' scheme, providing
the 'evil' British government didn't get in their way.

The next tape included a section titled 'Jihad Conference' and the
date 12 March 2000 was displayed. It was held in the city of Derby
in the north of England and appears to have been an unadvertised
event. Hamza told Glen that these were 'special' tapes that he didn't
bring to the mosque. I was beginning to appreciate why: these were
very rare insights, records of private meetings held by someone who
had been branded as one of al-Qaeda's leading mouthpieces in
Europe.

Time and time again he used the phrase 'kaffir', which means
'infidel', but, because of the virulent way he used the word, it came
across as derogatory in the way that kaffir is used in South Africa to
describe black people. Azzam's 'no negotiations' philosophy also
shone through: jihad was the only answer. He branded Muslims
who joined the British establishment as 'traitors' who are used by
the government to infiltrate and oppress militant Islamic groups. He
held up a Muslim Labour peer, Lord Nazir Ahmed, as a figure to be
derided.

He was not going to help oppressed Muslims, he claimed.

What you going to do then? Choose Lord Ahmed to go to the Parliament and say, 'these people are terrorists', I'm going to kiss the Queen's hand, and kiss the Queen's legs, and I'm going to give her chocolate, Quality Street, and everything will be all right?

There was some tittering from the audience at this point.

These people, they only choose them because they are a future investment . . . So this man is a bagman for the kaffirs, that is why they give him a chair, to be a Lord, to stand on people like us, because he is a future investment.

These kaffirs impose their devil work. But jihad is more comprehensive, but we must all go to the support of the Mujahideen: the people who are going to do the final work. Allah has made jihad obligation, he has made fighting also an obligation, he has made inciting also obligation. Inciting? Obligation? Yeah. But these people call it terrorism, but we call it obligation . . . If they call incitation a terrorist [act], we're still going to incite.

The slogan that emerged from this talk was 'fight and incite' and he proclaimed: 'Allah is happy when a kaffir gets killed.' The invective against his adopted homeland and his fellow non-Muslim residents, who he described as 'like cattle', also continued: 'This society caters for thieves and prostitutes, and they like it that way', and, according to Hamza, Christian churches were used to teach homosexuality.

The lecture was interspersed at regular intervals with grainy and old-looking jihad video clips from Palestine, Kashmir and Bosnia. One showed scenes of what appeared to be a massacre of Serbian civilians in a village in Bosnia. The camera roved around the scene, focusing on the corpses that littered the ground. Some of the bodies were being taken away on stretchers by distraught relatives. A jihad anthem wailed in the background on the soundtrack.

Hamza stated to climax: establishing an Islamic state in Britain will be 'a means to dominate earth'.

Who's going to rule America, who's going to run all these countries, England, France? It's you!'

> You all know who are the enemies of Islam. What are you
> waiting for? Go and work. Go and do some work. See who
> are opposing Allah most and get rid of them!

I'd hardly started, but it was already clear that this was recruitment material. He was certainly inciting his audiences to participate in an armed struggle against all infidels, and he had described suicide bombings as 'the peak of jihad'. The question was: was he actively recruiting Mujahideen fighters and suicide bombers? The next section appeared to confirm that he was.

The tape cut to a masked man, who was clad in black and holding an assault rifle aloft. The landscape in the background looked desert-like. An arm with a microphone extended towards him and he introduced himself as Abu Ibrahim: a 21-year-old third-year medical student from Golders Green in London.

He started by talking about the satisfaction of seeing 'hundreds of dead bodies' in Bosnia. As he spoke, it was clear that he was suffering from a cough or a cold:

> To begin with, as I said to you, that I am a medical student
> and I come here and I see that in the West many brothers
> they say to us that the Muslim ummah needs doctors, they
> need lawyers, they need scientists, they need engineers, and
> I disagree with that, because there is enough Muslim
> doctors, there is enough lawyers, scientists, engineers. But
> what we lack here is Muslims that are prepared to suffer and
> sacrifice.

Where 'here' was meant to be was unclear; it could have been Bosnia, well that was the impression that was being conveyed anyway. Abu Ibrahim was obviously a false name, or else he was one clueless terrorist. Golders Green was an unlikely breeding ground for a jihad warrior, as it was home to one of London's largest Jewish communities. I'd chased up stories previously about named Britons who were supposed to be fighting against the US in Afghanistan, but they were all false names.

Donating money to Islamic charities was not enough, he said; physical participation in jihad was not only manly, it was downright enjoyable.

What I see here when I come here is a sense of satisfaction. Because when every time that I'm in Britain, I go to study circles, I go to lectures, I go to talks, and I see in my heart that something is empty. I watch the TV and tears roll down my face when I see the Muslims in Bosnia, the Muslims in Palestine, Muslims in Kashmir, and then I come here and you feel a sense of satisfaction; you feel that you're fulfilling your duty, you feel that you are doing what the Prophet Mohammed and his companions done 1,400 years ago.

You feel that you've achieved something. When you come here, people they think, 'Why are you going to Bosnia?'; you're sitting down and there's shells coming down, there's firing everywhere around you. They don't know that we sit here and we have kebabs, they don't know that we have ice cream and we have cake here, they don't know that we can telephone or fax anywhere in the world, they don't know that this is a nice holiday for us where you meet some of the best people you've ever met in your life, people from all over the world, people from Brazil, from Japan, from China, from the Middle East, from America, north, south, Canada, Australia – all over the world you meet people.

And the most important thing, you feel a true sense that you achieved something. That you come here, and you achieve something – you see gains in front of your very eyes. You come here and in a matter of a few weeks you free maybe 200 villages. You see the Serbs, the same people that rape our brothers and sisters, you see their dead bodies lying around in the hundreds, you feel that you've achieved something and something was achieved here in a short amount of time.

The tape then faded to an interview with another alleged British jihad fighter. He was dressed in the same way as the ice cream-eating colleague. Although he was masked, he was a large, podgy chap and very conspicuous. He shifted from foot to foot as he talked, as if he was in a state of agitation. By the confusing way he spoke, I could tell that he was not as well educated as his friend. I couldn't make out his first name, but the rest of it was Abu Anan and he claimed to hail from south London.

He had a similar message: merely attending conferences and talks is a poor way to perform jihad.

And what happens after that? And after the talk they go back home and they sleep . . . they carry on watching *Coronation Street*, they drink their coffee, they eat, they stuff their faces: what life is this?

If you want to see true groupism, if you want to see true people, true Muslims with unity, come to this place. Then you'll see.

A third Briton was interviewed. This one wasn't masked and he sported a beard. He was sitting in a car with the door open. These interviews seemed to date from some time after the NATO invasion of Kosovo in 1999, as he said that some people were questioning the need for the Mujahideen now that the Serbs had been forced to withdraw. That was wrong, he said; people are needed because the battles still go on.

So for people that are sitting at home and say, 'Well, they don't need people there any more', it's not true, it's not true. Because we need as many people as we can that it takes to push these people back, these Serbs, these enemy of Allah, so we need as much, as many people, and as much money, and everything that the people can send us to help us in this task.

That these people, Mujahideen, come from all over the world, not just from one Arab country, but many brothers from France, from England, from everywhere, from Uganda, from Philippines, everywhere, and they come to fight here not for money, but . . . for religion and Islam. So this will be a good time for them . . . so they can come back to their religion.

Whilst the guy in the car looked like he was on location in Bosnia, there was something about the two masked gunmen that wasn't quite right, and neither Glen nor I could quite figure it out. We both had a feeling that we were looking at something and not seeing it. It transpired that we were not hearing it. We were told months later by a TV producer exactly what it was. We sat down to go through the tapes with him and as soon as we got to the interviews with the gunmen he said straightaway that the interviews had been recorded inside a building. He could tell by the sound that it wasn't recorded outside, and he said they were probably taped inside a studio against a backdrop to make it look like they were on location.

He was absolutely adamant about it. The guy in the car looked real enough, but it seemed that the other two were faked. The only logical explanation seemed to be that the producers of Hamza's video were struggling to find footage of Brits performing jihad abroad and they decided to 'stage' two interviews. The story took on yet another twist many months later.

The Palestinian terror group Hamas released a video in March 2004 showing two Britons it said had died in a suicide bombing a year previously. Asif Hanif, 21, from Hounslow in west London, killed three people and injured fifty-five when he blew himself up in Mike's Place, a beachfront bar in Tel Aviv. Omar Khan Sharif, 27, from Derby, is thought to have fled from the scene when explosives strapped to his body failed to detonate. He was later found dead on a beach, presumed drowned.

The video, which had been shot in a flat in Gaza, showed the two men brandishing assault rifles and calling for God to punish Prime Minister Tony Blair and US President George W. Bush. Sharif said he'd visited a farm to the north of Gaza that had been destroyed by an Israeli incursion. He addressed the camera directly and asked: 'What are we doing to help?'

It was a familiar appeal. Hanif was a large man and I noticed that he was shifting from foot to foot while he was talking. A thought occurred to me and I phoned Glen.

'Glen, I think the British Israeli suicide bombers are the same two as on the Hamza tape,' I said.

He thought I might well be right and said he'd take a close look at the clips and compare them. Later he emailed me to say that he thought I was right. Hanif's body language, mannerisms and the way he talked were all very similar to the fat masked 'Bosnia' gunman. They may have faked it on Hamza's video, but they'd finally achieved fame as Britain's first suicide bombers, well, Hanif had anyway. It was a powerful reminder that these people were committed and utterly single-minded, and sooner or later they would get through.

It later emerged in the press that Hanif was a pupil of Hamza's colleague, Sheikh Omar Bakri Mohammad, and he frequented Finsbury Park mosque. The police later raided Bakri's house and the offices of his al-Muhajiroun organisation, although no arrests were made. The group reacted angrily to the raids and issued a statement warning the government that it was 'sitting on a box of dynamite' and claiming it was in danger of violating the 'covenant of peace' that existed between both sides.

Before I had had a chance to go through the tapes in such detail, the *Sunday Times* had printed an initial article on 17 November based on the video clips on Glen's website. They plumped for an angle about a section on the tape of a meeting where Hamza urges his followers to commit terrorist attacks. 'Kill them. It's OK,' he said. I thought the recruitment story was a better one, but they wanted the incitement angle, and I was in no position to argue. They also wanted to talk to Glen, but I advised him against that. It's always a dilemma and normally I would concede, but this time I sensed that he was too good a contact to just hand over like that. I stalled them, and I'm sure they realised that, but I was thinking of the bigger picture. We had the BBC's *Newsnight* programme to think of next, as reporter Peter Marshall had been on to me and there would surely be many other possibilities after that.

The *Sunday Times* headline was: 'LONDON CLERIC TOLD FOLLOWERS TO KILL'. In this section of the tapes, Hamza described kaffirs in Muslim countries as like cows who could be bought or sold into slavery or killed. He also praised the twin 1998 bombings of the American embassies in Kenya and Tanzania as 'legitimate'.

Newsnight broadcast a long report about the tapes a month later, which was along similar lines to the *Times* article, except that Hamza was there at the end of the film for a live interview with Jeremy Paxman. Paxman was regarded as the toughest interviewer in the business, although he failed to land a sucker-punch this time.

When tackled about a statement in which he had said that it was permitted for Muslims to rob banks in the West, because non-believers are not protected by Allah ('I say go and do it, take, shoot and loot'), Hamza stood his ground. Paxman then probed him about his contempt for the British government and he declared that the only government in the world he respected was that of the Taliban in Afghanistan, because it was the only pure Islamic state in the world. The interviewer expressed something close to incredulity, but Hamza again stuck to his guns.

The *Times* article said that he could well be arrested now, because of the emergence of the tapes – he wasn't, although it did serve to turn up the heat on Hamza, considerably.

The website where Glen had placed some clips from the videos was mentioned in the story and he showed me the massive spike in the site logs that marked the day of publication. One senior tabloid journalist told me that Hamza had been regarded as a bit of a harmless buffoon up until that point. His various denials ranged from claiming that the quotes from the tapes had been fabricated and denying that he'd been involved in recruiting British Muslims for al-Qaeda, to claiming that he'd been quoted out of context unfairly. He claimed that his former associate Ujaama was facing a 'kangaroo court' in the States.

From that point on, Hamza started to became a major bogeyman for the media. Officialdom started to focus on him and some 150 police officers raided Finsbury Park mosque in January 2003. The mosque was closed and Britain's charities watchdog, the Charity Commission, won a court order that banned Hamza from preaching there. It had been investigating him since 1998, after it received allegations that he and his associates had effectively usurped the trustees and had taken control of the place. The Commission noted that the stated aims of Hamza's group, Supporters of Sharia, 'are not charitable'. He lost his disability benefits and he was subsequently stripped of his British citizenship by Home Secretary David Blunkett in April 2003, under the new Nationality, Immigration and Asylum Act which had just come into force. He had the right of appeal, though the Home Secretary pointed out that any appeal would focus on:

> the way in which people are encouraged to take part in the jihad and fight us overseas. I want to deal with people who our intelligence and security people believe are a risk to us. If you encourage, support, advise, help people to take up training, if you facilitate them, then, of course, that takes you right over the boundary.

Hamza resorted to holding his meetings in the road outside the mosque and continued with business as usual. A press release was issued on the Supporters of Sharia website that called for the execution of Coalition troops who might be captured in Iraq. It said:

As has been highlighted, this crusader war does not even conform to the kuffar's own criterion, thus making the crusader rabble war criminals. Therefore, any kaffir mercenary captured should either be executed for war crimes or preferably be exchanged for the blessed Muslims being held in the Guantanamo Bay concentration camp.

The plug was pulled on his website after that, after the hosting company was flooded with complaints. At the same time, his brothers in arms in al-Muhajiroun issued a call on its Pakistan-based website calling for British Muslims to rush to the defence of Iraq. 'Muslims are fighting a battle. A battle which we are seeing the worst of,' it said. 'Oh, Muslim men of Pakistan, India, UK, US where ever you [are], what is wrong with you? Wake up and work with al-Muhajiroun . . . It is a time for action, revolution, a time of strength and honour.'

The whole Hamza furore caused the *Sunday Times* to revisit the tapes. One of the editors called me and we talked through what more there was that could be reported. There was a lot, as the first story didn't come anywhere near to scratching the surface, really. As I now had the tapes in my possession, I spent a lot of time going through the sections that he said he was particularly interested in and transcribing them, as well as doing the usual donkeywork of background checking. *The Times* also now asked for a copy of the statement Glen had given to the police and this went to the legal department, to ensure that the story was watertight. It was going to be a major investigative news piece, which are usually afforded a generous amount of space towards the front end of the paper, often with an opener on the front page.

After tying up a few loose ends over the phone, and trying to fit this in with a family barbeque that was in full swing, it made for a rather hectic afternoon, and I was eager to see the piece the following day, 21 July 2003. It carried the headline: 'WEB STING LINKS HAMZA TO TERROR CAMPS'. If the Grand Jury investigation in New York into the US jihad camp plot that Ujaama was testifying about did prove links to Hamza, then sources close to the case told the paper that they would press for his extradition. The removal of his citizenship was seen as a move to prepare the ground for this eventuality.

I sold the story on to the *Washington Times* a day later, and they ran a piece that went along much the same lines. I joked to Glen that President Bush might read it at breakfast and gag on his cornflakes. He said that he hoped the director of the CIA would see it and it would send his blood pressure soaring and he'd fly into a rage and smash up his office. The reality was that a phoney war would probably ensue for the next few months, as Hamza hadn't exhausted his right to appeal against being stripped of his citizenship, and there were no murmurs about charges emerging from the New York Grand Jury probe. It was a secret process and no one really knew what was going on. We weren't done with Hamza yet, however; not by a long chalk.

MEETING MRS GALT

Glen kept sniggering on the phone and dropping hints that something big was under way. Nothing to do with Hamza, this time, well, not directly, he told me, though he said he couldn't tell me any more about it just now, as things were at a delicate stage. Whatever it was, I'd love it, he assured me. I didn't like to be left out of the loop, and after a few days of badgering, he finally told me what was going on.

He and I had established a good level of trust by this point. We were in a bit of an interregnum period after the Hamza videos stories. He also had 19 audiotapes, but he'd turned the material over to an intelligence contact a few months earlier and they'd been spirited out of the country for analysis. He said that there were around 30 hours of material recorded inside Finsbury Park mosque and their intelligence value far exceeded the videos.

He said he had listened to them constantly for about two weeks, and the thought of having to listen to them again made him feel sick. He filled me in on what was on them, and he made some hair-raising allegations that convinced me that we needed to get hold of them as soon as possible. I couldn't do anything until then and, according to Glen's description, they were sheer dynamite.

Glen's contact (who cannot be named) was now trying to retrieve them, although he said initially that there wasn't much hope of getting them back. They'd been sent to a branch of an intelligence agency that was devoted solely to scouring through militant Islamic propaganda for information. He said he'd try in any case, although a series of official requests would have to be made and there was a mire of bureaucracy in the way.

I spoke to this guy on the phone myself, after we hadn't heard from him for a while. I explained that they sounded vitally important and that we could make a big splash with them, to the benefit of everyone concerned. He said that there were some worries at the top about sharing intelligence externally, and he confirmed that the tapes had been of great use. They'd already been transcribed and analysed, and they were just lying in a file somewhere, so he couldn't really see why they shouldn't be returned. It would take at least ten days to get them, although, by the way he said this, I gathered that it would in all likelihood take a lot longer.

I talked to Glen afterwards, and he said he'd talked to his contact separately. As I suspected, there was an internal debate going on about the wisdom of releasing them, but our contact was batting for our side. Glen was completely confident that we'd have them shortly: 'Don't worry. We'll have them soon. He won't let us down.' There was no doubt in his mind, and I had a sneaking suspicion that things would pan out, even though on the surface the odds seemed to be against it.

Glen kept sending me emails when he remembered important details about what he'd heard on the tapes, and this just served to give me a 'must have' knot in my stomach as I worried that this one might get away. That's always a good sign.

While I waited, there was the new project to be getting on with. I couldn't report anything about it yet, because it would blow it out of the water. Glen explained his reasons, and I could appreciate why he was being cautious. It was another audacious sting operation, but this time the targets were al-Qaeda operatives in Pakistan. He'd been commissioned by an embassy contact to digitally infiltrate militant Islamic groups there, and everything was going swimmingly. That's what he'd been cackling about on the phone.

He'd scoped out some likely target areas and then he'd tasked one of his 'web workers', an American lady, with getting in on the inside track. He'd mentioned her before, but I wasn't really sure what her role was within the circle. Glen started copying me in on their correspondence, and it appeared that she was a protégé of his. He said he'd met her soon after 11 September during his Internet travels and, being of a similar mindset, she'd gradually become part of the team. Her prime role in the early days was to maintain the websites, as she was an accomplished designer. Now she'd graduated to becoming a real spy.

Her mission was to engage likely al-Qaeda suspects in online conversations and become a trusted confidante. The information she elicited would be fed back to the contact who'd commissioned the project and they'd do what they had to do with her findings. Whilst her real name cannot be disclosed, Glen decided that, should her story be told in print some day, she should be referred to as 'Mrs Galt'. It was a bit of a joke, because it would sound like she was related to the scourge of online jihadists, Johnathan R. Galt.

She'd been boning up on Islam and Muslim customs and practices, and she'd developed several different aliases and cover stories. Glen said she'd succeeded in penetrating an al-Qaeda cell in Pakistan and was doing spectacularly well. He told her to copy me in on the transcripts of her conversations when she reported back every few days, and I waited eagerly to see the first one come through. They'd give me a unique insight, he said, as I'd be able to see an intelligence operation unfolding in real-time.

As always, it sounded a bit fanciful, but I'd already learnt that Glen meant what he said and I could easily appreciate how it would be possible to do this. It was at the cutting edge as, instead of sitting back and soaking up the information/disinformation, she was setting out to actively solicit information whilst mingling with the enemy. They were combining the benefits of using modern technology and instant communication with traditional espionage tradecraft. It was a hugely ambitious plan and potentially a very dangerous mission.

Mrs Galt was talking on a daily basis to several highly suspicious characters who were members of a notorious al-Qaeda-affiliated group in Pakistan called Lashkar-e-Toiba (Army of the Pure). Others were well-placed members of Jaish-e-Mohammad, Jamaat-e-Islami, Jamaat al-Dawa and other jihadist groups. Lashkar was said to be supported by Pakistan's ISI intelligence agency in the same way as the ISI supported the Taliban in Afghanistan. It was known to operate mostly in Kashmir, although it was now reportedly taking care of al-Qaeda operatives who'd fled into Pakistan from Afghanistan after the battle of Tora Bora.

Terrorist groups and their operatives are surprisingly easy to spot, once you 'get your eye in'. Mrs Galt found her targets in a Microsoft Network discussion forum called JihadKashmir. She was told later by one of her new contacts, however, that all of these factions had recently agreed in secret to work under the same umbrella and the new organisation was called Shahbaz.

Though they might be easy to spot, being accepted by the group as an honorary member was a different matter. Her opening gambit was to make out that she was looking for her brother, who had left to fight jihad in Kashmir, and she asked around to see if anyone had any information about him. They didn't, of course, but she latched on to the people who'd answered her call for help and started to build a rapport with them. She spoke to them in real-time, using instant messaging, as well as traditional email. Mrs Galt sent me a few samples of her discussions so I could familiarise myself with what was going on, before her next update landed in my in-box. The subject lines were interesting, to say the least: 'my brother is trained in chemicals'; 'we must conduct the meetings in secret'; 'al-Qaeda demands from Mujahideen'.

Although they didn't know her brother, they assured her that they would ask and see if anyone else knew him. She made it clear that she supported what her brother was doing, and she offered to support the brave Mujahideen in any way she could, perhaps by helping to enhance their Web presence. This marked the point at which the bait was swallowed. The information she was getting indicated that the group was very poorly funded. Later, she found that they hadn't been paid their regular stipend for some time and there was unease in the ranks about that. They seized on the offer, as it represented a significant boost to their resources and opened up the prospect of raising revenue from e-commerce. As she was a woman, the barrier of proof that she needed to surmount was lowered, because it's a well-known fact that military men love to talk to the ladies.

There were around 100 members of the JihadKashmir group, and some of them had included revealing information in their group profiles, although most of them had the good sense to leave everything blank. One member betrayed his political colours by listing his favourite quote as: 'It burns me up that the life of a Muslim is very much cheaper than a Dog. Killings of Muslims is very much easier than a Chicken.' Oddly, the administrator of the group was a 25-year-old guy called Abu Hamza, who helpfully listed his location, the Kapwara district of Kashmir. Now I knew what Glen had found so amusing: it was the name. Mrs Galt soon found out that Hamza was actually a heavily armed jihadi who doubled up as a press officer for Lashkar, and he had no connection with the Finsbury Park Hamza.

The group wanted to raise funds by selling their jihad videos and tapes online, and they asked Mrs Galt if she could help with that. She could, of course, and she set about creating a site for them called Victorious Mujahideen. One of their showcase products was a 30-minute audiotape of the screaming and burbling of various unknown people having their throats cut. It was number one in the hit parade in Lashkar-e-Toiba and they were very proud of it.

Pakistan Hamza talked about his favourite tape and said he could probably convert it and send it by email as a digital file.

'It will be a very good experience to listen to that sound on the Net,' he said.

'They have to be under one megabyte to go on the site, OK?' replied Mrs Galt.

'OK, God willing, I will try. Thank you so much for your help, sister.'

'No problem. I just hope it works.'

'You will be very happy when you listen to it. It also has the sound of cutting throats.'

'Cutting throats?'

'Yes – aarrrrggh, arrrrgggh, oooohhh, don't kill me, etc., etc.'

She was also asked to help them to better understand various email messages that were written in English. One of them was a formula for making mustard gas, along with part of a discussion about extracting viruses from vaccines. One response to that message read: 'This is very good research. I will print it and read it. In time, God willing, you will see the works of the Mujahideen, because the kuffar doesn't even know what's coming . . . you will see, it is true, Allah is the best of plotters.'

One of the group's leaders, who called himself Abou Qitaal An-Nizzi, responded saying: 'The brothers say that you must do the searches for the chlorine gas also, because this is a very good method for smaller kaffir targets.' I knew this was serious, because he referred to a gas attack that had been planned for the 1993 bomb attack on the World Trade Center: 'but they did not have the proper knowledge'. It was a reference to the failed attempt to generate a cloud of cyanide gas at the 'Yahoodi [Jewish] towers', as he termed it. He also revealed that Muslims who worked at the WTC had been warned to avoid the place on 11 September, although 'one or two' had not heeded the advice.

Mrs Galt was inside the proverbial goldmine and she was starting to piece together the wider picture. Early on, the email addresses on private correspondence had already highlighted links between the Pakistani groups and jihad circles in the UK, Italy, Australia, Germany, Canada, Mexico, Afghanistan, Chechnya, Uzbekistan, Palestine and Burma. Most people kept their location disguised by using free Hotmail-type accounts. One interesting point to emerge was that, in some cases, several different people were using the same ID.

A jihadi calling himself Abu Umar emailed her to say that he was using Hamza's email account, as he was away and probably would be for some time. The entrepreneurial streak was coming out in all of them, and they were having grand visions about raising their profile and generating income at the same time. He said:

> Tell me how to make a website and I can help you making the site, because we have had a discussion that we should have a website to promote things about our operations and other things about our business. Talking about the business, he said something about you wanting to be a partner in the business . . .

They were also soliciting money from Mrs Galt, and he gave her the details of an account at the Faisal Bank. It seemed that they were desperate for money and he asked her to help with the fundraising drive, although their needs were surprisingly meagre. They'd drawn up a list and their most wanted items were extremely mundane: socks, hats and other clothing, and batteries. The group was also using an account at the Muslim Commercial Bank in Lahore, although she was warned that they were in the process of opening a new account, for reasons that weren't clear. She could use the Lahore account in the meantime.

One of the biggest revelations, to me, came in an email that she had received from Hamza on 26 June 2003, after about a month of talking to them. She was busy designing the websites, and her targets were completely relaxed with her. They were very chatty, and she was even in on the everyday gossiping. On this particular day, the jihadis appeared to be very excited, as they had hot news about bin Laden. The terror chief had paid a morale-boosting visit to al-Qaeda's relocated headquarters in Pakistan, near a village called Angoor Adda in the South Waziristan tribal area, just over the border from Afghanistan.

There were many in the Western media who still maintained that bin Laden was dead, and it seemed that the jihadis themselves were starting to wonder whether that was true. It sounded as though bin Laden had broken a long period of complete isolation and that this had been the first time he'd been seen among his people in a very long time. You could almost feel the relief and happiness caused by the news. Hamza described the South Waziristan base as 'our operational command centre'. Indeed, the US had carried out an air strike against a *madrassa* (religious school) there, after an army patrol had unexpectedly come under fire in the area a month previously, according to a recent report.

It was a great coincidence, because the same region had been suggested by an intelligence source three months earlier after I'd been commissioned to write an article about the latest intelligence on whether bin Laden was alive and, if so, where he was at the moment. It was the second time that I had possibly pinned him down to a precise location, in Pakistan this time, so I was feeling a little elated about the news myself. I didn't think he was dead, as there was no sign of memorial activity: no banners commemorating the deeds of a great leader, no eulogies. Dead martyrs are usually praised to high heaven and heavily promoted in recruitment material as shining examples for the Muslim youth to follow. There was none of that. On all of the Arabic jihad boards, the health of bin Laden was *the* hot topic of discussion. The replies from those who appeared to be in the know were equivocal. Be patient and it wouldn't affect the jihad if he had been martyred, anyway.

Mrs Galt's friend had given me the ideal first paragraph. There had been lots of sightings in the previous few weeks, some more believable than others. The reports that did seem to tally indicated that he'd recently moved from north to south along the entire border between Afghanistan and Pakistan and he'd covered great distances. More anomalous jihadi chatter placed him in the city of Qom in Iran, where he owned property, and the mountainous north-east of Iran, which borders the Baluchistan region of Pakistan. Kashmir and the Kunar province of Afghanistan came next, and there was even speculation that he'd recently paid a flying visit the holy city of

Medina in Saudi Arabia, to be near his son, Hamza bin Laden (would you believe), who was getting married in Mecca.

Glen's pet theory was that bin Laden had been hiding out in Chechnya with his old buddies from the 1980s, who were now fighting to create an Islamic state there. He said he was convinced that he'd seen a dry river bed in a Chechen Mujahideen video that looked remarkably similar to one seen in the background of a recently released bin Laden video. No one had suggested that before, although I looked into this possibility and found an article that claimed that his deputy, Ayman al-Zawahiri, had visited Chechnya before the 11 September attacks.

As webmaster of the Victorious Mujahideen site, Mrs Galt fielded many interesting email queries. One was from a guy in Azerbaijan who was trying to sign up for jihad in Chechnya, and he said he had many friends who also wanted to go. He got very, very excited when Mrs Galt asked for his email address and personal details. When he'd coughed them up, she told him he should expect to receive instructions soon. Well, he'd probably be receiving a less than polite knock on his door early one morning, anyhow.

A 39-year-old from Agadir in Morocco, who called himself Abderrahmane, contacted her to ask how he could volunteer to fight against US and UK troops in Iraq. She advised him to spell out his intentions in a message in a private discussion group that she'd set up, called SoldiersofAllah, where she and her new chums were now talking. Part of his message said: 'I really wish that you can help me, as I feel sad about what the US Army and Britain are doing to our brothers in Iraq, and the Muslim kuffar who are helping them. I really wish to go to Iraq and help them, as I'm really ready to go to jihad and kill more US army.'

A guy called Gihan contacted the group to appeal for donations so he could continue to expand a 'well-organised and trained resistance' in Australia, where he lived. He even sent in his bank account details: 'Account number: 10117390, Branch: Summer Hill NSW, Bank State Branch number: 062257'.

Mrs Galt's relationship with Abu Hamza Pak, as she called him, started to blossom in beautiful way, and she was completely in his confidence. It started after he'd returned to the group's base after a lengthy, unexplained absence and joked that he was still in one piece. She said she had recently injured her knee, and he was concerned about her health. The whole thing was rather touching, and it was hard to believe that here was a battle-hardened terrorist pouring his heart out to a spy in the very best Mata Hari tradition. He even sent her a picture of himself. A heavily built bearded bear of a man, he was smiling at the camera and holding a huge snake; it looked like a boa constrictor. She suggested putting his tape on a CD and he thought that was a very good idea.

A few days later he apologised for not sending the disc, and he asked her for her help in tracking down formulae for making explosives. 'A few days ago, a brother who is in the training department asked me to get some formulas for explosives. We have very many formulas, but they are only those which the ISI gave us and we are searching for more. Can you help us in this?'

Mrs Galt was caught in a dilemma: sending the material by email could easily leave her open to charges of aiding the enemy, but she also couldn't afford to ignore his request and risk arousing any suspicions. I think in the end she fudged it and pointed him towards a website where she thought that kind of information might be available.

He was pleased with the results of the fundraising drive, as the group had raised more money than they'd seen for years. As he opened up, he revealed that he'd been trained in Afghanistan by an Arab Mujahid called Abu Umar from Jordan. He sent her copies of two newspaper articles about recent terrorist attacks and implied that he'd had something to do with them. One was about the beheading of a suspected Indian army informer in Kashmir and the other was about a rocket attack on an Indian army battalion, also based in Kashmir, in which seven Indian soldiers had died.

She was also told about militant attacks that were being planned, as well as attacks that had just happened but had not yet been reported by the media. One of these involved a rocket attack by al-Qaeda forces against two US bases in the Uruzgan province of Afghanistan. Another concerned an ambush of an Indian army convoy in Kashmir, and he also appeared to know all about a bombing campaign that was being waged against Shell petrol stations all over Pakistan. He claimed that this was because Shell 'is a Jewish company'.

One day he received bad news:

> Today, I cry very much in my prayers, because my very close friend, who was also with me in training, got killed. His

pocket-sized Koran (which we all take with us everywhere) was filled with blood. Brothers came here with all of his belongings − gun, Koran and other things that they took from that place to give those things to his family. I'm trying to get a single page of that Koran so that I can scan it and email it to you and other brothers.

When he was hit by the mortar, his blood flowed and entered the Koran which was in his pocket. And Sister, you won't believe it, but when the Koran was opened in our headquarters, the whole building was filled with a sweet smell. I haven't smelled that kind of smell in my whole life. It was very sweet.

Their live online chats were the most revealing. Mrs Galt sent me transcripts of hours of conversation they'd had. At first they looked like a load of gobbledegook, but this was down to the poor English and the mobile phone texting-type shorthand that tends to be used in live online chats and can make them difficult to follow. I've cleaned up the following example to take account of this:

'Sister, how are you?' said Hamza. 'Have you heard about the Temple attacks?'

'Greetings, how are you?' replied Mrs Galt.

'I'm fine.'

'Yes, I heard about it earlier. Seven people got killed − is that right?'

'Yes, it was our attack and there's still one more to be done, God willing. A much bigger one.'

'OK. What, bigger than hitting the temples?'

'No sister, we didn't attack their places of worship. The temple was their headquarters. The previous attack was the same as this one.'

'Oh, they say a lot of different things in the media. Was it near Kashmir?'

'Sister, do you remember the attack on the temples in Gujarat [India]? Well, this was in revenge for the brothers and sisters killed by them.'

'I only caught the end of the story.'

'It was the same kind of attack. Two brothers were killed and one is injured.'

There had been a spate of attacks against churches and temples in

Kashmir and northern India at the time, and it seemed as though Hamza's group was responsible. It was later realised that this conversation took place one hour after the attack. It was astonishing to think that a terrorist in some filthy hole in Pakistan was committing terrorist atrocities and then hot-footing it back to his hideout to tell a woman in America, whom he believed to be a jihad-supporting Muslim, all about it. But there it was in front of my very eyes; there was no getting away from it. I knew I was witnessing something unique happening here: spying in its purest and most traditional form, yet done entirely digitally. I was sure it was a first of some kind.

Later on, they had a chat when he was in Karachi, and he talked about an FBI-directed raid in the city. Two Arabs were captured and later released. Whatever he was up to, it didn't sound good: he said he was suffering from deafness caused by 'you know, bang bang'.

Another rather touching moment came when the news headlines had been dominated by a story that US special forces allegedly had bin Laden surrounded in the province of Baluchistan.

> MG: So, Brother, what's going to happen if Sheikh bin Laden is caught?
> AH: God willing, he will not be caught.
> MG: I'm very glad you are safe. Brother, I can't even type now.
> AH: Why sis, is everything OK?
> MG: Just upset about the news about Sheikh Laden and the fighting going on and the stupid kaffir war.
> AH: Don't worry. Nothing will happen to him, because millions of Muslims are praying for him.
> MG: Maybe I just need a break and go to the lake and think for a while.

He sought to reassure her that if bin Laden was captured, then another leader would take over and the jihad would continue. It was one of the last conversations she had with him, because he seemed to suddenly disappear. However, she was also talking to a local newspaper reporter (MQ) who was an associate of Hamza and he'd interviewed many of the leaders of militant Islamic groups in Pakistan. He had promised to send Mrs Galt a CD with Mujahideen video clips on it.

MQ: Did you hear about bin Laden? He is alive and he's moved to Chechnya.

MG: Who told you that?

MQ: First, you tell me whether you've heard that or not.

MG: No, I haven't heard that news.

MQ: The situation is that he's now moved there.

MG: Yes, and yesterday they though they'd almost caught him.

MQ: I don't think anybody can catch bin Laden.

MG: Isn't Chechnya too hot for bin Laden to be there?

MQ: Yes, it is hot, but many places are.

MG: So, did you hear about bin Laden's sons being caught [in Iran]? Is that true?

MQ: They are not bin Laden's sons. He is alive and he's moved to Chechnya. I had arranged a meeting with him, but suddenly the situation turned critical in Afghanistan and I was not allowed to meet him.

MG: So, what's new?

MQ: The FBI is trying to arrest more people in Pakistan, maybe. Tonight, they captured some people. This week some Pakistan agents captured my CD that I sent to you and asked me why I sent that. They questioned me for hours.

MG: Not good . . .

MQ: The ISI is watching my activities on a daily basis.

MG: Did they ask you anything?

MQ: Yes, but I can't tell you.

MG: How did they get the CD?

MQ: I think they checked the post office in Islamabad.

MG: So, they must be checking things out.

MQ: Yes, they also took my personal computer and I haven't got it back yet.

MG: Your computer, the one you have at home?

MQ: Yes. They think that I have links to al-Qaeda or other religious groups.

MG: Not good.

MQ: Oh please. It is a part of life. I don't care about that. They are also checking my home phone and my mobile phone. He said I have close relations with Hekmatyar [Afghan warlord aligned with the Taliban] – do you remember that the last time I told you I'd interviewed Hekmatyar?

MG: You shouldn't be in trouble for just knowing someone.

MQ: I don't care about it. My office will stand by me.

MG: Remember we were talking about bin Laden a couple of times? They might be looking at that.

MQ: Yes. I'm not worried about it, but please do not break off contact with me.

MG: When are they going to give your stuff back to you?

MQ: I don't think I will get it back. You know about the attitude of intelligence agencies. I think it's beginning, but I don't care about it. If they took me, they would pay a high price.

MG: What did your family say?

MQ: Nothing.

MG: Are you at work or home now?

MQ: Home.

MG: Did you get another computer?

MQ: No, I'm using my cousin's computer – he's been staying at my home for a few days. There is information on my laptop, but it is safe.

MG: Good, I'm glad it's safe.

MQ: You are very clever.

When I read that last line I started to think that maybe he'd realised that something was wrong. I had a strong feeling that, in fact, he'd rumbled her. He'd been detained and was under surveillance, Hamza had disappeared, people were suddenly being arrested left right and centre, and computers were being seized. In any case, her friends in Pakistan suddenly became reticent, and they started to gently question her. If a group like that thought they might have a mole in their ranks, I'm sure they'd behave in exactly this way. It wasn't hard to imagine that the chatty lady in the USA might appear on the list of suspects. They would want to disguise their suspicion in an effort to try and find out more about their mole and start feeding him/her with disinformation: turn the tables. That's what it looked like to me and, sure enough, as I was having these thoughts, I got a copy of an email from Glen saying that the project was terminated.

Glen pronounced that the operation had been a major success. Mrs Galt had been doing a fine job trying to gather 'actionable intelligence'. I noticed that she always asked where they were when they were chatting, what their telephone numbers were and what their plans were. Every word was being fed back to the contact who'd commissioned the project, and I knew her questions were designed with him in mind. Whether all the attention that the jihadis were attracting was down to her activities was impossible to tell. I talked to the contact, and he said even he wouldn't know. The intelligence went up the chain and that was the end of the matter; there was never any feedback, because that's just the way agencies operate.

The end of the mission was marked in a typically high-profile way. The transcripts were uploaded to a website called 'Online Chats with al-Qaeda in Pakistan' and promoted on numerous websites that Glen was controlling. It was marketed in a 'jihadis outwitted by American housewife' manner. I asked Glen why he did this: why make a song and dance of it instead of keeping it under wraps? It had shades of the 'jihad is crap' stunt.

It served two purposes, he told me. First, it ensured that all the Internet addresses, email accounts, bank accounts and names would appear high on the search results page of anyone researching into this area. It was a just very simple way of making sure that the information was disseminated as widely as possible to the people who needed it, circumventing the procedural and bureaucratic hurdles of going through the official channels.

The second reason was to just have a laugh. He was an intelligent guy who liked to wind people up. He wanted to maximise their embarrassment, and he came up with the name Mrs Galt to make out that she was the wife of his jihadi-hunting collaborator, Johnathan Galt. The story he came up with was that they were a husband-and-wife team. They weren't, of course; Glen said it was just a wind-up to give the opposition a dose of paranoia and this gave me an idea for a good angle for a possible story about all this.

He had no objections because, he said, the intelligence had already been acted on, so why not? He asked Mrs Galt to help me out. I hadn't really had an in-depth conversation with her up until then, and I was curious to know more about her and her motivations for doing this. She was 42, married with children, and she did it as something of a hobby-cum-duty. She said she had been shocked to the core by 11 September and had used the Internet to try to find out why those people wanted to kill Americans. Before long, she bumped into Glen and others like him, and realised that there were a lot of well-intentioned people out there who wanted to 'do their bit'. This was a story I'd heard several times before and it was similar to the path that I'd trodden myself.

Part of the reason that she'd managed to pull off her deception and appear authentic was that she'd read up on Islam and had a crib sheet of crucial sayings and incantations that she needed to inject into conversations. Traditionally, you should praise the Prophet even when you mention him in passing, and not doing this would have shown her up as a kaffir straight away. She was surprisingly casual about it all. It was something she did in the evenings, and she was just pleased to be helping out in any way she could. Her husband had no idea that she was talking to terrorists live over the Internet until the story reached print. She'd even had tentative proposals of marriage from two of the jihadis.

She told me: 'Glen told me to cut the line, as they had no more good information to give. It was his idea to put the letters on the website, so that's what I did. I would have loved to have seen their faces when they saw the messages on the Web. All I can do is hope that some of the terrorists I talked to get picked up. After all, they are not terrorists until a court says they are. In about a week or so, I'll have another ID and start all over again, hitting the Web looking for jihad supporters. It's a never-ending battle.'

Mrs Galt forwarded on some pictures that her 'friends' had sent her. They included large bearded men who were criss-crossed with ammunition belts and posing for the camera with impossibly huge machine guns. One showed a group of people standing proudly next to the rear of a red pick-up truck and, though it would have been easy to miss if you didn't look closely, one could see several severed human heads piled up near the tailgate.

It all amounted to an inspiring tale of derring-do at the very least, and calling her an amateur didn't seem fair. She was clearly an expert at this and online espionage was a new kind of phenomenon, so I guess 'independent operator' is a better description. I used 'Cyber-Mata Hari' in the headline of the first draft of the story, although I was worried that people might not remember who Mata Hari was. I pitched the story at several UK newspapers, and I think it's fair to say there was some healthy incredulity. Also, because she was an American, it wasn't immediately viewed as a 'must have'. I had anticipated that her nationality might be a problem and so I looked to the States for an outlet there. They'd love something like this, surely.

I eventually got on to my friends at the *Washington Times* and there was a positive initial reaction. I sent the copy of the draft story over and there was a day of emails and telephone conversations. They wanted to be absolutely sure that this fantastic story was true. I directed them to a website where they could see the messages for themselves and answered many questions about Glen, Mrs Galt, who they were, where they lived, what they did and why, and I did everything I could to provide them with the answers. I even got a call to tell me that they thought the name 'Galt' had been taken from a book called *Atlas Shrugged* by Ayn Rand. It was apparently a very well-known book in the States and I felt like a bit of a philistine for not knowing about it. They were obviously thinking very deeply about this, because he told me that a phrase that occurs repeatedly in the book is: 'Who is John Galt?' I was a bit baffled, so I asked Glen. To my surprise, he confirmed that, yes, it had been inspired by the book. It was another one of his jokes.

The *Times* published the story the following day, 9 August 2003, under a headline that read 'MOM AIDS IN HUNTING TERRORISTS OVER WEB'. The first paragraph read:

> Referred to by her spymasters only as 'Mrs Galt', she is by day an unremarkable American housewife and mother. But after her two children go to bed, she plunges into a secret world of Internet chat rooms and websites populated by some of the most dangerous people on earth.

I was inundated with queries from the media as soon as the story was published. The *Times* was forwarding emails and telephone messages from all sorts to me. They were all asking: 'Who is Mrs Galt?' Several TV news programmes wanted to do a live interview with this heroic soccer mom. The story appeared on numerous websites, and contacts were emailing me to say well done. It was fascinating to see what people thought of the story on the Web, and I browsed through all the comments. They polarised down into the 'way to go Mrs Galt!' brigade and the 'come on, it's clearly a Pentagon disinformation effort' camp. Great fun.

Predictably perhaps, the responses matched the two prevailing views on the situation: pro-Israel right-wing and pro-Arab left-wing. I was tempted to post some warnings of impending legal action in reply to some of my more virulent detractors, but I managed to stop myself.

A couple of journalist friends cribbed the story and ensured that it received even wider dissemination on the Net than I'd bargained for, but I didn't really mind. It was a seminal story, and I was glad that I was the first to get it out. Those are the only stories that have ever really interested me: the groundbreakers. I then had a new experience as I watched in real-time as the story spread around the world. One of my intelligence contacts told me early on in my journey that slip-ups by al-Qaeda can be exposed at the speed of light, thanks to the Internet, and I was watching a case study.

I monitored who was following up the story with nothing more than regular Google searches. I didn't undertake an in-depth survey, but this would show up the most obvious coverage. It was circulated on many US websites, and it reached as far away as Italy, Norway, India, Pakistan, Taiwan, Russia and China – huge audiences. *La Stampa* wrote an article about the story and it was accorded the accolade 'best of the web' on the *Wall Street Journal* website. Not a bad haul, all in all, considering that there must have been other coverage that hadn't been picked up by Google.

Now we had the TV interviews to contend with. We had a choice of *Good Morning America* or *Fox News,* which was an interesting position to be in. I asked Glen and Mrs Galt what their feelings were; Glen was up for it, but Mrs Galt was wary. She really didn't see what the fuss was about and didn't think it was worthy of TV coverage. I guess she was also worried about security, although she'd joked before about being well armed. She was eventually persuaded to agree to an interview in principle, as long as her identity was concealed, and we agreed to proceed on that basis. If we just stuck to the story that was in print, everything would be fine.

We plumped for *Fox News* in the end, purely for mercenary reasons: it had a huge worldwide reach and we could make some good contacts there, in a way that was unlikely with *GMA*. I phoned the researcher with the good news, and he said they wanted me to do a live interview as soon as possible, then interview Mrs Galt, Glen and myself live again for a weekend show a few days later. I said 'fine' and was booked in for an interview live from London in the late evening.

A car whisked me down to a studio at Westminster, and I was questioned live for about five minutes on prime time. I was tempted to hold up a hand and say, 'Good evening, America' at the beginning, or get in a quick, 'Bush is a tosspot', for the hell of it, but instead I just stuck to the script and tried to forget about exactly how many millions of people might be watching, which was quite easy really. I'd done TV interviews in the past and I knew the drill.

They started by flashing up captions highlighting quotes from the *Washington Times* article. 'She's a true American hero,' I told them, as I recounted the story and they played some footage from an al-Qaeda training video. I was asked what people out there should do if they wanted to 'do' a Mrs Galt. I replied that without professional advice, people were likely to get themselves into serious trouble, but if they were determined to do it then they should just ask around on the Internet and they'd soon find people who'd be able to help them. I even managed to get a plug in for a book that I said I was planning to write.

Mrs Galt's appearance in a couple of days was going to be the main event. In the meantime, David Jones, the foreign editor of the *Washington Times,* said he wanted to write a profile about me. There had been an amazing reaction from the readers to the story, and he wanted to cover more of the background to the story in a longer, feature-length piece. The tale of the brave mom had struck a chord with many people, it seemed. There were many reasons why – the clandestine James Bond aspects and the obvious patriotic benchmarks she had set, for example. But I think, ultimately, although it worked on many levels, the prime reason was because readers could easily identify themselves with Mrs Galt.

Glen and I met in the Westminster studios late on a Sunday night ready for the big climax on *Heartland*, a show hosted by John Kasich, a former Ohio congressman and the current managing director of Lehman Brothers' investment banking division. We'd run things through with Mrs Galt the day before, and, though she was a bit nervous about the prospect, she was willing to play along. Fox had agreed to keep her identity concealed, and we'd done our best to placate her fears.

It was only the second time I'd met Glen in person, but we greeted each other like old friends in the green room. When Mrs Galt appeared on screen, it would be the first time that we'd all seen each other, albeit that we were unlikely to see much of her; but she'd see us. We debated whether they'd go for pixellated, full-facial blackout, or quarter-face illumination with wig.

The surroundings were less than glamorous. The studio was deserted, and it looked like the cameraman and the production assistant had been called in unexpectedly. We had at least a half an hour before we were due on air, which gave Glen and I the opportunity to smoke a few preparatory cigarettes and have a good chinwag. He told me he had some hot news. He'd heard that a guy called Abu Hamza had been killed in a shoot-out.

It happened in a town called Rajouri in Kashmir, where four Lashkar-e-Toiba militants and an Indian army officer, Captain Rohit Reddy, perished during a gun battle that lasted for more than two hours. It was suspected that the four were planning to attack VIPs in a nearby housing compound. Soldiers had suddenly surrounded them and a night-long siege ensued. It ended with a fierce firefight involving AK-47s, grenades and mortars before the militants were eventually overcome. A diary was found near one of the bodies. Glen said it might not be the same person, but it did sound like Mrs Galt's friend. He'd finally achieved his aim of becoming a martyr, it seemed, and it was an appropriate and very final ending to the story.

Glen asked me what I thought he should say in the interview, and I shrugged my shoulders. Just run through the story, really, was all I could suggest, and try to relax and be succinct. We'd each done pre-interview interviews with researchers on the phone the day before, so that had given us a bit of a practice for the real thing. My pre-interview was rather tough, though, and I was just getting to the 'now, look here' stage with her when it was over. She'd been playing devil's advocate with me – and had played her part very well. Almost without me realising, she forced me into launching a forceful defence of the story, and that had been her plan. She said she'd look forward to seeing me on the show.

We finally got the sign that they were ready to roll, and we were led to our seats in the studio. It was arranged so that the Houses of Parliament loomed in the background – and the building was looking particularly spectacular under the floodlights. I marvelled at it for a few very brief moments. Mrs Galt was thinking the same thoughts thousands of miles away, as she emailed me later to say: 'London sure looks pretty at night.'

After a quick sound check from the producer in New York in the earpiece and final confirmation of the spelling of our names, we were on. We could see Mrs Galt on the monitor out of the corner of our eyes. All we could discern was a blacked out face and cascading long blonde hair. Most of the broadcast was devoted to her, naturally, and she proceeded to tell her story, which went along the lines of the *Times* article, as planned.

I was asked a question, but I can't remember what it was now. Attention then turned to Glen and he seized the moment. He introduced himself as a former intelligence operative, and he praised Mrs Galt for the marvellous job she'd done and the quality of the information that she'd provided.

He also took the opportunity to address the American people to tell them that the next project he'd been working on was some explosive audiotapes that would expose Abu Hamza in London for who he was. It was a little off the subject, but he wagged his finger and declared menacingly that the next targets in the crosshairs would be: 'Abu Hamza and the al-Qaeda idiots in London.'

THE HOIST

'The tapes have arrived,' said Glen. I broke into a wide smile. It was the news that we had been waiting for and I was flooded with a sense of relief. His contact had stayed true to his word; they'd just arrived from foreign shores securely contained in a diplomatic bag and Glen was going to go and pick them up from his office the next day. I was right to have had full confidence in him. 'They're top-notch intelligence. You can't get better than this,' he assured me.

My initial elation after the phone call was quickly tempered by the realisation that I was now going to have to listen to around 30 hours of Abu Hamza talking and ranting while taking accurate, professional notes. It was the transcribing that was going to be the tedious part, and I mentally winced at the thought. Making notes, stopping and starting the tapes, playing and replaying would mean I was looking at 90 hours of feverish work at least. In effect, there'd be two full weeks of him being piped directly into my ears: wired to Hamza, barring meal breaks and essential sleep.

There would be no time to do anything else, and it was a very hefty commitment. Glen said the thought of listening to them all in one go again, as he'd done initially, made him feel sick – and he hadn't been making notes then. Bloody hell, what was I doing! Who knew what kinds of psychological ill-effects might flow from being exposed to Hamza for such a long period. The more I thought about it, the more the Hamza mind-meld project seemed like one of those nightmarish *A Clockwork Orange*-type secret military medical experiments from the 1960s, like clamping soldiers' eyes open, giving them LSD and exposing them to films of killing and butchery for hours in an effort to desensitise them to the horrors of war and turn them into efficient killing machines. Hamza's followers seemed to find him very persuasive, and I was slightly concerned, though not seriously so, that he might cast some sort of magic spell over me and get me to sign up for jihad.

The time commitment would be unprofitable in the short term, but I was gambling on the work paying dividends further down the road. I was taking the risk that Glen's sometimes hazy recall of the contents of the tapes would prove to be close to accurate, but I had full confidence in him. It wasn't something that I needed to ponder on for very long, because he had nothing more to prove to me. He'd come up with the goods at every turn. Now it was time to prove that I could deliver my side of the bargain.

In actual fact, I put off listening to the tapes for as long as I could, right until the last possible moment. That came when I signed the contract for this book and there was no getting away from it. I dusted off my old Technics tape deck, fished out a pair of headphones from a box in the cupboard and got on with it. Up until then, Glen kept asking me whether I'd listened to the tapes yet and what did I think of them, and I kept fending off his questions by saying I'd sampled some of them, but none of them in any great detail yet.

He told me the tapes that sounded as if they had been recorded before 11 September 2001 were much better than the ones recorded after that date, as in the later ones Hamza appeared to be much more careful about what he was saying. I decided to go through one of the tapes marked 'World Trade', then try an older-looking one to see if I could discern the difference. I put a tape in, started a new Word document on the laptop and waited. Hamza live at Finsbury Park mosque: it would be like I was in the front row.

After some loud talking in Arabic, Hamza started to speak in his own peculiar broken English: 'My dear brothers and sisters . . .' As the label indicated, he started with the attack on the World Trade Center and claimed that a videotape found in Afghanistan, which purportedly showed bin Laden talking about the 11 September attacks, was a fake produced by the 'United Snakes of America'. In his opinion, as a former engineering student, the destruction of the twin towers had been a professional demolition job.

> The reality is they done it themselves.
> And maybe because they know that those who done the

operations are the Zionists . . . we haven't seen them try to investigate how many Jews have died on the day, or why Jews did not go to the World Trade Center or its surrounding area. Who gave them that tip? They don't want to investigate that. All what they are interested in is to add more suspect names to the list. They are not interested to find out who done the operation; they are only interested in what they are going to gain from the operation at the expense of Islam.

On another tape, he elaborated on this:

Coming to Osama bin Laden: did he do it? No, he didn't do it. How do I know? Number one: this man, short ago, and you witness that, have given allegiance to [Taliban supreme leader] Mullah Omar and he cannot do anything without the order of Mullah Omar otherwise he is a disobedient Muslim and he can go to the fire. It shows that it was a fresh cell made in USA. They had no experience whatsoever about explosives, or money, or smuggling anything inside the aeroplane. All what they knew, these people, was how to drive an aeroplane and which tank was full, at most.

He added that America would soon attack Somalia and Iraq, and that the White House was apparently planning to publish its own approved version of the Koran. He didn't appear to be speaking from notes, and it seemed that this mentally prompted him to plug his own book, called *Allah's Governance on Earth*: 'It shows how much the earth needs the sharia. The book is a masterpiece, *inshallah* [if Allah wills/God willing].'

I doubted that this was going to be a light read and, in any case, it seemed a bit naughty to be elevating the status of his 400-page tome to something approaching that of the Koran.

He then moved on to Afghanistan, 'the only Islamic nation on Earth', and, specifically, the prison siege at Mazar-i-Sharif in late November 2001, during the war in Afghanistan. It was the incident where Taliban fighters, who had been captured by Northern Alliance troops under the command of the notorious Afghan warlord General Abdul Rashid Dostum, mutinied and took over the prison in which they were being held. CIA agent Johnny 'Mike' Spann died in the initial fighting, and John Walker Lindh, 'the

American Taliban', and a handful of survivors finally emerged from the ruins of the compound after a long siege.

Hamza was very angry about it:

> So, if we forget about what happened to our brothers in that prison, in Afghanistan, and in other places as a whole, our children will not forget. And they will do as we did not do and they retaliate to them. So George Bush, the father and the son, they are both tricked by Allah by their own evil.

When rumours surfaced in early 2002 that Tony Blair and George W. Bush might win the Nobel Prize for peace, Hamza was incredulous:

> Look at whom they recommended for the Nobel Prize for peace. Look, if I tell you, you will not believe. It's George Bush and Tony Blair. Would you believe that? The people who are spreading terror all over the planet; the people who have sanctioned children they are killing them for tens of years; the people who have killed millions of children; the people who have killed Muslims by tons and non-Muslims and weak people and sanctioned Africans and they starve them and give them weapons to kill themselves. They starve people, they've caused a lot of corruption and they're still going to do more and more. How much they degrade mankind . . . if you give these people, these two people who are warlords, international warlords, if you give them this prize, then it is a meaningless prize. Then it's a corrupt prize. It doesn't mean a thing.

One thing that struck me was the enormous amount of ground he was covering. He attacked the Pakistani government for wanting 'to suppress jihad in their land' and then there was a tirade against the 'fat-bellied' clerics in Mecca and Medina in Saudi Arabia who had spoken out against jihad. (This was quite ironic, considering that Hamza himself clearly wasn't going to win Slimmer of the Year any time soon.)

> If they don't want the brothers to do an armed struggle, what is their struggle? Let them show us another way, if they disagree with what the Mujahideen are saying and doing.

Allah . . . he's not going to finish these people, because Allah
wants *us* to finish them.

He started to wind up by claiming that attacks on the World Trade
Center were part of a US plot to find an excuse for invading
Afghanistan. Curiously, he warned: 'And that scenario will repeat.'

On another tape, which looked like one of the pre-11 September
ones, judging by the cracks and scratches on it, Hamza had issued a
similar warning. He didn't express the exact nature of the coming
great event that would provoke Muslims into action, but he was
hinting heavily that it was just over the horizon.

Firstly, we have to believe in the news which is coming and
we don't abuse that news or reject that news. After we
believe in that truth, then we have to do – what? Then we
have to apply it. We have to apply the orders. If this news
comes, there's orders that we have to apply, the orders which
came with the news. We have to make sure that we fear the
hereafter and we prepare for the hereafter.

After he'd once again finished roundly criticising the fat-bellied
imams, and before leading prayers for 'the Mujahideen', he said:

Let us all raise one banner which nobody dispute about it.
We ask Allah to make us Mujahideen. We ask Allah to make
us *shaheed* [martyrs]. We wish more success for the brothers.
They [non-Muslims] are jealous of us. They hate us! Because
we have so-called stupid scholars, they underestimate, they
undermine, our Mujahideen brothers.

The next tape also looked like an older one. The subject of the
lecture was the social fabric of the UK: how it was 'diseased' and
needed to be changed. There was an appeal for funds: 'So, inshallah,
don't forget your contributions, by effort and by money, to those
who organise such things, at least if you can't do it, they can.'

Who 'they' were wasn't made clear. It didn't look like the money
would be used for peaceful purposes, however, and he soon
launched into an attack on the kaffirs – 'They will suffer the fire-
hell and in their graves as well' – and then moved on to jihad, again.
There was no equivocation about the meaning of jihad: 'The

meaning of the word jihad here means fighting.' According to Hamza's view of the world, jihad was more than simply fighting – it was 'the highest form of Islam'.

Apparently anyone who strayed from the path of jihad would be punished by Allah, and he used the Aids pandemic as an example: 'Before it was VD. Next time, we don't know when, Allah gave them a suitable punishment, because the way of life provokes the way of punishment. And this is how it goes.' The same was true of crack addicts. Conversely, those who performed jihad would be rewarded.

There next followed a vicious outpouring of hatred and bigotry. There is no other way to describe his remarks, and I wondered how media pundits who try to claim that he is really a friendly and well-meaning person whose only fault is being perhaps a bit of a hothead would explain this away.

According to Abu Hamza, Jewish people were subhuman and no further up the evolutionary scale than monkeys. It was Allah's will that they should be exterminated. He even seemed to suggest that Adolf Hitler had been sent to earth by Allah to carry out the task. 'Not only did they become monkeys, but Allah put a law on Earth that wherever always Allah will send in people to humiliate them, to kill them, and to punish them. And Hitler is not far from us,' said Hamza.

He even had some advice for young pregnant mothers: don't educate your children too much. It's preferable that they sell tapes and perfume on the street than become a doctor and look down on you. 'Don't run after certificates,' he implored. It's 'evil' to send a child to a non-Islamic nursery; young children should devote their time to memorising the Koran. And care should be taken to make sure that they weren't taught to respect gays and lesbians, like in State nurseries. 'Don't trust the kuffar with your children,' he warned them.

A reference on the next tape to the Jenin massacre showed that it was a more recent recording. A further reference to a report by the Charity Commission suggested it was some time on or after 24 April 2002. What followed was a fascinating insight into the power struggle going on within the Finsbury Park mosque. Officialdom was moving decisively against Hamza at this time, in the wake of the *Sunday Times* story, and, although it was one of the less important tapes in terms of controversy, I listened eagerly.

The 24th of April was the day that he was suspended from his position as cleric at the mosque. The Charity Commission issued a press release:

> The Commission has taken this action following a number of political and inflammatory statements made at the mosque by Mr Hamza, which his subsequent representations have not allayed. The suspension is a temporary measure pending consideration of the permanent removal of Mr Hamza from his role within the charity. The Commission is aware of the Bank of England's recent directive to freeze any bank accounts held in Mr Hamza's name following a recent meeting of G7 finance ministers which has given the Commission additional cause for concern.

It was like bugging the mosque and listening to the reaction to that. The tape started with an announcement by an unfamiliar voice:

> Brothers and sisters, there's a problem with the finances, and the Charity Commission, with the finances. Please do not give a penny to the *masjid* [mosque] until further notice and we'll explain afterwards why, inshallah. Do not give a penny until we explain to you why.

Hamza gave a long speech in Arabic before going on to explain the situation in English. He started by informing the audience that the mosque had not been paying its bills for the past five years and claimed that the problems lay with the trustees of the mosque, who the Commission had failed to investigate properly. Hamza also claimed that the trustees had been involved in skulduggery during the recent sale of the building next to the mosque and branded members of the board as 'government agents'.

He sounded like a man who was struggling to contain his fury, claiming that the Commission's move had been inspired by his allegations of conspiracy surrounding the 11 September attacks. His followers were urged to vent their anger on the media scrum that had gathered outside the mosque waiting for Hamza to appear. The media was apparently to blame for reporting his comments and trying to 'hijack the camera from any Islamic issue'. There was going to be a demonstration outside after the meeting to protest about the actions of the Commission. He said: 'Look at the media outside. Go and spit in their faces. Go and tell them "you crooks, you . . . ".'

There also seemed to be a growing concern that his comments had set off a chain reaction that could ultimately land him behind bars, so he was at least aware that he was sailing close to the wind, although he claimed to be unconcerned. 'So what if a preacher go to prison? People go to prison for anything. So the main reason is not the commentary about the 11 September, it's about Palestine,' said Hamza.

The spectre of Hitler was again invoked, although this time the Jews, using the pretext of 11 September, were apparently 'doing a Hitler' against the Muslims. He refused to be swayed from his mission in life: 'It's about winning the Europeans' hearts to support our causes. It's about exposing these Zionist Jews who are now doing the work of Hitler against ourselves and the nation.'

Some of his assertions were ghoulish and downright silly, even. Christians were killing Muslims in Indonesia and practising cannibalism on them, apparently. Hamza declared quite solemnly: 'I've seen a video of Christians there eating the flesh of Muslims.' Christmas was described as 'evil days' and, referring to the scandal of child abuse in the Catholic church, he said:

> Why once these people they know that these priests are abusing people, why they leave them? Shall I tell you why? Because they are all abusers. These are devil worshippers who are using churches only for black magic and for sexual relations.

After announcing the demo about to take place outside the mosque, an unidentified associate proceeded to give the audience a run-down on the state of the mosque's finances in which they claimed that no accounts had been drawn up for five years: 'Basically, they've wasted your money for years. We don't know where the money has gone.' Money had been spent like water on legal fees as the trustees had attempted to oust Hamza from the mosque, he alleged. Cash from the sale of the 20-bedroom building next door had disappeared and, in all, £360,000 was missing from the coffers, said the announcer.

The voice reminded the audience that Sheikh Abdullah el-Faisal, a Jamaican-born preacher who was very much in the Hamza mould, had just been imprisoned for soliciting murder. In fact, both he and

Abu Hamza were said to have been inspired by the preachings of Abu Qatada, who has been described as Osama bin Laden's ambassador to Europe. Qatada was wanted in eight countries for questioning in connection with terrorism and he was said to be directly responsible for recruiting shoe-bomber Richard Reid and the '20th hijacker' Zacarias Moussaoui. Videos of his speeches were found in the Hamburg flat of lead 11 September hijacker Mohammed Atta. He went on the run hours after the Anti-Terrorism, Crime and Security Act – which gave the police emergency powers to indefinitely detain foreigners suspected of involvement in terrorism – came into force in December 2001. He was finally captured in October the following year, during an armed police raid on a flat in Bermondsey in south London, and he was interned in Belmarsh Prison.

'Sheikh Faisal has been taken to prison and we don't want Sheikh Hamza to be taken to prison either,' said the announcer on the tape.

El-Faisal was convicted at the Old Bailey and sentenced to nine years in jail after being found guilty on three charges relating to tape recordings that he'd made of his talks and then sold. They included calls to kills Jews and Hindus, and claims that the Koran justifies the use of chemical and nuclear weapons against unbelievers. Hamza had been due to appear as a defence witness for el-Faisal and he appeared before the judge during a pre-trial hearing, but el-Faisal's legal team eventually decided not to call him when the trial got under way. Afterwards, it was revealed that the judge had received a letter from Scotland, sent by person/persons unknown, offering him a £50,000 bribe if he'd let el-Faisal off the hook.

Hamza claimed that the official crackdown on his activities was further proof that the so-called war on terrorism was in fact a war against Islam. He was clearly a master at deflecting criticism and using it for his own ends. Condemning anti-terrorism legislation that was introduced soon after 11 September, he said:

> Let us see what they are going to do about it now and let us see how they can attack the standards of these so-called honest and fair British. These laws are coming one after the other. And the main goal is to distract Islam and Muslims from Islam, because Islam now is what makes their life difficult.

They don't want Islam. They'll have to fight Muslims . . .
and the first to be kept in the quiet are the militant Muslims,
those who are speaking out, those who are willing to
sacrifice, and maybe they chose some people to scare others.
This is their policy. They've always done it like that.

As always, it seemed, this was the jumping point for going on about
jihad once more. I wondered how many times I'd already heard that
word and how many more times I would hear it. Transcribing all
this was just as torturous as I'd imagined, and I'd slipped behind
schedule. I'd started working into the early hours of the morning to
catch up. It seemed like a mad thing to be doing, although I tried to
comfort myself by telling myself that the pain would be worth the
long-term gain. This seemed like a very empty promise at times, as,
despite hours of work, I'd hardly made a dent in the material. I took
to scowling at the pile of tapes on the table that I'd yet to listen to.

Hamza had a wide repertoire and he spoke like he was a world
statesman. On one section I was listening to, he was advocating
training new Mujahideen in Kashmir, at a time when the Taliban
was well on the way to being ousted from Afghanistan. Now, he
suggested, was a good time to threaten the president of Pakistan,
General Pervez Musharraf. He called for Muslim scholars and the
army to oust him. He urged his followers to travel there and
'defend Pakistan before it's too late'. I was thinking that he was
being perhaps a bit presumptuous about the weight carried by his
views, when he said something very startling, even by his
standards.

Many brothers they want to be Mujahideen, but they are so
oppressed in their own countries, they want to leave their
own countries. They want to do jihad in Kashmir, they want
to do jihad in Chechnya, in Eritrea, in Afghanistan, but they
wouldn't dare to do jihad in their own homeland. But it is
more rewardable and it is more obligatory.

Was he inciting people to perform violent jihad in the UK? I listened
on, and, sure enough, he expounded on this ten minutes later: 'So
our immediate duty now is to correct our own homeland.'

He continued:

> So let us open our eyes, let us not go for jihad which is far
> away from our countries, although it's good, but it's not as
> good as you do in your own door. You don't have to travel
> thousands and thousands of miles to become a shaheed, you
> can be shaheed right on your own doorstep.

This was the 'best' jihad.

> May Allah open our eyes for what's good for us, so we don't
> waste our efforts and our Muslim blood far away, without we
> do it and we use for our own country.

Hamza appeared to be inciting his followers to conduct martyrdom
operations in Britain. He approved of them elsewhere in the world,
so it wasn't as much of a shock to hear this as it should have been.

He emphasised the inevitability of an attack on the UK on another
tape:

> The Mujahideen have succeeded in Syria against the regime,
> and have succeeded in Egypt, and it becomes compulsory
> with them now to carry on and do it in Saudi Arabia, and do
> it in Yemen, and do it here.

Hamza approved of suicide bombings in Israel, targeting 'evil Jews'
and their 'satanic methodology'. According to Hamza: 'They cannot
protect themselves against a Muslim who really wants to take them
– really, really wants to take them – to the fire.' It was a question of
numbers, he explained. The more barriers the Israelis put in the way
of suicide bombers, the more bombers would be sent on such
operations, as at least one of a group would be bound to slip
through. 'You go if you want to be a real martyr. Go for that.
Because that's what hurts the kuffar.'

Indeed, on the next tape he opened his speech with a word of
thanks for the 'brothers' who had recently died in a suicide
bombing mission in Jerusalem, claiming that 'this is the only way
for Islam to come back in dignity'. He referred to the guy killing
seven people, so I tried to find a report of the event to see if I could
date the tape. That was easier said than done, as there were several
recent Palestinian attacks in and around Jerusalem that had resulted
in the deaths of seven people. In one particularly nasty incident, an

armour-plated bus had been damaged by a roadside bomb and the attackers stayed at the scene, opening fire with machine guns and lobbing grenades at the surviving passengers as they tried to scramble from the wreck.

Later on, he reminded everyone: 'Every time you pay money to the mosque you pay money for the Mujahideen.' It seemed to be a brief but clear admission that funds had been flowing from the mosque to Islamic terrorist groups, although he had an annoying habit of not elaborating further on these kinds of points.

Looking back to the videos, there was always a cassette recorder or two on the table in front of him to remind him that he was being recorded. Perhaps he had this at the back of his mind. He couldn't have been short of legal advice, as a result of his tussles with the authorities.

He regarded the armed struggle between Israel and the Palestinians as a vision of the future. If he was right, the streets of London would soon be littered with burnt-out buses and dotted with craters. It was a subject that he returned to time and time again, railing at the Zionist 'murderers of children'. Israeli-type hi-tech weaponry was of no use in this kind of war: 'These weapons cannot defend themselves against martyrdom bombers.' For those who only know violence (the West), the sword is the only answer. He summed up this vision quite succinctly in this prayer:

> May Allah ignite in our hearts, in the Muslims' heart . . . the love for fighting, the love for sacrificing, and may Allah put terror in the hearts of the kuffar, in the hearts of the enemies of this ummah, and may Allah make this ummah united in one thing: sharia only. And this is the time when Allah will remove humiliation from this ummah and this the time when Allah will elevate and venerate the people of this ummah so they become leaders of earth.

Maybe the difference between el-Faisal and Hamza was that Hamza had stayed just on the right side of the line, by luck or judgement. He was advocating the murder of Jews, like his colleague: 'All the Israelis are fighters. They all fight. That's why anybody over 15 he is a warrior and he should be killed!'

There was also the possibility that he was working for the Security Services. His mentor Abu Qatada claimed that he'd pretended to co-operate with MI5 during an attempt to recruit him as an informer; perhaps they'd actually succeeded with him and/or Hamza. One wag on a jihad discussion forum, one that was frequented by Hamza and his followers, posted a message saying that this theory must be true because it was funny how Hamza's friends had all ended up in prison while he remained free. The site administrator chastised the poster, telling him it was a grave allegation to level against such a respected Muslim figure and one that was unworthy of further discussion.

Back on the tape, Abu Hamza went much further than calling for the murder of Jews – he started encouraging the audience to obtain false travel documents and to actively participate in the fighting in the Middle East. 'And here we should help and support,' he began.

Yasser Arafat is an Israeli agent, he said, so care must be taken to ensure that money and help goes to the militant groups who were doing the real fighting.

> The money goes for Arafat to stop the intifada and his people. Make sure you don't give these people this money. If you can take it there, take it. If you can't, prepare yourself that you will be a helper, a mujahid for the intifada where you can smuggle yourself in. Don't tell me about 'I don't have papers and I don't have' – you're all clever, you can make papers for yourself. It doesn't matter. You go and make your own papers; you fight. This is also a part of jihad, this is also a part of the preparation.

Undergo training, practice, then return to your constituencies ready to play your part in the coming global jihad, was how I interpreted all this. He underlined the point by talking about 'exporting' the Palestinian intifada. 'So, my dear brothers and sisters, it's time for earth to be clean. And who's going to clean it? It's Muslims,' he said.

The big questions about Hamza revolved around the closeness of his ties, if he had any, to the Taliban and al-Qaeda. The tapes provided some clues, as he seemed to have an insight into the thinking of the Taliban's leader, Mullah Omar. He referred to the destruction of the two giant Buddhist statues in Bamiyan in Afghanistan, which had stood there since 2 AD. Supervised by the Taliban's defence minister, the statues were destroyed using two truckloads of dynamite in March 2001 after a panel of international experts had approached the regime to seek permission to renovate the monuments.

On the tape, Hamza says the request was offensive, as the statues were idols and 'the enemies of Allah'. I was intrigued as to why he thought he should cover this and it wasn't until months later that I realised the significance of this remark. An Indian website published a purported interview with Mullah Omar in April 2004, which was conducted by telephone. During the interview, he was questioned about his reasons for wrecking the statues. He said he didn't want to destroy them, but he was shocked at the 'callousness' of the expert group who were more concerned about non-living objects than the suffering of the Afghans. That's why he gave the order.

Hamza expressed his 'love' for Mullah Omar on the tapes. Like bin Laden, he regarded Afghanistan under the Taliban as the only truly Islamic nation on earth. This seemed to be a recurring theme, as I'd watched a curious discussion on a jihad forum where senior members of al-Qaeda appeared to be slotting in members of the group for cabinet positions in Saudi Arabia after bin Laden had achieved his goal of toppling the Saudi royal family and taking over the country. Mullah Omar would become president, bin Laden's deputy, Ayman al-Zawahiri, would become prime minister and bin Laden himself would be minister for defence and jihad. The proposed new name for Saudi Arabia was Mohammedon. Hamza perhaps had this scenario in mind when he said:

> Why do we love Mullah Omar of Afghanistan and we want to kill our own leaders, Saudi Arabia leaders and Egyptian leaders, why? Because this man have more love and loyalty for the sharia of Allah than what we see in the crooks ruling our countries.

He had similar warm feelings towards bin Laden and he talked glowingly of bin Laden pledging *bayat* [allegiance] to Mullah Omar. '. . . Sheikh bin Laden is not a normal person. He is an example for all the Mujahideen, with his past experience, goals and achievements.' Hamza told his followers that he had a videotape of the ceremony where bin Laden put the full resources of al-Qaeda at Omar's disposal. He offered to supply a copy of the video to anyone who wanted to see it.

Bin Laden was portrayed as a saviour figure – 'a beautiful man' –

who'd been wrongly blamed and framed for the events that occurred on 11 September. He said:

> Allah sends every 100 years for this ummah somebody to renew its religion. It could be a person, it could be many people, it could be a group, it could be everywhere. And the only people who are renewing the religion are the Mujahideen and the scholars who are saying the truth, even if they get killed for it.

Pledging bayat to Omar or bin Laden was seen by the courts, in the US at least, as proof of membership of a terrorist organisation. All al-Qaeda operatives make the pledge before undergoing training. Hamza told his audience that they should follow bin Laden's lead.

> Maybe you cannot give bayat by tongue, because you can't shake the Emir's hand, but you can do it by heart, you can do it by action. By intending to help this Islamic state, by paying *zakat* [charitable tax] to them, by collecting funds to them, by going . . .

He seemed to suggest that, when the UK is attacked by al-Qaeda, the atrocity will be committed by foreign volunteers rather than indigenous fighters. They were, however, quite likely to be recruits from another European country, as the West's so-called war on Islam has resulted in a recruiting bonanza in Western countries. All through the tapes he was scathing of the lack of commitment to jihad by British Muslims. I'm not sure how much of that was actually true or to what extent these kinds of statements might have been designed to goad people into action with a bit of crude reverse psychology. According to Hamza:

> . . . more Westerner Mujahideens go everywhere. In fact, sometimes they're not going to go everywhere. They're going to do it here. And this is what they are worried about. Muslims in this country are very weak. They are not anything here. They are not going to do anything anywhere.

He estimated that it would take up to 500,000 suicide bombers before the earth would be completely Talibanised. The guy had obviously thought about this very deeply, and this was his conclusion and firm conviction. He was predicting a long global guerrilla war that would eventually see the final and permanent victory of Islam. Every single living person on Allah's planet would be forced at gunpoint to become a practising Muslim. It sounded like the mother of all James Bond plots, but this was *real*. This was the game plan. What about the people who didn't want to play along? It didn't take much thought to foresee that perhaps hundreds of millions of dissenters, those who would not be enslaved, would be exterminated in an accompanying genocide: the mother of all nightmare scenarios.

'The real weapons of mass destruction are the desire for martyrdom,' Hamza explained.

> Half a million martyrdom shaheed is enough for Muslims to control the whole of earth forever. Our people should know that we should have intifada also, uprising in our own countries, more than Palestinians do in their own country.
>
> In the end of day, Islam must control earth, whether we like it or not.

There were several options for putting the tapes to work. With so much material to hand, I knew that it would be a waste to hand them over to a newspaper. I wanted to avoid the situation whereby a paper would run a little 250-word story on them and then they would become untouchable. Other media outlets would then view the tapes as old news and the totality of the material – 30 hours of it – wouldn't be fully exploited. Besides that, the money would be poxy and wouldn't pay for the two weeks that I'd devoted to researching and transcribing them. They deserved a full page at least, or a special 'inside Finsbury Park mosque' series. The chances of securing such a deal were very slim, I knew. I felt strongly that they merited something more than a quick and dirty news story, though, and my thoughts turned to TV possibilities.

Packaged up with the videos and other material I'd gathered was a documentary waiting to be made. I decided to hold off from going to a newspaper and explore this possibility first. I had offered them to a press contact just before we actually received them, but the response was lukewarm. Audiotapes didn't intrinsically sound like they were going to be as exciting as videotapes, basically, although I stressed that the disclosures on the audiotapes were much more exciting than the videos. My man was unmoved, though he said he'd like to know about the contents once I'd gone through them.

I'd also tested out a TV contact, and he was much more interested. He asked me to call him as soon we'd got them, but again there was going to be very little money involved, though we could expect to secure a decent chunk of airtime.

I started ploughing through listings of TV media contacts and production companies to draw up a shortlist of possibilities. It wasn't my usual territory, and it was a bit baffling to start with, because, on the face of it, there were a multitude of possible outlets. My initial enthusiasm was tempered by a realisation that 'bumping into the right person' might not be as easy as I first thought.

I finally narrowed the list down to three possibilities and sent off introductory emails to three senior executives. After one 'I don't think it's for us' kind of catch-all response (I hate those), a second came through expressing positive interest. The development director asked me to call her. We had a long chat about the exact nature of what I was proposing, and she said she was definitely interested in meeting to discuss the project. She also explained that the managing director had recently filmed a documentary that explored the phenomenon of Islamic terrorism in general, and it sounded like something that might be right up their street. We set a date, and she said it would probably be a good idea if Glen also attended.

I set off for the meeting the following week. I bombed down the motorway on a beautiful summer's day, wishing I was doing something other than work. I might have been a bit excited about the prospect a few months previously, but was too battle-hardened for that now. I viewed it almost as a mundane task, as I knew that we were a long way from reaching first base even if the meeting went well.

It did go well, for the most part. As we chatted and munched sandwiches, the MD and the company seemed to have the kind of pedigrees that we were looking for. He was a very bright guy who I thought might have been an Oxbridge graduate; Glen thought his highly polished shoes betrayed an ex-military man. He was very interested in Glen's story and quizzed him closely about his spying activities. Glen coped with the 30-minute grilling quite admirably, and the MD, who we took to referring to as just 'M' for security purposes, declared: 'OK. I'm in.' We all beamed smiles at each other, shook hands and moved on to sketching out how the film might pan out.

The meeting was wrapped up with a discussion about finances and a promise to send us a letter of agreement with confidentiality assurances. My task was to draft a document that could form the basis of a script, and M's task would be to tickle up his contacts and to set up a preliminary meeting with one of the major broadcasters. He suggested that the project was sensitive enough to justify the establishment of a secret production office. They'd suffered a number of suspicious break-ins when they were working on a controversial film about terrorism a few years back, he explained. This is why we decided to refer to him as M in emails and on the phone.

Producing the draft script was an enormous undertaking. I fished out a book proposal I'd put together the previous year for inspiration and this was when I decided to open a second front and produce a new book proposal at the same time. The intention was to get that in the works simultaneously to maximise the chances of getting the story out into the public domain. I groaned at the thought of starting a new book project, but it seemed like the obvious thing to do.

I completed the draft film outline over the course of a couple of weeks and sent it over to the production company when I was done. It was a waiting game after that, as M set to work organising meetings to discuss securing a commission from a broadcaster. Reviewing all the material I had written and collected since I quit the rat race was an eye-opener. I hadn't done it before, and I marvelled at the quality and volume of information I'd unearthed. That spurred me on to complete and polish up the new book proposal, which I'd already roughed out. I set out to find a new literary agent and started mentally preparing for a long haul. After a few hours of research spent drawing up another shortlist, I approached one of the literary world's leading agents. He liked what he saw, but he said that the major multinational publishers weren't commissioning books about terrorism at that time. The cynical business reason was that they were saving their money ready to commission a rash of quickies about the next 11 September-style attack.

He did, however, refer me to an independent publisher that he thought might be interested in the project. It was fantastic advice, because the publisher was indeed interested, and after a meeting and some revisions to the outline, I was offered a contract.

It was a relief, although the celebrations were brief after I calculated the words-per-day rate that I'd need to stick to in order to get the job done. The TV company had all of the tapes, so I cancelled our agreement and asked for them to be returned, to safeguard the book project. I also felt a sense of irony, as, despite all the technology that had been deployed in gathering the material, the paper book had triumphed over all other outlets – newspapers, TV and Internet – as the best vehicle for disseminating the information to as wide an audience as possible.

Glen had delivered his side of the bargain, and now I'd fulfilled my side of the agreement. He was over the moon at the news and was as relieved as I was. Now the public could decide for themselves if Hamza was a threat to national security or simply using his right to free speech to the fullest. Perhaps he had the right to incite his followers and tell them it was their 'compulsory' duty to mount terrorist attacks in the UK. Perhaps there was no harm in letting him instruct people that performing violent jihad in Britain and provoking an armed uprising by Muslims is 'obligatory'. Perhaps he was right to warn that a devastating al-Qaeda attack on his adopted homeland was unavoidable; his allegiance was to bin Laden and Mullah Omar – he should know. All the way through the tapes I don't think he ever uttered 'al-Qaeda'; he always referred to 'the Mujahideen'. In most people's minds, 'the Mujahideen' can mean only one thing.

Is it illegal to urge people to forge documents and carry out suicide bombings in Israel? I don't know. Inciting people to kill Jews and Europeans, sending money to terrorist groups, directing people to carry out jihad in Pakistan, telling people they should pledge allegiance to Mullah Omar, praising bin Laden and welcoming terrorist attacks on the West, accusing Tony Blair of murdering millions of children – maybe he had every right to say all that. I'm not a lawyer. I'd heard from police sources that there was widespread incredulity about why he was still a free man in this country. One military contact seethed and almost growled when I talked to him about Hamza and it was a good measure of the pent-up anger there was inside the closed world of law enforcement and the military.

It felt like the book was setting the seal on the first phase of my new career.

Glen told me in March 2004 that he had tried to hand the Hamza audiotapes over to the police, but, despite several telephone calls, they didn't seem to be interested in them. Perhaps, as I'd found with the media, it was down to an assumption that audio couldn't match video. That attitude changed in April 2004, as Hamza's appeal against being stripped of citizenship was due to be heard towards the end of the month. My media contacts knew that I had the tapes and they wanted to do a story before the appeal hearing. Several newspapers were running campaigns calling for his deportation, but none of them could find the knockout punch and they were starting to run out of steam.

Suddenly, there was great interest in the tapes, but I had to disappoint them. 'I can't, because it will undermine the book,' was my standard reply. One particularly tenacious journalist wouldn't take no for an answer and tried to get me to name the TV company that I'd been dealing with. I wasn't naive, however; his plan was obviously to get hold of their copies of the tapes. 'It's confidential,' I said. They shouldn't have any copies of the tapes and our agreement barred them from handing them over to third parties in any case. In the end, he resorted to offering me money to just leak a few choice quotes to him in an 'under the counter' fashion.

I phoned Glen to remind him to hold the fort, in case he got a call. He told me that he'd had a journalist working for the *Washington Post* magazine on to him. He wanted to do another interview with Glen and Mrs Galt and, initially, I wasn't too happy to hear it. This kind of exposure might be damaging, although it could be a good way to create a pre-publication buzz in the States, as it was one of world's most prestigious media titles. The journalist also seemed like one of the good guys, and I relented. It was a good call, because he was friendly with a Congressman who'd taken an interest in the Hamza Tapes and the activities of Mrs Galt. The Congressman, in turn, had some very high-level intelligence contacts and he wanted copies of all the tapes, so he could cause a stir in Washington. He wanted to use Hamza as a case study to illustrate the asymmetrical nature of the threat that the world is facing.

THE HOIST

I met up with Glen after he had finished the interview. We shared
a feeling of satisfaction that everything had come together as
planned. He was going abroad for a holiday in a couple of days, and
he said he could relax more than he normally would, now that his
work on Hamza was almost done.

'We'll have to come up with another scam for the next book,' I
suggested.

He paused in the way he usually does when he knows something
I don't and is wondering whether to tell me or not. Perhaps Mrs Galt
had already been at work on something big.

Glen eventually gave me a cheeky smile and said: 'We'll have a
talk about that when I get back.'

There was still one major outstanding issue and earlier we'd
weighed up the chances of it coming off while he was away. Weeks
earlier, and because of the calls I was getting from journalists in the
run-up to Hamza's immigration appeal hearing, I had the idea of
offering a newspaper exclusive early access to the tapes for a news
story, in return for the paper agreeing to serialise the book when it
was published. I'd cleared it with the publisher and set about selling
them to the highest bidder.

I spent a week meeting reporters from different national
newspapers, after they'd signed confidentiality agreements, and
guiding them through the material I had. It would be an ideal way
to finish off their campaigns, I argued, because he was surely going
to be in very hot water when news of the tapes was finally broken.
Of all the reporters I met with, I got on best with the *Daily Mail*'s
crime correspondent Ben Taylor. He immediately appreciated the
parallels between what Hamza was saying on the tapes and the case
of Sheikh Abdullah el-Faisal, who'd received a lengthy prison
sentence. I could tell that he was genuinely intrigued and we spent
a few hours going through the transcript and listening to key
passages. I hoped that the *Mail* would make the winning bid,
because I was sure that Ben would do justice to the story.

The *Mail* did come out on top, and I got a call telling me that a
motorcycle courier was on the way to pick up the tapes. They
wanted to get an acoustics expert to go through them and confirm
that it was Hamza talking, just to be on the safe side. I felt a little
uneasy about handing them over and ceding control, but the deal
depended on the outcome of the expert analysis.

It was a long wait, as the expert had been tied up giving evidence in a court case and, as he was one of only two people in the country with the requisite skills, he was in high demand.

After three weeks, I finally got a call to say that the expert was satisfied that it was Hamza and that the deal with the *Mail* was signed and sealed. Soon, I was talking to Ben about the story he was writing and helping him resolve a few issues, mainly with regard to Islamic terminology. A few days later he called to read me the story over the phone to check that I was happy with it and to say that it was due to be published in a couple of days' time. From what he was saying, it was clear that they were going to give Hamza the full treatment and he was being lined up for a 'monstering'.

The story wasn't published on time, and I wondered if something had gone wrong until Ben phoned to say that it had been put on hold at the last minute. Everything was fine, but a decision had been taken to use the story at a later date, when it would have maximum effect. Hamza's appeal hearing was due in about three weeks' time, and I assumed that this would have played a part in the decision.

Glen jetted off on holiday during this period, not knowing when the story would be published. I didn't want to be a pest and I refrained from calling the *Mail* every day for an update. After a couple of weeks of silence, Ben finally phoned, the day before Hamza's appeal hearing, to say that the story would be out the following day, Monday, 26 April 2004. It came as a huge relief, and I was anxious to know if it had made the front page.

I planned to get up early the next day and see what the *Mail* had done, but my mum phoned and woke me up to give me the rundown. It had indeed made the front page: 'HAMZA'S CALL FOR SUICIDE BOMBS IN BRITAIN'. There was extensive coverage spread over pages four and five inside as well. It all sounded exactly like the story Ben had read to me. I felt relief and pleasure in equal measure, as well as an overwhelming sense of satisfaction, as everything had panned out as it should have.

I had just enough time to read the *Mail* coverage and scan the news headlines before I started fielding phone calls. It was certainly the best front page of the day. It was one of those rare occasions when every newspaper splashed with a very different story. Aside from the Hamza tapes story, the subjects included an exposé of abuse of pensioners in nursing homes, a warning of an impending flood of asylum seekers from eastern Europe, the possibility of more UK troops being sent to Iraq, and the introduction of ID cards.

The next call, at 9.30 a.m., was from an Anti-Terrorist Squad detective at New Scotland Yard. He said, matter-of-factly, that he was calling about the story in the *Daily Mail*, obviously, and he just wanted to confirm that the tapes and the transcript that the newspaper had handed over to them had originated from me. He explained that they'd known about the story since Friday and that they'd taken a statement from Ben Taylor, who'd turned the tapes over to them. I confirmed that the tapes came from me. He said that that was all they needed for the moment and that a colleague of his would probably be in touch with me later in the day. I offered to help in any way I could.

Then all hell broke loose. Ben phoned to ask if it was OK to give my mobile number out to journalists wanting to follow up the story, and I agreed. Within minutes, I was at the centre of a media storm and inundated with calls from newspaper reporters wanting to know more and TV news broadcasters requesting interviews. I just kept jotting people's names and numbers down in my notepad and wondered how I was going to fulfil all my promises. I switched off my phone so I could have a shower in peace and get ready for a round of interviews and I had 15 new voicemail messages by the time I got out of the bathroom.

Hamza didn't bother to turn up to the appeal hearing, and his case was adjourned until 10 January 2005. The *Mail* had timed it to perfection. The article set the media agenda and the tapes story was *the* story of the day. It filled the vacuum left by his no-show, though the government's barristers had taken the opportunity to outline the case against him – for the first time in any great detail.

Ian Burnett QC, acting for the Home Secretary David Blunkett, told the Special Immigration Appeals Commission in London that Hamza should be stripped of his nationality because he had provided support and advice to five terrorist groups: the Algerian Armed Islamic Group (GIA), the Islamic Army of Aden, Egyptian Islamic Jihad, a Kashmiri group called the HUA, and 'of course' al-Qaeda. Hamza had 'encouraged and supported the participation in jihad, including fighting overseas and engaging in terrorist acts'. He'd also provided a safe haven for Islamic extremists and a sense of extremism at Finsbury Park mosque and promoted violence through his teachings, the barrister added.

I then scrambled to tidy up the house and get ready for the arrival of a BBC TV news crew. I promised the producer of *Tonight with Trevor MacDonald* that I'd then head to the ITN building in Gray's Inn Road in London in a cab that they'd sent. *Channel Four News* then wanted an interview as well, as did *ITV News,* and they were all based in the same building. A BBC Radio Five Live car was heading for the ITN building to meet me outside, as was a France 2 camera crew.

The BBC TV news crew duly turned up at my house and immediately started setting up in the front room. The report was scheduled to go out on the main *Six O'Clock News* evening news bulletin, and I answered all the questions they fired at me, though I must say I didn't take a shine to the reporter. After I bade them farewell, I got into the waiting cab and headed into central London.

I had 39 voicemail messages when I switched the phone back on while I was in the car. I made further arrangements for cab pick-ups and interviews with *ABC News* and the *Richard and Judy* show on Channel Four, and talked to several regular newspaper contacts who wanted to know what scope there was for follow-ups.

I recorded an interview with *ITV News,* which the *Channel Four News* producer said he could use instead of doing another interview, whilst I was at a tape machine going through copies of the tapes trying to find a Hamza soundbite that *Tonight with Trevor MacDonald* could use. They wanted to use a specific quote from the tapes, but I couldn't find it in time, because the copies of the tapes were all in blank boxes without labels and there was no quick way of zeroing in on it. Still, they kept me there for an hour and a half looking for it, so I missed the Radio Five Live car and there was no hope of making it to the *Richard and Judy* show in time. Glen was lazing around in the sun on some beach somewhere, blissfully unaware of what was going on, otherwise I am sure he could have taken up the slack for me.

The France 2 crew should have been waiting outside, so I set off to find them when I was done. They weren't hard to find: I guessed they must be the three people smoking and casually lounging around a camera that was sitting on the floor. I did a kerbside interview with them and arranged to meet up with the reporter at his company's offices to record a lengthier interview the following day. I then jumped into a waiting cab and headed for the UK studios of the US broadcaster ABC in Hammersmith in west London. I was there for a few hours with the producer in charge, going through the tapes and recording a lengthy interview. Bruno bought me a Thai takeaway meal, and we chatted at length about how I might be able to contribute to their terrorism coverage in the future. It was my final port of call for the day and I got home just before midnight.

The interview went out on the early evening *ITV News* bulletin and the Hamza story was also covered later on *Tonight with Trevor MacDonald*. I found out that the BBC report didn't go out because the lawyers were jittery about possibly being accused of prejudicing Hamza's appeal hearing. I was told that this was largely down to an atmosphere of ultra-caution that now existed at the Corporation, after it was savaged in the Hutton Report over Andrew Gilligan's notorious story alleging that the government had 'sexed-up' a dossier making the case for war in Iraq.

There was to be more of the same the following day, as I had appointments with NBC News, France 1, France 2, and Fox News Channel and CBS News had also been in contact. All in all, it was a good showing – and the book hadn't even been published yet.

The investigating officer at the Anti-Terrorist Squad in London called me on the Tuesday to go through the basics of the story of what was on the tapes and how I got hold of them. The poor chap had been given the task of listening to them all, and he said he might come and see me soon for a chat. On the day the tapes story was published, Scotland Yard had issued a statement saying: 'On receipt of the tapes, the Metropolitan Police will work closely with the CPS [Crown Prosecution Service] to establish whether a crime has been committed. We will seek legal advice on what course of action is appropriate.' On the Thursday, the issue was brought up in the House of Commons by Labour MP Andrew Dismore. The Solicitor General, Harriet Harman, said in response:

> A file from the police is with the Crown Prosecution Service at the moment. I cannot say more about that case at this stage . . . My Honourable Friend will be aware that the CPS is independent, and when it is actively considering a case such as this, it would be wrong for me to pre-empt or prejudice

any decision about to be made. I do not think that the House would thank me for that.

I probably derived the greatest satisfaction from the story featuring at the top of *Have I Got News For You* the following day. Being a BBC show, that in itself seemed to make a mockery of the lawyers' decision to pull the report from the *Six O'Clock News*.

Glen was back in the UK by then, and I filled him in on the events of the past few days. The matter was now out of our hands, we agreed: mission completed.

The Anti-Terrorist Squad officer had been given two weeks to listen to the tapes, and the file that had been passed to the CPS must have largely consisted of my transcript. Ben at the *Mail* had handed it over along with the tapes. The *Mail* ran another story: 'YARD STUDIES TERROR TAPES' – and we waited to see what would happen. It was a crucial moment, because it would surely seem to be a big green light for all militant Islamic groups and their leaders in the UK to continue inciting people to commit mass murder if no action was to be taken against Hamza.

After the two weeks were up, Glen called a police contact to see if he could find out what was happening. He said he could tell that something was up by the tone of his voice. I called Ben a few days later to see if he'd heard any whispers, and he also said he'd been given the impression that something was on the cards. He'd been told that there had been some unspecified movement on the American side.

At around 6 a.m. on 27 May 2004, I was woken up to be told that Hamza had been arrested.

'Fuck,' was my response. I tumbled out of bed and scrambled to get dressed.

He'd been detained in a police raid on his home in Aldbourne Road in Shepherd's Bush, west London, three hours earlier. The US had issued a warrant for his extradition. He was being questioned at Paddington Green police station. I switched on the TV and watched the smiling policemen in fluorescent jackets guarding the entrance as the media circus started gathering outside the building. The precise charges that were being levelled against Hamza wouldn't be known until he appeared before a hearing at the magistrates' court inside the high-security Belmarsh Prison in south-east London at 3 p.m.

I emailed Glen to congratulate him and said: 'Presumably the knighthood and the reward money are in the post.' It was a serious point. Glen's acquisition of the videos marked the start of Hamza's downfall, as his former associate who'd become an FBI supergrass, James Ujaama, had originally pleaded not guilty to charges of aiding the Taliban. Glen had turned the videotapes over to the authorities and that clip of the meeting involving Hamza and Ujaama was shown in court, causing Ujaama to change his plea to guilty and agree to testify against his former associate. It apparently all boiled down to that one scene where Hamza talked about the Afghanis not knowing how to fire RPGs correctly. That had sunk Ujaama and it had now caught up with Hamza.

Yet, despite three years of work and considerable personal expense, not to mention personal risk, Glen has not received so much as a thank you from the authorities – absolutely nothing. He started making enquiries about claiming a reward from the US for providing information that led to the conviction of Ujaama, after getting hot under the collar when it was reported that the Iraqi informer who betrayed the whereabouts of Saddam Hussein's two sons was immediately paid $30 million, but he got no response. The US ran a scheme called Rewards for Justice, and Glen put a big headline on his websites that declared 'NO REWARDS FOR JUSTICE'.

What was already a big story was sent into orbit, as Hamza's court appearance was accompanied by a simultaneous press conference in the US held by the US Attorney General John Ashcroft and New York City Police Commissioner Raymond Kelly. Ashcroft, standing next to a huge blow-up photograph of Hamza waving his hook, detailed the 11-count indictment that had been returned by a New York grand jury investigation on 19 April and unsealed on his arrest. He was charged with providing support and resources to terrorists. 'Hamza is the real deal,' Commissioner Kelly told the media. 'Think of him as a freelance consultant to terrorist groups worldwide.'

The indictment read: 'United States of America v. Mustafa Kamel Mustafa, a/k/a "Abu Hamza," a/k/a "Abu Hamza al-Masri," a/k/a "Mastafa Kamel," a/k/a "Mostafa Kamel Mostafa".' It wasn't referred to in the court document, but one of the main charges could only have come from the testimony of Ujaama. It alleged that he'd provided material support to al-Qaeda by conspiring to set up a jihad training camp in Bly, Oregon, and stockpiling weapons and ammunition inside the US. Ujaama appeared to be the 'Co-Conspirator 2', a US citizen, who was referred to throughout the document: the recruitment material on the videotapes must have been related to this project.

It also claimed that Co-Conspirator 2 collected money from worshippers in mosques in New York and brought it back to Finsbury Park in London to swell the funds of the mosque there. He then used the money to fund his travelling expenses when Hamza asked him to escort one of his followers to a jihad training camp in Afghanistan in 2000 and to organise safe houses in Pakistan and transport over the border. Hamza, 'along with others known and unknown', also supplied 'funds, goods and services' to the Taliban in Afghanistan. He'd discussed the establishment of a 'computer lab' in Kandahar in Afghanistan for the use of Taliban officials and he gave C-C2 £6,000 to lease a building and fund some of the start-up costs.

So it seemed that Hamza was being deadly serious when he said on the audiotapes: 'Every time you pay money to the mosque you pay money for the Mujahideen.' It occurred to me that the Taliban money may have accounted for part of the £360,000 that went missing from Finsbury Park mosque funds, which was also mentioned on the tapes.

The other charges claimed that, prior to this, he'd been directly involved with the Abyan faction of the Islamic Army of Aden in conspiring to kidnap hostages in Yemen in late 1998. He allegedly supplied the leader of the militants with a satellite phone and topped it up with £500 of pre-paid airtime. Three calls on that phone were made to Hamza's home when the group took 16 Western tourists hostage in the country on 28 December 1998. He provided advice on hostage-taking and agreed to act as an intermediary, according to the document. Four of the tourists – three Britons and an Australian – were killed and several injured during the firefight that ensued when Yemeni security forces mounted an attempt to free the hostages.

Hamza shrugged his shoulders and laughed when he was asked in court if he'd like to agree to be extradited to America. 'I don't really think I want to, no,' he replied.

Just after the charges were announced, I set off for Hamza's house in Shepherd's Bush, to give a live on-the-scene interview for *London*

Tonight. He lived in a very nondescript street and many of his neighbours were unaware of his presence; several people stood in front of the police cordon and phoned friends and family to give them the news. I could see figures going in and out of Hamza's house in the distance, which was still being searched, but there was no urgency in the movements. I chatted with a couple of journalists from *The Sun* and the *Daily Express* while I was waiting for the crew to set up, and they had orders to get an interview with Hamza's wife when the cordon was taken down.

'I don't rate their chances,' I thought, while I was standing just out of shot and waiting to go on-air. Then suddenly I spotted a black taxicab cruising slowly past us. Sitting in the back was Hamza's son, Mohammed Mustafa Kamel. He had a mobile phone clamped to one ear, and he was leaning forward and glaring menacingly out of the window. His eyes seemed cat-like, I thought, as we stared at each other for a few moments.

His old man had been remanded in custody at Belmarsh Prison. His famous hooks were detached from him, as they were judged to be a security risk, and I wondered if he'd be able to turn the pages of the Koran without them. There was some confusion over the sentence that Hamza would face if convicted: Ashcroft said he could face the death penalty, though Home Secretary David Blunkett said that an agreement had been reached with the US over a year ago that he wouldn't be executed. Assuming there was such a deal, he might be looking at around 100 years behind bars.

The notion of Hamza spending a century in prison reminded me of a prediction I'd read in a book that I'd been given as a gift at the end of a meeting with a senior diplomat in London just before the tapes story broke. It was an analysis of the West's struggle against terrorism by a senior army officer. He predicted that the war against Islamic terrorists would carry on for a century or more. I also remembered one of the key quotes from the audiotapes, in which Hamza estimated that it would take 500,000 suicide bombers before Islam gained dominance over the West and took control of the earth.

I did the maths: Hamza's half a million divided by the army man's 100 years, equalled 5,000 suicide bombings every year on average. It equated to just under 14 attacks a day, and that appeared to be the benchmark for deciding whether the West really was engaged in a war on terrorism or not. Both sides seemed to agree on one thing: it was going to be a very protracted struggle, and it would slowly escalate. If they are right, then what we've witnessed so far are only the initial skirmishes.

EPILOGUE

The final report of the National Commission on Terrorist Attacks upon the United States was published as this book was going to press. It contained few major surprises about how the 11 September attacks were executed on the day, though it did contain some thought-provoking new snippets of detail. The panel found that institutional failings at all levels allowed the hijackers to get on with their big job in New York, despite numerous signals in the preceding years and months warning that al-Qaeda was planning a spectacular against America. 'The system was blinking red,' reads the title of one section in the report, but few in officialdom expected the targets to be inside the borders of the USA.

The publication of the report was almost overshadowed when one of the law firms working for relatives of the 11 September victims, Motley Rice, released new video footage of hijackers being taken aside for questioning by Dulles Airport security staff in Washington. That was the final thin line of defence being breached, and it was an eerie sight. The footage shows Khalid al-Mihdhar and Majed Moqed setting off the alarms; Moqed was searched with a handheld metal detector after tripping a second alarm. After a thorough search of their hand luggage, they were allowed through to board American Airlines Flight 77 – and crash-dive it into the Pentagon. Five hijackers boarded, and only Hani Hanjour, the presumed hijack pilot, escaped inspection.

The report also reveals that Mohammed Atta, who steered Flight 11 into the north tower of the World Trade Center, was selected by computer for special screening in Portland, though this only meant that his luggage, containing the stolen uniforms, was held back from his flight. The man himself was allowed to board unimpeded. It also confirms that Atta phoned the hijacker of another flight, Marwan al-Shehhi, after this, and the two spoke for three minutes, most probably to check that everything was set.

On Flight 175, the details of additional phone calls made by passengers has now been revealed, and it seems that the hostages were aware that they had been caught up in a suicide mission. Peter Hanson told his father that the plane had been hijacked: 'I think they intend to go to Chicago or someplace and fly into a building.'

The panel concluded that Flight 93, which crashed in Pennsylvania, was deliberately ploughed into the ground by hijacker Zaid al-Jarrah. The cockpit voice-recorder indicates that the passengers were fighting back and getting very close to gaining entry during the final minutes. After rolling and pitching the plane in an unsuccessful attempt to throw the passengers off balance, al-Jarrah can be heard to exclaim: 'Allah is the greatest! Allah is the greatest!' He then asks a fellow hijacker: 'Is that it? Shall we finish it off?'

His colleague responds: 'No. Not yet. When they all come, we finish it off.' After another series of violent manoeuvres, the hijackers appear to judge that they are about to be overpowered. Jarrah says again: 'Is that it? I mean, shall we put it down?'

The other hijacker replies: 'Yes, put it in it, and pull it down.'

The commissioners were also able to question senior al-Qaeda operatives who are being held in custody. These included Khalid Shaikh Mohammed (KSM), regarded as the mastermind of the 11 September project, who was captured during a police raid in Pakistan in March 2002. His nephew is Ramzi Yousef, the chief planner of the 1993 World Trade Center bombing. Together, both men had developed the aborted 1995 Operation Bojinka plan, which would have seen multiple aircraft en route from Asia to the US blown up in mid-air.

In the spring of 1999, KSM said, he was summoned to a meeting with bin Laden to develop a list of American targets to be attacked using aircraft as weapons. Under interrogation, he revealed that the original plan involved ten aircraft and targets on the east and west coasts of the US. Nine were to be crashed into landmark buildings and nuclear power plants, but he had special plans for the tenth airliner.

He would pilot this himself and take the passengers hostage. According to the commission's report:

> Rather than crashing the plane into a target, he would have killed every adult male passenger, contacted the media from the air and landed the aircraft at a US airport. He says he then would have made a speech denouncing US policies in the Middle East before releasing all of the women and children passengers.

Bin Laden later scrapped that idea and the whole plan subsequently underwent several revisions in the years that followed, until it became the 11 September plan that we know today.

Among its many and varied recommendations, the 9/11 Commission panel said that the American people should be told in no uncertain terms: 'No president can promise that a catastrophic attack like that of 9/11 will not happen again.' Indeed, Britain's anti-terrorism minister recently advised people to stock up on food and medical supplies in case of an attack, and the chief of the Metropolitan Police, Sir John Stevens, has revealed that 'four or five' major terrorist strikes in the UK have been thwarted since 11 September.

Al-Qaeda's core leadership remains intact, it has been reinforced with battle-hardened recruits and its supporters have been emboldened by its activities in Iraq. We now await bin Laden's promised backlash.

Further reading and sources
www.neildoyle.com

INDEX

Abassi, Feroz 170
Afghanistan
  Bamiyan Buddhist
    statues 215–16
  bin Laden's base 39, 41,
    44–5, 48, 50–1, 105, 107
  bin Laden's nuclear
    cache 77–8, 83
  Coalition war against 47,
    51, 57–8, 65, 74–5, 95,
    161–2
  jihad camps 66, 92, 97,
    155, 168, 171, 191, 230
  Mazar-i-Sharif prison
    siege 205–6
  military intelligence
    search for bin Laden
    71, 74
  Pashtun people 48–9, 52
  Tora Bora caves 65, 185
  war with Soviet Union
    66, 141
  see also Taliban
aflatoxins 130
Aftergood, Steven 76
Ahmed, Lord Nazir 173
Ahmed, Sarmad 163
al-Fadl, Jamal Ahmad 78–9
al-Hazmi, Nawaf 104,
  119–20
al-Jarrah, Zaid 233–4
Al-Jazeera 47, 51
al-Jihad 155
al-Liby, Anas 148
al-Masri, Abu Hamza 155,
  229 see also Hamza,
  Abu
al-Mihdhar, Khalid 104,
  119–20, 233

al-Muhajiroun 178, 181
  see also Mohammad,
  Sheikh Omar Bakri
al-Neda 69, 149
al-Omari, Abdul Aziz 103
al-Qaeda
  in Afghanistan 45, 65–6,
    75, 168, 170
  allegiance to bin Laden
    67
  blamed for 11
    September 43
  in Chechnya 81
  goals 57, 94–8
  global network 68, 93,
    168
  and Iraq 129, 131, 147
  in Jordan 91
  manuals 138–45
  nuclear capacity 78,
    81–6, 89
  in Pakistan 86, 184–5,
    189, 196
  in Philippines 118
  pseudonyms 60–2, 64
  risk posed by 14
  sleeper agents 91, 94
  in Sudan 79
  in UK 180, 202
  use of technology 65,
    69–70, 91, 92, 135,
    150–1, 185, 199
  World Trade Center
    attack, 1993 53
al-Qassam Martyrs'
  Brigade 142
al-Saud, Crown Prince
  Abdallah bin Abd al-
  Aziz 127

al-Shehhi, Marwan 104,
  234
al-Suqami, Satam 104–5
al-Zarqawi, Abu Musab 62
al-Zawahiri, Ayman 69,
  155, 190, 216
Algeria 143 169, 171, 225
Amalgam Virgo 01 116–18
America West Airlines 118
Amundson, Ryan 102, 120
An-Nizzi, Abou Qitaal 187
anthrax 45, 59–61, 63, 96,
  112, 130, 133
Anticev, John 53–4
Anti-Terrorism, Crime and
  Security Act 211
Anti-Terrorist Squad 63,
  159, 225, 227–8
Arafat, Yasser 41, 215
Armed Islamic Group
  (GIA) 143, 225
Armitage, Richard 108,
  111
Ashcroft, John 100, 229,
  231
Assad, Bashar 64
Aswat, Haroon Rashid 168
Atta, Mohammed 61,
  103–5, 118, 120, 171,
  211, 233–4
Attaturk, Kemal 166
Atomic Demolition
  Munitions 82, 98 see
  also nuclear weapons
Australia 176, 188, 190
Azerbaijan 190
Aziz, Abdel 143–4
Azzam, Sheikh Abdullah
  141, 169, 173

236

INDEX

Bank of England 163, 209
Belmarsh Prison 211, 228, 231
Berg, Nick 62
Bigum, Wing Commander Randall K. 137
bin Laden, Hamza 190
bin Laden, Osama
 and 11 September attacks 35, 38–9, 61, 105–8, 110, 112, 233–4
 in Afghanistan 39, 41, 48, 50–3
 Afghan–Soviet war 48
 family business 39
 goals 57, 94–8
 interviews 87
 and nuclear weapons 77, 83–7
 obtains US military software 135
 pseudonyms 62
 rumours about 45, 65–7, 75, 90, 189–90, 193–5
 as saviour figure 57, 216–17
 search for 46–8, 50–3, 67, 71–2, 74
 in Sudan 48, 79, 92
 and Taliban 45, 57
 US attack on, 1998 44
 use of technology 69, 92, 148–9, 151
 videos 47, 51, 68, 204
bin Laden, Shafig 104
biological weapons 45, 83, 96, 117, 129–33, 142
black space programme 71
Blair, Tony 41, 152, 178, 206, 221
Blunkett, David 180, 225, 231
Boren, Senator David 105
botulinum 130, 133
British Olympic Association 125
Buckingham Palace 159
Burma 188
Burnett QC, Ian 225
Bush, George W. 36, 43–5, 76, 86, 99–104, 106–12, 115, 125, 147, 155, 161, 178, 182, 200, 206

caesium 80
Canada 110, 166, 168, 176, 188
carbon tetrachloride 139
Card, Andy 45
Carlyle Group 104
Castro, Fidel 100
Center for Arms Control and Non-proliferation 89
Charity Commission 180, 208–9
Charles, Prince of Wales 159–60
Chechnya 68, 81, 166, 188, 190, 194, 212
 Chechen separatists 80, 147, 165
chemical weapons 77, 83, 87, 96, 117, 129–34, 136, 142–3, 211
China 82, 127, 176, 199
CIA 23–4, 43, 69, 72, 105–8, 110–11, 113–14, 116, 118–19, 139, 150, 172, 182, 205
Clark, General Wesley 110
Cohen, William S. 117
Cold War 40, 86, 110
Command Emergency Response Training 115
cotton poison (methyl parathion) 139
Cruise O'Brien, Conor 14
Cuba 100
Cuomo, Mario 30
cyanide 54–5, 139, 187
cyber-terrorism 89–93, 135, 150

Decision Support Systems 94
Defence, Press and Broadcasting Advisory Committee 80
Delta Airlines Flight 1989 107
Department of Homeland Security 99
Department of Trade and Industry 126
Dinkins, David 30
dirty bombs 80, 83, 86
Dismore, Andrew 227–8
doomsday devices 78, 83, 87

Dostum, General Abdul Rashid 205
Dulles International Airport 104, 116

Egypt 59, 95, 132, 169, 172, 213
Egyptian Islamic Jihad 155, 225
el-Faisal, Sheikh Abdullah 210–1, 214, 223
EMAP 36–7
EMAP Digital 37
Empire State Building 21, 34
Encyclopaedia of the Afghan Jihad 69, 140
Encyclopaedia of Jihad (Mawsu'at al-jihad) 141, 143, 145, 147–8
FBI 24, 27, 43–4, 51, 53–4, 63, 101, 106, 110–11, 119–20, 129, 151, 156, 164, 168, 170–1, 193–4, 229
Fedayeen 129, 131, 134
Federal Aviation Administration 106
Federal Emergency Management Agency 113
Federation of American Scientists 76, 86, 98
Felt, Edward 108
FieldSoft 115
Finsbury Park mosque 42, 155, 163–4, 178, 180, 183, 187, 204, 208, 218, 226, 230 *see also* Abu Hamza
Florida 45, 103–4, 117, 119, 137
Floyd, Nancy 54
'The Fortress' 148
Fulton, John 116

G7 summit bomb plot 171
Galt, Johnathan R. 163, 185, 196
Galt, Mrs 185–93, 196–202, 222–3
Gandhi, Rajiv 159
gas gangrene 130
Georgia 86, 108
Germany 188

Giuliani, Rudolph 30, 110
Gulf War, 1991 18, 27, 58, 97, 130, 133, 136, 143, 148
guerrilla warfare 94, 140, 142

hackers 87–8, 134–5, 138, 145, 151
Hamas 146, 152, 178
Hamza, Abu (Finsbury Park) 42, 155–6
appeal for funds 207, 214, 215
arrests 170, 228
audiotapes 156, 165, 183–4, 202–18, 229
Bank of England sanctions against 163
British citizenship 180
on Catholic Church 210
on Christmas 210
criticism of UK 174
on Hitler 208, 210
on Israel 213
on Jews 208, 210
jihad training camp 168, 230
Jihad UK 164, 174, 214
links to al-Qaeda 155, 168, 173
pseudonyms 163, 229
recruitment for jihad 174–5, 179
study circles 164, 176
on suicide bombers 213
support for bin Laden 163, 168
support for Taliban 168, 173
videotapes 156, 160, 165, 167, 169, 171, 173, 218, 229
on Western education 208
Yemen kidnapping 163, 230 167–74, 178–82
see also Supporters of Sharia
Hamza, Abu (Pakistan) 186–93, 195, 201–4, 206–18, 221–25, 227–31
Hanif, Asif 178
Hanjour, Hani 233
Hanna, Conor 52
Harman, Harriet 227

Hanson, Peter 234
Hekmatyar 144, 194–5
Hezbollah 146
Home Guard 150
Hoon, Geoff 85
Hotmail 145, 165, 188
HUA 225
Hubble Space Telescope 73
Hussein, Qusay 129, 134
Hussein, Saddam 27, 46, 72, 97, 111, 123–6, 129–30, 134, 147, 229

Ibrahim, Abu 175
Ikonos satellite 129
India 165, 181, 192, 199, 216
Indonesia 210
intelligence community 64, 74, 120, 156
International Olympic Committee 125
Internet 36–8, 42, 46, 56, 64, 68–70, 79, 89, 103, 122, 144, 146, 148–51, 160–1, 165, 184, 196–200, 221
intifada 215, 218
Invisible Web 68
IRA 18, 152, 159, 161–2
Iran 85, 125, 127, 157, 189, 194
Iran–Iraq war 157
Iraq 62, 66, 80, 85, 95, 123, 125–7, 129–34, 136–7, 143, 147, 158, 166, 169, 180–1, 190, 205, 225, 227, 235
Iraq Communist Party 133
Iraqi National Congress 130
Iraqi missile programme 132
Islamic Army of Aden 163, 225, 230
Islamic Jihad 64, 155, 225
Islamic Media Centre 146–7
Islamic-News.co.uk 163
Israel 49, 60, 64, 98, 126, 165–6, 169, 199, 213–14, 221
Italy 103, 188, 199
Izzedine Al-Qassam Brigades 146

Jaish-e-Mohammad 185
Jamaat-e-Islami 185
Jamaat al-Dawa 185
Japan 136, 176
Jenvey, Glen 155–9, 163–5, 167, 169, 171, 173, 177–86, 190, 195–204, 219, 221–4, 226, 228–9
Jones, David 89, 200

Kamel, Mohammed Mustafa 163, 231
Kashmir 164–6, 174, 176, 185–6, 189, 191–3, 201, 212
Kassir, Oussama 168
Kazakhstan 81, 86
Kelly, Raymond 229
Kennedy, President John F. 100
Kenya 79, 147, 179
KGB 139
Khattab 147
Khodada, Sabah 129–30, 132–3
Kolchuga early-warning radar system 85
Koran 57, 192, 205, 208, 211, 231
Korean Air Flight 85 110
Kosovo 177
Kuchma, Leonid 84
Kurdish PKK 159
Kuwait 95–7, 130, 133

Labsi, Mustapha 171
Lashkar-e-Toiba 185–7, 201
Lebanon 95, 146
Lebed, General Alexander 82
Lewin, Daniel 104
Liberation Tigers of Tamil Eelam (LTTE) see Tamil Tigers
Lindh, John Walker 205
Logan Airport 103
London 13–14, 18, 38, 40, 42, 130, 152, 155–6, 158–60, 163, 168, 170–1, 175–6, 178, 200–2, 211, 214, 225–8, 230–1
Los Angeles Airport 91–2

INDEX

Mahmood, Sultan
  Bashiruddin
  86
Majid, Abdul 86
Metropolitan Police 156,
  227
Mexico 188
MI5 139, 152, 215
MI6 139, 150
Microsoft 151, 185
*Military Studies in the
  Jihad Against the
  Tyrants* 148
Mineta, Norman 111
Mir, Hamid 87
Mohammad, Sheikh Omar
  Bakri 171, 178
Mohammed, the Prophet
  57, 176
Moqed, Majed 233
Mossad 84, 111
Motley Rice 233
Moussaoui, Zacarias 163,
  211
MP3 91–2
Mujahideen 50, 70, 141–3,
  145, 153, 165, 170–2,
  174–5, 177, 186–7,
  190–1, 193, 206–7,
  212–14, 216–17, 221,
  230
*Mujahideen Poisons
  Handbook* 142, 144,
  152
Muntaqim, Abdul 143
Murtada, Dr Ahmed 131
Musharraf, General Pervez
  45, 212
Myers, Air Force General
  Richard 105

NASA 31, 57, 76
Nash, Major Daniel 111
National Command
  Authority 137
National Commission on
  Terrorist Attacks upon
  the United States 233
National Military
  Command Center 109
National Reconnaissance
  Office 71, 116
National Security Agency
  108, 150
National Security Council
  111–12
NATO 110, 177

Nautilus Institute 136
nerve agents 139
nerve gas 130, 133, 140,
  148
New Civil Engineer 28
New Jersey 111, 116
Newark International
  Airport 104
Nidal, Abu 132
North America Aerospace
  Defense Command
  [NORAD] 103–4, 106,
  110, 116, 118, 121
North Korea 125, 128, 136
North London Central
  Mosque 155 *see also*
  Finsbury Park mosque
Northern Alliance 50, 57,
  65, 205
Norway 199
nuclear weapons 40–1,
  77–87, 89, 95–8, 111,
  117, 136–7, 142, 211
nuclear suicide bombers
  78, 96
NYPD 10, 24

Odigo 103
oil 57, 96–8
Old Bailey 211
Olson, Barbara 107
Olson, Ted 107
Olympic Games 123, 127
Omar, Mullah 45, 69, 173,
  205, 215–16, 221 *see
  also* Taliban
Operation Bojinka 118, 234
Operation Northwoods
  100, 102
Organisation for the
  Preparation of
  Mujahideen 145

Pakistan 45, 48, 51, 54,
  66–7, 69, 77–8, 90–1,
  95, 169, 181, 184–5,
  189, 191, 193–5, 199,
  206, 212, 221, 230
  Directorate of Inter-
  Services Intelligence
  (ISI) 44, 105
  nuclear capacity of 86,
  96
Palestine 38, 56, 59, 61–2,
  126–7, 132, 142, 161,
  166, 174, 176, 178,
  188, 210, 213, 215

Palestinian Liberation
  Organisation (PLO) 158
Pentagon 39, 41, 66, 102,
  105–7, 109, 112,
  115–16, 118–20, 198,
  233
Pentagon Mass Casualty
  Exercise [MASCAL]
  115
Petronas Towers 169
Philippines 118, 177
Phoenix Air flight school
  118
'Phoenix Memo' 119
phosgene 139
plutonium 86
Popular Democratic Front
  for the Liberation of
  Palestine 38
Port Authority of New
  York 25–6, 32
Potorti, David 101
Powell, Colin 111
Presidential Emergency
  Operations Center 106
Project Echelon 52
PROMIS military software
  135

Q8crackers 151
Qatada, Abu 211, 214

Rahman, Omar Abdel 53,
  120, 169
Rand, Ayn 198
Reagan, Ronald 104
Reddy, Captain Rohit 201
Reid, Richard 163, 211
Rewards for Justice 229
Reynalds, Jeremy 146
Rice, Condoleezza 111
ricin 130, 143, 152, 171
Rogers, Professor Paul 85,
  98, 133
Romero, Dr Van 110
Ronan Point 39
Royal Navy 153
Rove, Karl 43
Rumsfeld, Donald 105–7,
  109–11
Russia 68, 84–6, 135,
  166–7, 199
Russian mafia 81, 83

Salem, Emad 53–4
Samaranch, Juan Antonio
  126

Sarasota-Bradenton International Airport 107
Saudi Arabia 46, 62, 95–6, 98, 127, 132, 172, 190, 206, 213, 216
Sears Tower 118
Secret Army for Justice 58, 60–1
September 11 (9/11) 13, 36, 44–7, 56, 58–9, 65, 86, 103, 115–16, 118–20, 147, 163, 168–71, 188, 197, 217
American Airlines Flight 11 101, 103–5, 233
American Airlines Flight 77 104–7, 109, 116, 233
claims of responsibility 38, 60–2
conspiracy theories 100–1
hijackers 43, 45–6, 103–4, 106–8, 111–12, 118, 120, 129, 171, 211
hijackers' flight training 44, 118–9
timeline 103–12
United Airlines Flight 93 43, 100, 104, 107–9, 119, 234
United Airlines Flight 175 104–6, 234
victims' relatives 101–2, 109, 112, 120
see also World Trade Center
Shahbaz 186
shaheed 207, 213, 218
Shaikh Mohammed, Khalid 234
sharia 57, 205, 214, 216
Sharif, Omar Khan 178
Shell 191
Shepley, Linda 108
Sherman, Robert 86, 98
Shin Bet 139, 152
Shroder, Professor Jack 50–1
Sinn Fein 88
Smalley, Darrick 168
Somalia 132, 169, 205
South Africa 79, 173
South Korea 128, 136

Soviet Union 72, 82
Space Imaging 66
Spann, Johnny 'Mike' 205
Special Air Service (SAS) 144, 147, 153
Special Boat Service (SBS) 153
Special Branch 152, 171
Special Immigration Appeals Commission 225
Spectrum Astro 75
spy satellites 53, 71, 73
see also National Reconnaissance Office
Sri Lanka 158–60
stealth bomber 71
steganography 92
Stevens, Sir John 235
Sudan 39, 48, 78–9, 92, 169
Supporters of Sharia 163, 168, 180 see also Abu Hamza
Sweden 143, 168
Syria 64–5, 94, 95, 127, 213

Taiwan 199
Taliban
Abu Hamza's support for 168, 173, 179, 205, 215–16, 230
Coalition war 57–8, 65, 67, 75, 83, 168, 205
collapse of 77
links to Pakistan's ISI 105, 185
Mullah Mohammed Omar 69
President Bush ultimatum to 45
protecting bin Laden 45, 48, 51
Tamil Tigers 158–9, 163
Tanzania 83, 179
Taylor, Ben 223, 225
Tenet, George 105, 110–11
Thompson, Dave 75, 77
Tillman, Colonel Mark 109
see also Air Force One
Transamerica Tower 118
Turkistan 82

Uganda 177
Ujaama, James 156, 167–71, 180–1, 229–30
Ukraine 82, 85–6
United Airlines Flight 23 106
United Arab Emirates 95
University of Bradford 85, 133
University of Nebraska at Omaha 50
US Air Force 74, 121, 137
US Army 109, 115, 142, 190
US Attorney General 229
US Marine Corps 144
US Navy 39, 110
US Secretary of Transportation 39
US Strategic Command 111, 157
USS Cole attack 157–8
Uzbekistan 78, 86, 188

Vandy, Ray 112
Vigilant Guardian 103–4

Wallace, Alan 107
Washington Dulles International Airport 104, 116
Weisburd, Aaron 149
Williams, Kenneth 119
Winter Olympics 87, 125
World Cup 127
World Trade Center
attack, 1993 17–35, 39, 53–4, 95, 120, 139, 170, 187, 234
attack, 2001 36, 39, 41–2, 85, 101, 103, 105, 107, 119, 205, 207, 233
Building Six 23, 114
Building Seven 111, 113–14
see also September 11
Wright, Bill 108

Yemen 132, 157, 163, 213, 230
Yousef, Ramzi 54, 234

Zubaydah, Abu 92–3, 168